Five Standards for Effective Teaching

JOSSEY-BASS

Five Standards for Effective Teaching

HOW TO SUCCEED WITH ALL LEARNERS, GRADES K–8

Stephanie Stoll Dalton

BICENTENNIAL
1807
WILEY
2007
BICENTENNIAL

John Wiley & Sons, Inc.

Published by Jossey-Bass
A Wiley Imprint
989 Market Street, San Francisco, CA 94103-1741   www.josseybass.com

Jossey-Bass books and products are available through most bookstores. To contact Jossey-Bass directly call our Customer Care Department within the U.S. at 800-956-7739, outside the U.S. at 317-572-3986, or fax 317-572-4002.

Jossey-Bass also publishes its books in a variety of electronic formats. Some content that appears in print may not be available in electronic books.

Library of Congress Cataloging-in-Publication Data

Dalton, Stephanie Stoll, 1979-
    Five standards for effective teaching : how to succeed with all students, grades K-8 / Stephanie Stoll Dalton.
        p. cm. – (Jossey-Bass teacher)
    Includes bibliographical references and index.
    ISBN 978-0-7879-8093-1 (alk. paper)
1. Effective teaching–United States.   2. Teacher effectiveness–United
    States. I. Title.
    LB1775.2.D35 2007
    371.1020973–dc22   2007019659

Printed in the United States of America
FIRST EDITION
PB Printing 10 9 8 7 6 5 4 3 2 1

Jossey-Bass Teacher

CONTENTS

PREFACE

For the era in which I was taught to be a teacher, I was formally well prepared, with multiple degrees, including a content major, and state certifications; but I soon realized that I had not been prepared for the students I would meet every day: diverse youngsters from traditionally underachieving groups, new immigrants speaking many languages, and inclusive classes of every achievement level. I love teaching, and like all teachers I wanted to be a spectacular influence on every one of my students every day. This desire drew me to work with teams that were systematically studying how to be successful with *all* students. By working with organizations from the Kamehameha Early Education Program (KEEP) to the Center for Research on Education, Diversity & Excellence (CREDE), I was able to teach, consult, research, and write about the new demographics of the classroom: diversity in culture, language, readiness, and resources (Dalton, 1995). These efforts helped me to develop systems and routines that supported quality content teaching by using a variety of effective strategies. This approach made classroom instruction time more predictable, controllable, productive, and most important, enjoyable for students and teacher.

Adopting a systematic approach increased my opportunities to teach in order to meet the instructional goals I set. Teaching no longer meant leisurely lecturing or floating about from one student or group of students to another, commenting and questioning for a minute or even less; instead, it now included regular in-depth conversations with first graders about narratives such as *Three Billy Goats Gruff* or with twelfth graders about epic poetry such as Milton's *Paradise Lost*. I now guided students to be the discussants and writers, to produce learning outcomes that helped us build ourselves into a community of academic learners.

Central to this approach are five pedagogy standards that have provided a framework for me, and for all other teachers who have applied them, to think systematically about the essential components of classroom teaching. This framework is especially useful for identifying and organizing the components in ways that support and strengthen teaching. This book presents these standards, along with scenarios, examples, and engaging activities that can promote learning for the broad range of students in today's classroom by making teaching responsive to all students and to the unique needs of each student.

I use the term *pedagogy* to refer to the *system* in which teaching and learning are embedded. When the teaching standards work together, they create a system—a specific pedagogy—and thus also become standards for pedagogy. This system is effective across content areas, from literacy to mathematics, from science to art. The standards enhance the compatibility of classrooms with diverse cultural and linguistic groups, with all age and ability levels, and with the high numbers of students that our classrooms must accommodate.

Of course traditional classrooms also have a pedagogical system, though it is rarely recognized as one. It is a system that relies on a cycle of assign and assess, assign and assess. It depends heavily on assigned texts and on teacher talk and lectures; it demands highly individual performance, although instruction is not individualized; and it requires student silence and acquiescence. Opportunities for students to apply concepts or obtain assistance from peers are unavailable or sporadic and covert. The system is teacher dictated rather than teacher guided. Teaching is often focused on the most academically talented, while those with other strengths manage on their own or suffer the sad consequences of academic failure.

The system you will learn from this book is very different. It provides teachers with predictable and frequent teaching occasions on which to assist students' academic understanding. It ensures that students regularly interact with one another and with the teacher for academic purposes; that they have regular performance opportunities that develop language and promote complex thinking; and that throughout the process teachers and students develop relationships of trust that lead to learning and to patterns of participation that make the classroom an experience of real community for every member.

The idea of setting standards for effective teaching is overdue. Teachers understand the value of content standards, which give us benchmarks to guide our instructional goals and raise the bar for student achievement such that these standards are in constant view and guiding inspirations. Likewise, pedagogy standards for teaching can spotlight our ideals for teaching, reminding us to secure classroom conditions that enable teaching that produces student achievement and joy in learning.

CONTENTS OF THE BOOK

Five Standards for Effective Teaching articulates how standards-based teaching supports achievement for all students. It describes the five standards; discusses their rationale, theory, indicators, and supporting research; and provides examples of their implementation from real K–8 classrooms. It explains how standards guide teaching and build classroom compatibility to support all students' academic success.

The five standards for effective teaching are as follows:

1. Teacher and Students Producing Together
2. Developing Language and Literacy
3. Connecting Learning to Students' Lives
4. Teaching Complex Thinking
5. Teaching Through Conversation

The book prepares teachers to organize their classrooms as communities of learners, design innovative instructional activities, encourage student interaction, provide positive classroom management, use a variety of grouping formats, and use dialogue to teach directly to goals. The effectiveness of this system for all cultural and linguistic groups and for all age and ability levels in typical classroom settings is shown by example and by an outline of research results.

In these chapters, teachers will find extensive guidance for setting up and maintaining a system that maximizes face-to-face teaching in small groups, increases students' learning time and opportunities, and establishes a rhythm of productivity in the classroom. A wealth of real classroom examples and learning activities demonstrates how teachers using the standards transform teaching in classrooms into participation in academic learning communities. In these settings, frequent and substantive teacher and student interactions supported by rich application and extension opportunities culminate in deep content understandings that can be measured.

The book is organized into two parts. The two chapters in Part One present introductory material and the research basis for the five pedagogy standards. Part

Two contains six chapters, one for each pedagogy standard, and a concluding chapter, which focuses on the integration of all five standards into a system that supports and expands classroom teaching, followed by appendixes.

SOURCE OF THE PEDAGOGY STANDARDS

Like other standards, the standards for effective teaching are derived from a consensus process in addition to evaluation and research. The researchers of CREDE, and its predecessor, the National Center for Research on Diversity and Second Language Learning, conducted the process. It involved analysis of the literature on teaching and learning produced by researchers and program developers working with a broad range of the nation's majority and minority students in K–12 classrooms. The five standards focus on features of teaching that are widely associated with student success and on ways to boost the use of these features in classrooms across grade levels, content areas, and cultures. The work presented in this book is based on implementations of the standards in numerous classrooms serving diverse and at-risk students across the nation.

AUDIENCE AND INTENDED USES

This book is written for teachers, students preparing for teaching, teacher educators, administrators, teacher professional developers, and others who are interested in the practices of effective classroom teaching, especially with diverse and at-risk students. It can serve as an informative text for university teacher preparation courses and for district professional development workshops and programs.

The book is intended to expand the reader's conceptual and practical knowledge of effective teaching using the five standards of pedagogy. Its comprehensive presentation is research based and anchored in examples of teaching and classroom practice from a broad range of classrooms serving many student populations. It describes how the five pedagogy standards can be implemented in diverse classrooms of thirty or more students in ways that support making a difference in every student's performance.

ACKNOWLEDGEMENTS

Talented teachers have been my colleagues, partners, mentors, and coaches from the start of my career. In the schools where we taught, their teaching models were thoughtfully and creatively designed to meet their students' needs. Fortunately they extended their teaching to include students of teaching, like me. They deepened my understanding of *how* to teach the curriculum while meeting both the teaching standards and my students' needs. They made it clear how I could help every student learn in my classroom. Accomplished teachers themselves and extraordinary coaches, Doris Fujimoto, Sarah Sueoka, Lynn Vogt, and Karen Bogert challenged and strengthened my professional competence in guiding students to achieve.

In my experience, every teacher questions his or her efforts to assist students' learning, reflects deeply, and tirelessly seeks to improve. Thanks to my fellow teachers' commitment to continuous improvement, I have had many partners in studying teaching approaches such as student-generated activities, instructional conversation (IC), and classroom social organization. As a talented beginning teacher, June Sison used IC to teach mathematics to her high-need English language learners. Her work continues to be an example of focused teaching based on her high expectations of students' success. Excerpts from some of her ICs are used at the beginning of most of the chapters of this book. Of my student teachers, Cynthia Waters is an extraordinary classroom organizer whose ICs with Native American students continue as models to emulate. Many other teachers have contributed to the development of the approaches described in this book.

Many colleagues have helped in the writing of this book. A primary collaborator has been Vanessa Lee, an associate of CREDE. Her extensive observations and support of teachers performing in diverse classrooms make her a rich resource on teaching. Her experience and understanding enabled her to provide many examples of teachers' efforts in a variety of classrooms, and her analyses of teachers' performances were helpful in describing how teachers use pedagogy to support their teaching. She continues to apply her skills in classrooms.

I have heard my teacher colleagues say that they enjoy the conceptual part of teaching as much as the challenge of its implementation in the classroom. Many of us have been fortunate to learn from and be mentored by those whose work has advanced the concept of teaching. I have learned more than I ever thought I could from Roland Tharp, my husband, and Ronald Gallimore, my mentor. They have influenced not only me but also a generation of teachers across the nation through a new definition of teaching as responsive assistance and through the conceptual framework that supports it. Reports on the concepts and application of responsive assistance, particularly for diverse students, continue at CREDE (http://www. crede.org).

I appreciate the enormous help I have received from reviewers and editors who have worked to improve the book. Teachers who have contributed have themselves developed systems for teaching that are exemplary models. Thank you to my daughter, Jessica Stoll Dalton, for her emotional support and her confidence in the value of this writing effort. It has also been a pleasure and a learning experience to work with the editors at Jossey-Bass.

THE AUTHOR

Stephanie Stoll Dalton has enjoyed a career in education that began with teaching eleventh and twelfth grade high school English. After becoming a secondary reading specialist, she taught elementary school to learn more about early learning and literacy processes. As a teacher mentor, she has coached teachers at every grade level. Her international experiences include teaching English in Tokyo, serving as an advisor to the Iraq Ministry of Education during her tenure with the Coalition Provisional Authority, and consulting in Mexico and Greenland. As a teacher educator, she codesigned and coordinated an alternative-route teacher preparation program at the University of Hawaii at Manoa.

In addition to teaching, Dalton has been a researcher, research administrator, and author for more than twenty years. Her research has focused on the social organization of the classroom, the role of activity in teaching and learning, and students' opportunities to learn through dialogue with teachers, particularly sustained interaction on academic topics. She writes from her experience teaching African American, Asian, Latino, Middle Eastern, Southeast Asian, Native American, and Hawaiian and Pacific Islander students in multilingual and multicultural classrooms. It is on these populations in particular that both her teaching and her research have focused. Her students continue to inspire her work, her writing, and her reflections.

Dalton's formal education includes a bachelor's degree in English from the University of Maryland, a master's degree in reading from the University of Miami, and a doctorate in administration and reading from the University of Hawaii. She is currently an education program specialist for the U.S. Department of Education.

Five Standards for Effective Teaching

PART ONE   Understanding
the Standards

ONE

In a modern tale, Thomas Edison returns to visit an American home where a teenager is submitting her physics homework on the Internet. "Ahhh," he sighs, "How far we've come with electricity!" Not long after, Wilbur and Orville Wright follow Edison into the family home, where the younger son is watching a space shuttle launch on TV. "Ahhh," they sigh, "How far we've come with flight!" The next day, John Dewey visits the boy's classroom. "Ahhh," he sighs, "Exactly as I remember it."

—Jean Rutherford, University of Texas

Effective Teaching and Pedagogy

The dynamic of classroom teaching that is most vital to student learning is lost when classrooms function like cemeteries. The cemetery model of teaching enforces students' silence, solitary work, and permanent placement in an orderly arrangement of furniture, usually in rows and columns. This model has become emblematic of teaching. It appears whenever classrooms are portrayed in television programs and commercials. The model typically shows teachers standing in the middle of scrubbed and seated youngsters who look like the teacher and raise their hands, eager to participate. This view of classrooms lags behind current understandings of teaching and learning, and overlooks the rich diversity of students.

Teachers typically meet their students in numbers as large as their classroom will hold. Many of the students' home backgrounds and languages differ from those of the teacher. Classes include students who are poor, preliterate, and lacking in knowledge not only of the language of instruction but also of the expectations and procedures of school.

INCREASES IN U.S. MINORITY STUDENT ENROLLMENT

The percentage of public school students who are minorities increased from 22 percent in 1972 to 43 percent in 2004, with the largest growth among Hispanic students. In 2004, minority public school enrollment, at 57 percent, outpaced white student enrollment, at 43 percent, in the west of the United States (U.S. Department of Education, 2006).

Regardless of how the student population changes, teachers use the knowledge and skills they have been taught. They frequently use instructional methods that focus more on securing students' immediate attention to content than on building teacher-student relationships that support communication and learning. They may implement a cemetery model in their classroom because they were taught that way themselves and believe it is responsible for their own academic success. Even when teachers see their students struggle with and detach themselves from learning, they may lack the skills needed to shift to another approach or they may find other explanations for students' failure.

Because teachers are typically highly qualified and proficient in their content knowledge, the skills they lack are usually related to the knowledge and application of pedagogy. When teachers understand and use pedagogy, their teaching has the flexibility to meet students' vast array of learning needs. This book discusses pedagogy and its role in effective classroom teaching. Pedagogy, as much as teaching, ensures that all students are assisted in learning academic content as effectively as they learn in their worlds outside of school. Pedagogy can guide teachers to organize their classrooms, design activities, and communicate with students to support learning, but it is also a system for strengthening teaching in order to produce learning outcomes for all students.

This book is about a system composed of five pedagogy standards. The system supports teaching that encourages students to learn through activity and dialogue. Each standard emphasizes a component of teaching, beginning with activity and then focusing on language and literacy development; contextualization; thinking; and most important, teacher and student dialogue on academic topics. Together the standards support classroom teaching by organizing lessons and designing activity that supports the use of a variety of effective approaches, particularly dialogue. The major benefit of the five pedagogy standards is that they encourage teachers to use the premier teaching strategy: instructional conversation.

PEDAGOGY DEFINED

Pedagogy is commonly used as a synonym for *teaching,* referring to all the educational functions of classrooms and schools. More specifically, *pedagogy* is generally described as the correct use of teaching strategies. Dictionary.com (2007) associates it with *method,* the meaning often given to another education term, *instruction.* For our purposes here, *pedagogy* is defined as the system of principles and methods that supports and facilitates effective teaching. It is also implied in the use of the traditional term *instruction* and in discussion of instructional approaches.

In the classroom, pedagogy is as visible as teaching. Research supports the importance of teachers having knowledge of pedagogy and using it in their teaching (Allen, 2003). A close look at the dynamics of classrooms reveals components of pedagogy that are distinct from teaching: teacher-student interaction, classroom organization, social arrangements of students, activity design, schedule, setting and context, and management. Together these components constitute pedagogy that has been little recognized for its potential to support effective teaching in any classroom. In the same way that content standards set goals for teaching, pedagogy standards provide a system of support for teachers in meeting their teaching goals. The five pedagogy standards offered in this book express the system as a set of principles to be applied in every classroom. These standards are based on scientific evidence, effective practice, and theory (discussed in this chapter) about what teachers need to know to teach productively.

Although it is highlighted less often than teaching, pedagogy always accompanies teaching. Ignoring the relationship between pedagogy and teaching is usually a disadvantage in teaching and learning. Pedagogy is present in and an influence on teaching and learning whether it is explicitly planned for or not. For example, every day many millions of energetic youngsters throughout the world sit still and quiet in classrooms, performing rote and abstract tasks for hours, reflecting pedagogy practice that most nations assume best suits their teaching goals. The inescapable influence of this approach ruled many of our own youths in cemetery-like classrooms that used transmission models of teaching. When pedagogy is ignored, it is still at work, exerting a powerful influence and producing unexpected outcomes. Note the conditions in our most blighted schools, where content focus is negligible and pedagogy is ignored: pedagogy is as forceful in creating chaos as it can be in providing structure.

Specifically, pedagogy supports teaching through the physical arrangements of the classroom, time scheduled, activity designed, relationships defined, expectations and values set, and participation structures imposed. Teachers use pedagogy to prepare and guide their own and their students' participation in teaching, learning, and activity performance. Because students' learning processes are better understood than they used to be, the value that participating in activity with others has in developing knowledge is clearer. This awareness encourages teachers to try alternative models of teaching. The ability to shift to such models relies on understanding pedagogy's role in transforming teaching. For example, the power that pedagogy has to transform teaching into teaching for success through activity-based and interactive models is dramatic. The following list contrasts pedagogy that supports traditional or transmission teaching with pedagogy that supports activity-based and interactive approaches:

Transmission Pedagogy	Transformative Pedagogy
Individual tasks only	Joint productive tasks often
Whole group	Small groups often
Curriculum based	Activity based
Monotasking	Multitasking
Abstract	Contextualized
One size fits all	Differentiated activities

Transformative pedagogy is recognizable by how it supports teaching. It transforms the types of tasks and activities students perform; the social arrangements they use; and the pace, suitability, and familiarity of students' classroom experience. Transformative pedagogy also provides a system of support in the five pedagogy standards, which teachers use to guide students through increased levels of interaction, activity, and production toward their learning goals. Just as pedagogy can at times be broader than *how* to teach, teaching is not exclusively about *what* to teach, although in most models curriculum is closely associated with teaching. Because teaching is the source of all decisions made in the classroom and responsible for all of the classroom's effects, it is broader than *what*.

TEACHING DEFINED

There are numerous models of teaching and they are based in theories of learning, motivation, information processing, and cognitive and brain research. One model defines teaching as *assisted performance* (Tharp and Gallimore, 1988; Vygotsky, 1978). According to this view, learning occurs within the social interactions and settings of teaching and learning. The role of the teacher as well as of peers and parents in students' social groups is critical to learning. For example, peers who are proficient in language and the expectations of school influence students in classroom work through speech that models new ways of talking and thinking.

The role of activity is a component of the model. Teachers design tasks and activities to provide opportunities for learners to perform together, especially to accomplish joint outcomes. Activity is problem and reality based in order to prod students to think in different and deeper ways about solutions or outcomes. The activities aim to connect students' prior understandings to new knowledge for application beyond the learning situation.

In the model, teaching occurs when a learner is assisted in his or her performance by a more competent other. This means that students who can perform competently with assistance from the teacher are indeed learning. Teachers or other assisters, such as competent peers, continue to influence learning along a continuum known as the *zone of proximal development* (ZPD) until the student is capable of full independent performance (Vygotsky, 1978). Every student's ZPD, or learning zone, is different and requires a different amount of assistance. Teachers come to understand students' differing needs through interacting and working with them, not only through assessments. Teachers focus on what students can do as well as on what they cannot do by helping them perform tasks and through testing. Focusing on the learning zone allows us to see where teaching actually occurs—in interaction with a more competent other at different points within the learning zone.

Teaching—or assisted performance, according to the preceding definition—is composed of three processes of assistance. First, the teacher must access the student's learning zone through joint activity in order to stimulate the learning process. Second, the teacher must assist the student within activity to identify what the student knows or needs to know, as a hook for the unfamiliar and unknown. The teacher identifies a hook when students reveal something they already know that will serve as a link to new information, or the teacher uses a hook that all students can understand to serve as a bridge to new information. Finally, the teacher and student must work together to expand the student's understanding for use in new situations. To provide this quality of assistance, teachers must use pedagogical support in the classroom that allows interaction with students in situations small enough to influence individual learning. They must also have content area expertise that they can use when needed to assist knowledge acquisition within the student's learning zone.

According to the theory, the timing of assistance is also important. Assistance is most effective when it precedes the development of understanding and begins to awaken learning. Assistance is not limited to teachers but may also come from competent others, such as peers, parents, and experts. The teacher, the most valued assister, has a relationship with the students, and has many means of influencing students' learning. Entry into students' learning zones is a professional act requiring expertise that, like in the medical profession, according to its oath, must do no harm. The learning zone is where students' processes are activated and where teaching assistance can be most effective. The five pedagogy standards, when fully implemented, prepare students and teachers for productive work in students' learning zones. In other words, teachers have at their disposal the circumstances in which they can teach for understanding through dialogue, their most potent strategy.

THE ROLE OF PEDAGOGY IN EFFECTIVE TEACHING

Increasingly, U.S. public school students come from homes where language and culture may differ from the mainstream American experience, particularly the experience of the majority of those who teach them. This enormous change in the demographics of classrooms has outpaced every resource for preparing teachers. The five pedagogy standards facilitate teachers in assisting diverse and struggling students in instructional activity and in communication with their peers and their teacher.

Increasing interaction and activity in classrooms requires teachers to coordinate the components of their teaching. The five standards and their indicators provide guidance for teacher planning, relating, managing, designing, implementing, motivating, assisting, and assessing. The skills needed to implement five-standards teaching are not unique but they are powerful when they are polished and applied systematically. The following examples describe the role of pedagogy in teaching. Several classroom teaching models—transmission teaching, content-driven teaching, and performance-based teaching in a five-pedagogy-standards classroom—demonstrate pedagogy's evolving role in supporting teaching. The features of teaching and pedagogy in each example are identified and discussed.

Transmission Teaching

The transmission, or cemetery, model of teaching, which has been used continuously since before the twentieth century, has proponents and practitioners who keep it active today. The universal notion that teaching delivers knowledge intact to receptive minds is deeply rooted in tradition. Because over the centuries many talented students have succeeded within this model, its shortcomings for addressing all students' needs have been overlooked. Even when class sizes swelled during the twentieth century, the model was highly regarded because it was considered efficient for learning and low in per-pupil costs.

Do I Hear Talking?

It is fall. The twenty-eight third grade students in desks lined up in rows listen to and look at their teacher, Mrs. Daly, who is asking if there are questions about borrowing in subtraction. She has completed her problem demonstration on the board. With no questions asked, she assigns the students practice worksheets to complete at their desks. Not long after, some students look over at one another's papers. Mrs. Daly has returned to her desk in the front corner, where a student quietly waits. Students begin whispering across the aisles. Mrs. Daly looks up, rings a little bell, and asks, "Do I hear talking?" This brings startled quiet. She continues, "I asked for your questions during the lesson. If I hear more chatter, the entire class will miss recess. I was warned about your distractibility." The students return to their worksheets.

Mrs. Daly soon dismisses the student at her desk and sends him back to his seat, where he is admonished in front of the class to try harder even though he "is not the only one here who needs to listen better." Before accepting the assignment to this class, Mrs. Daly had heard it was a handful, but she knows how to handle that. She announces that she must go to the office for a few minutes. As soon as she leaves the room, several students begin to frolic, bumping desks out of alignment. Two students skip out of the room. The levity stops abruptly as the students from the hallway announce Mrs. Daly's imminent return. Silence is resumed, but furniture disarray gives away the students' antics. Mrs. Daly demands order and the furniture is noisily but quickly replaced. She circulates to check recent entries on students' worksheets. She observes little evidence of progress. Gloom sets in as Mrs. Daly barks that there will be no recess today because they already took it while she was out of the room. She collects the worksheets and marches to the board to demonstrate another borrowing problem. No one asks any questions. She assigns another practice worksheet to be completed within ten minutes. She sets her timer.

Mrs. Daly's students receive information in large-group and teacher-dominated discussion. The classroom is organized to support the orderly transfer of knowledge directly to students, which requires their quiet attention, accessibility, and undiluted effort. The large group of silent, passive students works quietly and separately on identical tasks at their own desks set in a cemetery pattern of rows and columns. The teacher controls the topic, task, talk, and turns of all the students. The teacher monitors students, judges them, and assigns more tasks until a preselected amount of knowledge is transmitted. After a limited number of sessions are devoted to teaching a topic, the students are assessed and graded. Those who require more explanation or repetition and are reticent to ask questions in front of their peers fail, are deemed "slow," or are told they just "didn't listen."

The teaching and pedagogy features of Mrs. Daly's classroom teaching model are as follows:

Teaching	Pedagogy
Curriculum driven	Teacher-controlled interaction and activity
Individual level of learning	Isolated tasks
Anecdotally driven instructional decisions	Whole-group organization
Varied learning outcomes	Individual- and curriculum-based tasks
	One size fits all
	Monotasking: single-session opportunity to learn

In Mrs. Daly's classroom, students' energy seeped into any crack it could find. Students gave one another answers on the worksheets and performed antics when she left the room. The openings to participate that Mrs. Daly provided were unused by the students. One brave student was desperate for help, but his approach to the teacher's desk resulted in criticism. The student energy that is suppressed in this model is lost as a resource for learning. Even though the transmission model works for some students, its capacity to meet all students' needs is unrealized.

Content-Driven Teaching

In international comparisons of classroom teaching and standardized test results in core subjects such as science and mathematics across industrialized nations, U.S. students have demonstrated mixed results. One of three international assessments that measure aspects of mathematical skills, the Trends in International

Mathematics and Science Study (TIMSS) assesses fourth and eighth grade students' mathematics and science knowledge and skills. It was administered in grades four and eight in 1995 and 2003, and in grade eight in 1999. Across that period, U.S. fourth graders' assessment results were stable. They showed no measurable change, which means the students fell behind the scores of improving students in several other countries. Partly as a result of these findings, requirements for content expertise in core subjects increased for U.S. teachers, and teaching and pedagogy skills were not addressed, although teacher-preparation "methods" courses that offered training in such skills were no longer considered necessary. Such policy mandated that all instruction in content be performed by content-expert teachers. This mandate produced the content-committed teaching model.

"What Is a Vector Anyway?"

It is spring. In an eighth grade classroom, the teacher, Mr. Kanter, can be heard in the hallway delivering a science lesson on vectors. Mr. Kanter pauses to say, "If you aren't paying attention to this information, you will not know it for the test." The threat reduces the noise level slightly, although several students continue to whisper together. The rest of the students are sitting in their seats, lackadaisically looking up at the teacher. They write and draw on materials at their desks, and noisily crumple papers to throw at the wastebasket. One student gets up to use the pencil sharpener. Another says he's leaving to go to the bathroom. Mr. Kanter slumps against the chalkboard at the front of the room. He picks up a marker, takes a deep breath, and continues:

"Let's talk about this first for a minute. Here's what a vector is. Listen. The first thing is, what is a vector anyway? It's a force in a direction, a specific direction. This is how you represent a vector when you're drawing it. [Draws lines on board.] If you're going to do this with the mathematics, you draw it with a dot, a line, and an arrow. That means there's this much force in this direction: 9.8 meters per second squared. This is the number for acceleration for gravity. If something is falling, gravity is pulling it 9.8 meters per second squared towards the center of the earth. That's the rate at sea level. If you go closer to the center of the earth, it's going to make a difference. If you go farther away, it's going to make a difference. The mass of the object you're talking about is how you adjust the gravitational pull. Gravity is pulling this block in this straight down at that rate [holding a block]. By changing those angles around, what we do is shift the direction of the vector, so the resultant vector comes back toward your finger instead of straight down. When you look at it, it doesn't look right. It looks like it should fall."

Mr. Kanter hands out worksheets on vectors. He tells the students that every student must complete the worksheet in the next twenty minutes or receive a zero. He returns to his desk in the back of the room. The students begin to read and write on the worksheets. They whisper and try to see others' papers, or they quietly bow their heads over their worksheets. When the bell rings they jump out of their desks to hand in their papers and race from the room.

Mr. Kanter's content-driven teaching is barely distinguishable from transmission teaching, except that he has content knowledge and the requisite degree. Content-driven teaching offers students new knowledge, usually textbook supported and logically presented. Mr. Kanter did not indicate that he based his content on data or individual students' needs. What makes sense to the teacher is assumed to compel the learner to understand, but students may not be able to assemble and connect on their own what they know, or follow the teacher's logic to new understanding. Mr. Kanter's teaching displays the following features of teaching and pedagogy:

Teaching	Pedagogy
Individual- and psychological-level model	Isolated tasks
Curriculum based	Whole-group instruction
Learning outcomes vary	Teacher controls talk and action
	Tasks are individual and curriculum based
	Abstract
	One size fits all
	Monotasking: single-session opportunity to learn

Without pedagogy that prepares students for new material through a variety of interactive and practical experiences with peers and teacher, few students can fully grasp new and abstract notions. Learning outcomes vary extremely and include failure. Without pedagogy that identifies and activates students in their learning zones, teachers cast about haphazardly for teaching moments and accept blank stares and silence as indicators of new knowledge gains.

Default Pedagogy

To understand pedagogy and its role in supporting teaching it is useful to examine its developmental stages as well as its full implementation. Teachers' instincts to use new approaches are praiseworthy and very brave when they respond to real student needs. Some teachers want to respond immediately by changing their approach in a single session rather than gradually introducing new activities and arrangements. Pedagogy is best understood and implemented as a system rather than as an alternative to employ occasionally. Because it is not uncommon for teachers to try new methods occasionally, even spontaneously, the following example is informative.

Seventh Graders Request Interactive Learning

It is October. In an inner-city seventh grade classroom, students argued about who was next to read aloud from the textbook. The new teacher, Ms. Tix, intervened and selected a student, who proceeded to read in a halting and unsure manner. The students fidgeted. They looked around and not at the text. Then one girl blurted out, "Can we have more discussions? That's what I want. I'm tired of listening to others read." Another said, "Can I have other work to do on my own?" Ms. Tix valued the rapport she had developed with her students and wanted to nurture it. By responding to the student's request for discussions, she hoped to invigorate the lesson and demonstrate her willingness to work with the students. She had already planned to follow up the reading with a debate assignment. This way she would just have them do it a day sooner.

She asked the students to break into groups of five to prepare debates on the topic of their reading. The students eagerly moved around the room, talking, joining, or being rejected by a group and dragging chairs noisily. After they had finally formed several groups, the teacher reminded the students to talk about their debate topic. They initially complied, but their talk gradually veered off, group by group, into nondebate topics, with increasingly louder exchanges that distracted and attracted others. After several other reminders did not return the students to the task, the teacher ordered everyone to return to their own desks.

The bell rang before Ms. Tix could review the experience with the class. The students ran out of the classroom into the hallway to continue the conversations they had begun in their small groups.

In this example, Ms. Tix seized an opportunity offered by her students to reorganize activity spontaneously. She imagined there was an advantage in doing so—that the lesson would be reenergized and expand to include discussion goals. As every teacher eventually learns, even a small change in classroom procedures has an enormous effect on students and on the learning environment of the classroom. As a result, impromptu or impulsive attempts to implement pedagogy are typically avoided.

Ms. Tix was intent on succeeding with her students, although she did not recognize that the model she used was teacher directed. When Ms. Tix changed the social organization of the classroom, she shifted it not only from teacher directed to student centered, but also from an individual-psychological level of teaching to a social-interactive level. At the social-interactive level, student interaction and activity increase enormously. Because Ms. Tix permitted an impromptu shift into a new model of teaching, she did not prepare her students for their roles and responsibilities, nor did she anticipate the social arrangements that were required to form the small groups. As a result, neither teacher nor students knew how to negotiate the social forces in a classroom that was no longer teacher directed.

When changes in teaching are attempted, even pedagogy intended to improve the learning situation can have the opposite effect. Like successful pedagogy, failed pedagogy is powerful, often loud, and always overwhelming for teachers. The dismaying effects of failed pedagogy drive most teachers to default abruptly to their previous model of teaching. Many never again stray from the stale comfort of traditional teacher-driven models.

Ms. Tix was completely surprised to discover that she was unable to guide the students to resume substantive discussion in their small groups. After the shift away from the teacher-directed, whole-group setting, she was unable to guide any part of the activity. In fact, she lost control of her class. Even the furniture in the room, which was also unsuited to support a multitasking classroom, contributed to the breakdown. Teaching at the social-interactive level succeeds in multitasking classrooms where teachers implement the five pedagogy standards as a system that guides learning through activity and interaction.

The differences between the teacher-directed model and the student-assisted model of learning are as follows:

	Teacher-Directed Performance	Student-Assisted Performance
Teaching	Individual-psychological	Interactive-social-community
	Curriculum based	Language and activity based
	Outcomes vary	Outcomes produced
Pedagogy	Lecture	Conversation
	Whole group	Small group
	Monotasking (single session)	Multitasking (multiple simultaneous sessions)

Dialogue Teaching

It is advantageous for teachers to hold conversations on academic topics with students in small groups. Most students engage in verbal exchanges several times in such a setting—far more than would be possible in a large group. In addition, students who would not participate in a large group may do so in a small-group setting. The teacher has the opportunity to probe students' rationales and to examine details and conceptual content of the material in relation to a lesson goal. The following example is a teacher-led discussion about planets with a small group of third grade students.

Third Grade Planet Dialogue

Ms. Macon: Planets, we know we have planets. What kind of planets do we have? We have two groups. We're writing about them in our essays.

James: Big planets, little planets.

Ms. Macon: No.

Avery:	Inner planets and outer planets.
Ms. Macon:	What are the inner planets?
Barbara:	They're closest to the sun.
Ms. Macon:	Let's try to put them in order.
Barbara:	Mercury.
Don:	Venus.
Avery:	Earth.
James:	Mars.
Ms. Macon:	Now we're going to go to the outer planets.
James:	Jupiter.
Barbara:	Saturn.
Don:	Uranus.
Avery:	Neptune.
James:	Pluto.
Ms. Macon:	OK, what else is in the solar system that you know?
James:	Meteorites.
Ms. Macon:	Good, meteors.
Barbara:	And comets.
Ms. Macon:	What else is in the solar system?
Avery:	The sun.
Don:	Without it we would be dead.
Barbara:	What would we do without the sun?
Ms. Macon:	What would we do without the sun?
Avery:	We'd be freezing.
Don:	We'd be a block of ice.
Ms. Macon:	We'd be a block of ice. And if we didn't have the sun, we wouldn't have the gravity to keep us in our—?
Barbara:	Orbit.
Avery:	It would always be dark and we couldn't see anything and the sun couldn't control any of us.
Ms. Macon:	Right. Now there's one thing you haven't thought about that affects us quite a bit, and other planets.
Don:	Inner cores.
Ms. Macon:	No.
Barbara:	Moons.
Ms. Macon:	Moons. Now, do all planets have moons?

Avery
[looking in
text book]:   Venus has no moons; Earth has a moon; Mars has moons; Jupiter, Saturn, Uranus, Neptune, and Pluto have moons.

Ms. Macon, unlike Ms. Tix, has developed the classroom organization skills needed to hold a small-group dialogue. The rest of the students were engaged in other activities while she dialoged with this small group. Because she had a manageable format, she involved all of the students in the conversation. She had the students review the facts of the planets' inner and outer placement. The students responded to their teacher's closed questions about the order of the planets. Ms. Macon's "No" response to a student's answer to the first question missed a language development opportunity. Later, in an instance of responsiveness, when she repeated a student's question, "What would we do without the sun?" what appeared to be an open-ended question meant to elicit students' knowledge of the topic rapidly became a search for a particular answer. When the answer did not come within two students' comments, Ms. Macon provided an oral cloze to prompt the answer she wanted. She barely responded to the next student's comment about the sun, then informed the students that they had missed something. To the first student to suggest a thought she replied no, meaning that he had not identified the answer she wanted. It is not clear whether Ms. Macon purposefully inserted the moon into the conversation or used it spontaneously. The instructional conversation's last statement was directly from the students' textbook, so its content was accurate.

Although Ms. Macon's goals for the dialogue were highly content focused, the social-interactive level of the dialogue shifted her teaching across the continuum into a transformative model. Her teaching was inclusive, but she used few opportunities in the dialogue to raise the level of the conversation by exploring students' thinking and understanding. This suggests that she was inexperienced in dialoging with students and was still developing her skills.

The following list summarizes the features of teaching and pedagogy that are present in the dialogue lesson:

Teaching	*Teacher-Directed Performance*	*Student-Assisted Performance*
	Individual-psychological	Interactive-social-community
	Ability- and IQ-based expectations	Standards-based expectations

(Continued)

Pedagogy	Curriculum based	Language and activity based
	Outcomes vary	Outcomes produced
	Transmission Model	*Student-Assisted Model*
	Lecture	Conversation
	Whole group	Small group
	Monotasking (single session)	Multitasking (multiple sessions)

With the addition of ability and IQ expectations that characterize teacher-directed performance, and of standards-based expectations that characterize student-assisted performance, the list of teaching and pedagogy features is completed. Finally, the addition of standards-based expectations is associated with content learning, which is observable in dialogue teaching. The teaching performance using dialogue with a small group of students, supported by pedagogy, provides an instance of teaching in the transformative model. The teacher achieved the learning outcomes in that all of the planets were correctly identified.

These models of teaching and roles of pedagogy make it clear that movement from one model and level of teaching to another requires planning and skills in pedagogy. Once the transition to a social-interactive level has been made, teachers find opportunities to assist students face-to-face in their learning zones. Teachers thus have occasion to interact on academic topics in ways that are not available in large-group and other teaching models.

In teacher preparation, pedagogy that complements and strengthens teaching is sometimes explained as coming from trial and error or, in other words, from on-the-job training. Although there is some evidence that teachers are more effective after five years of experience, it is misleading and simplistic to assume that teachers' skills in pedagogy or in teaching will spontaneously improve over time. Just as students must be taught concepts if they are expected to learn them, teachers must deliberately acquire skills that will enable them to succeed and that are based on what is now known about how students learn.

Performance-Based Teaching in the Five-Pedagogy-Standards Classroom

The five pedagogy standards introduced in this book provide a concise framework of guidance on *how* to teach, in contrast to state-mandated content standards and curricula that guide *what* is taught. These standards offer reliable methods for facilitating teaching that accesses, assists, and accomplishes knowledge development in students' learning zones. Teachers can use the five-standards pedagogy to prepare students to receive teaching assistance. This pedagogy uses numerous activities and practice sessions to introduce students to various learning concepts and skills. Then, when teachers turn to assisting students in actual content learning, the students will be sufficiently experienced and familiar with the material to expand their content knowledge.

Assisted Teaching Model for Fifth Grade Students

It is spring. Mr. Yode discusses a story with his small group of fifth grade students at a table in the front of the room. He refers to a chart where he has listed students' comments about the story's setting and structure. When the students return to reading for more information, Mr. Yode looks up to monitor the rest of the class. The other twenty-nine students are talking and sharing work at activity settings placed around the room. Languages other than English can be heard along with laughter. The five students in the stock market area use the newspaper to track, record, and compute the progress of their portfolios. In the library area, students read alone or with peers. Mr. Yode glances over to the science work area, where six students are planting seeds. He compliments them on making progress on their planting, and makes a note to check on their cleanup when he rings the bell for activity change. He scans other work areas where students are writing in journals, working on vocabulary development, playing games, and using the computers for content research, writing, editing, and stock market updates. Mr. Yode compliments the students on their work focus. He reminds them to be ready to travel to their next scheduled activity setting in ten minutes. He turns back to his small group and resumes the story discussion and the chart of their progress.

In Mr. Yode's classroom, teaching assistance to support learning occurs in many forms, at different levels, and in multiple locations. At thirty-five students, Mr. Yode's class is large, but he finds that having that many students increases his opportunities to assist. His students also enjoy assisting one another. His management is embedded in the activities and routines of the classroom community he has developed. Mr. Yode gradually introduced each of the activities described by involving his students in the planning and design. He explained and modeled or had students model how to approach and perform every activity. He found that his teaching was effective when he used the following pedagogy structures:

- *Multitasking,* which increases students' language and literacy practice with peers and teaching through dialogue
- *Routines,* which guide students through predictable sequences of activity
- *Activities,* which embed skill development within conceptual challenges
- *Work products,* which require knowledge application
- *Joint products,* which develop common understandings
- *Grouping,* which provides peer assistance for accomplishing academic tasks
- *Independent activities,* which ensure that students succeed across all content areas
- *Collaborative activities,* which involve the teacher in working with all students

Mr. Yode has developed his classroom to be a community of learners who view the classroom as their joint product. This community is an enjoyable experience, with students interacting; problem solving; and performing compelling hands-on activities, including those they design themselves or that their parents request and design. Throughout his years of experience, Mr. Yode has developed many joint products as well as other types of activities. Other activities have been created by his colleagues, some are commercial, and some are student generated. His criteria for activities have been that they must be compelling, language developing, and conceptual.

THE TRANSFORMATIVE TEACHING MODEL

The five pedagogy standards, when fully implemented, support effective teaching for academic outcomes. Mr. Yode's pedagogy supported his classroom's high activity and interaction levels and academic productivity. Using the five pedagogy standards, he developed the multitasking classroom that he prefers and that his students enjoy for the outcomes they can produce. In contrast, Ms. Tix was unable to finish her lesson because she lacked a pedagogy to support the social-interactive level of learning. Conversely, the third grade dialogue on planets reflected the teacher's considerable skill in organizing the students for an uninterrupted instructional conversation.

Mr. Yode assists students' performance through interaction with them, and students assist one another in the socially organized classroom. Mr. Yode's high expectations are standards based and embedded in discussion and multiple tasks and activities. He meets with students in small groups to assist their understanding, to discuss their work products, and to provide corrective feedback. He teaches within a system, which means he uses predictable routines and organizational formats to increase his face-to-face contact with students and to provide compelling activities that meet students' specific needs.

THE PEDAGOGY STANDARDS AND CLASSROOM IMPLEMENTATION INDICATORS

The five pedagogy standards express a consensus about common learning needs across all student populations. Because the five pedagogy standards are deeply rooted in human psychological and social processes, they can be applied in any classroom or learning situation to strengthen teaching and its effects on students' achievement. When the standards are enacted systematically by different teachers in different schools and different communities, their implementation may appear quite different on the surface. The similarities among the different systems are located in the standards' foundation in capacities that are known to underlie learning. The five pedagogy standards and their indicators can guide teachers to increase the power of their teaching to facilitate students' learning by implementing a system based on them.

The pedagogy standards are implemented through their indicators, which are based on effective practice. The indicators are valuable as benchmarks for enacting each standard. It is not, however, the presence or absence of specific indicators that defines quality pedagogy, but how the indicators are implemented to achieve an outcome. Specific pedagogy strategies and activities vary from one content area and particular situation to another, but all indicator implementations share the goal of aligning teaching practices with the broad statements of the standards.

In the following chapters, the pedagogy standards are discussed in numerical order, which reflects the logic of their sequential application. Although this order—especially beginning with the foundational guidance of the first pedagogy standard—is strongly recommended, the power of the individual standards does not require any particular sequence of implementation. However, the effects on student achievement are produced by fully adopting and systematically implementing the pedagogy standards in the context of daily teaching. A complete list of the standards and their indicators, in the recommended order, is presented in Appendix 1A.

Teaching must be redefined as assisted performance. Teaching consists in assisting performance. Teaching is occurring when performance is achieved with assistance.

(Tharp and Gallimore, 1988, p. 21)

Evidence: Scientific Support for Five Standards

This chapter discusses the theoretical and research foundations of teaching and pedagogy. Pedagogy is recognized as important to effective classroom teaching. Research on pedagogy is a relatively recent focus, but findings are accumulating. Progressively more evidence is available to inform teachers about the roles, interactions, and effects of teaching that are supported by pedagogy.

RESEARCH ON TEACHING

Concerns are rising from the literature about the ability of U.S. students to perform academically at levels necessary to meet the personal and national demands of the twenty-first century. Descriptive studies (Borko, Brown, Underhill, Jones, and Agard, 1992; McDiarmid and Wilson, 1991) have found mathematics teachers with a good grasp of the subject unable to make mathematical principles, rules, and concepts clear to their students. Furthermore, these teachers did not increase their proficiency as they continued to teach. In the Trends in International Mathematics and Science Study (TIMSS), U.S. teaching appears to lack key features used by teachers in other industrialized countries' classrooms (Hiebert and TIMSS, 2003). These and other findings about teaching and its effects on student achievement have increased interest in the qualities of teaching associated with student learning.

Research reports on teaching reveal a wide variety of ways in which teachers promote students' learning. Significant questions are asked about the most effective approaches and methods. The research supports the need for teachers to have strong content knowledge in the area of their teaching assignment (Wilson and Peterson, 2006; Allen, 2003). Yet findings vary about how much content proficiency is necessary to teach at various grade levels. The evidence suggests that an academic major may not be essential, and that beyond a certain undefined point, additional coursework is of small value (Goldhaber and Brewer, 2000; Rowan, Correnti, and Miller, 2002). There is agreement that teachers must be as competent as possible the moment they step into the classroom (Allen, 2003).

RESEARCH ON PEDAGOGY

Research variously defines pedagogy as centered on the art, practice, or profession of teaching, especially systematized learning or instruction concerned with principles and methods of teaching. Pedagogy, like the teaching it supports, is a relatively new and growing topic of scholarly study (Bransford, Brown, and Cocking, 2000). With such a slim literature, findings about pedagogy are often associated with studies on student learning, teacher learning and development, teaching, human development, linguistics, community studies, anthropology, and other areas of knowledge. In general, the research findings support pedagogy's relationship to student learning; that is, they support the idea of preparing teachers pedagogically in order to complement their content knowledge rather than only increasing that knowledge.

Research reports on the effect of pedagogically prepared teachers on student achievement vary from findings of a strong effect (Darling-Hammond, Berry, and Thoreson, 2001) to being dependent on teaching assignments (Chaney, 1995) to no effect (Goldhaber and Brewer, 2000). These findings offer limited support for preparing teachers in pedagogy, but they validate pedagogy as important in the study of effective teaching (Allen, 2003). On the whole, research evidence supports the complementary roles of pedagogy and content knowledge in effective teaching. A focus on how teachers are to acquire strong pedagogical skills has replaced concern about pedagogy's value to teaching and student achievement (Dalton, 2002; Tharp, Estrada, Dalton, and Yamauchi, 2000; Dalton and Moir, 1996).

The pedagogy system described in this book—the five pedagogy standards—draws on what is known about human intellectual development and learning to increase the impact of content teaching on students' academic attainment (Tharp, Estrada, Dalton, and Yamauchi, 2000). Teachers use the standards to strengthen classroom teaching—at any grade level, in any class size—that assists student learning on the basis of theory and research. There is a high degree of consensus about the standards, and there is evidence of effective use from preschool through grade twelve, including in highly diverse settings with at-risk students (Doherty, Hilberg, Pinal, and Tharp, 2003; Dalton and Tharp, 2002; Rivera, Galarza, Entz, and Tharp, 2002; Tharp, Estrada, Dalton, and Yamauchi, 2000; Dalton, 1998; Dalton and Youpa, 1998). This chapter discusses the standards' foundation in evidence, consensus, and effective practice.

The Five Pedagogy Standards

Standard I: Teacher and Students Producing Together Facilitate learning through joint productive activity among teacher and students using multiple classroom settings and student groupings.

Standard II: Developing Language and Literacy Develop competence in the language and literacy of instruction across the curriculum.

Standard III: Connecting School to Students' Lives Connect teaching and curriculum to students' experiences at home and in the community.

Standard IV: Teaching Complex Thinking Challenges students to think at increasingly complex levels.

Standard V: Teaching Through Conversation Engage students in dialogue, especially instructional conversation (IC).

PEDAGOGY THEORY

In the past, the predominant notion of teaching held that knowledge was conveyed directly from the teacher to the learner, with occasional assistance. Students were expected not to develop habits of mind and learning skills in the classroom but to already have them. Students were considered individual targets for learning, and their successes and failures reflected their particular attributes, talents, and efforts. In contrast, a contemporary view emphasizes that students' understandings are developed by participating in activities aimed at accomplishing joint goals. Individual attributes remain important, but this perspective also emphasizes the ways in which students' attributes play out in interaction and activity with others in a community of learners (Boaler, 1999; Tharp and Gallimore, 1988; Wells, 2000).

In a learning community, elementary and middle school students are encouraged to have a sense of ownership of and responsibility for the community and for the products and knowledge they develop within it. The aim is for students to develop reflection skills that inform the values they express, and critical thinking about the ways they apply those skills (Tharp, Estrada, Dalton, and Yamauchi, 2000). The complex level of critical thinking that informs literacy, technological, and other competencies characterizes self-directed learners who can both guide and learn from others in the community (Blumenfeld, Krajcik, Marx, and Soloway, 2001).

HOME AND COMMUNITY PEDAGOGY

Parents and competent others model and explain how to solve innumerable daily and practical challenges, even to the youngest children. Research shows that parents who talk to children beginning in infancy make a difference not only in their children's language development but also in their thinking. The consequences for children who are deprived of such early social experience are now known to be intellectual limitations regardless of their ability (Hart and Risley, 1995; Tharp and Gallimore, 1988; Vygotsky, 1978).

From kindergarten through third grade, when U.S. curricula are focused more on basic skill development than on conceptual challenges, students are nevertheless taught to use higher order thinking (Coley and Coleman, 2004). Studies have shown that throughout the world, youngsters and novices assume roles at the edge of society's activities and gradually advance through observation, modeling, and guided participation to assume higher competence (Tharp and others, 2001; Rogoff, 1990). Learners participate at the level of culture, community, home, peers, or individually when activity is interesting and important. Across the globe, youngsters acquire complicated skill sets for use in religious ceremonies, in producing crafts, in performing native and folk dancing, in utilizing the latest technology, and in communicating with peers, among other functions. For example, traditional cultures continue to convey their knowledge and value systems through forms of assistance in activities that support complex skill development and reflection beginning in early childhood.

Ancient Dances in Native American Tribal Religious Practice

The Zuni Pueblo in New Mexico continue to practice their traditional rituals, which include ancient dances performed by elaborately costumed male dancers of all ages, including very young boys. The entire community supports the ritual and the participants' extensive spiritual, mental, and physical preparation for the dances. Novice participants acquire skill in the dance and knowledge of its meaning from experienced dancers, while learning the community's beliefs, values, and norms [Dalton and Youpa, 1998].

Observational Pedagogy
> I am thankful for my mother teaching me to make the large [pottery] pieces. I watched her and tried to do like she did. And I did.

> (Native American potter Margaret Tafoya, 1983, p. 2)

School Pedagogy

Reports about students' learning indicate that students do not automatically transfer what they learn from one situation to another (Wilson and Peterson, 2006; Bransford, Brown, and Cocking, 2000). This finding supports the idea that knowledge is linked to the situation, or context, in which it was acquired. Teachers can use the learning context to affirm and value students' backgrounds and to create common reference points for learning. They can prepare learning experiences in contexts sufficiently robust to provide knowledge that students can use in new situations. Such pedagogy links school, home, and community.

Contextualization Explores Students' Worlds

The sixth grade at Zuni Middle School in New Mexico developed a contextualized unit on an activity the Zuni tribe has performed for centuries: going into the mountains to collect pinon nuts. After nut collection in the field, all of the unit's activities were carried out across content classes: cleaning, roasting, and salting occurred in home life class; measuring, bagging, and pricing occurred in mathematics and science classes; and dialogue, narrative, and expository writing in Zuni and English occurred in language arts classes. The pinon nut project provided common reference points for students to speak, write, think, and reflect. It provided numerous opportunities for students to develop and refine mathematics, science, language, and other skills in activity with practical meaning and application. Students expressed their new understandings about the topic in a variety of products: delicious nuts to sell, compelling advertisements to post, expenses and profits to track, art products to share, and other written descriptions of the experience [Dalton and Youpa, 1998].

Thinking Metacognitive approaches to learning can help increase students' awareness of their knowledge development. Using feedback and heightened awareness, activities designed to help students focus on their learning processes increase their capacity to evaluate and monitor their own learning (Bransford, Brown, and Cocking, 2000; Wilson and Peterson, 2006).

Zone of Proximal Development

Russian theorist Lev Vygotsky (1978) sought to understand how thinking, especially higher-order mental processes, develops. He studied the conditions for learning by observing interactions between adults and children. He described learning as a socially influenced process and provided tools for understanding how thinking develops through acting, saying, thinking, feeling, and connecting. These tools include engaging the learner with content in more complex ways than the learner could experience alone, and providing competent assistance to increase understanding. When these conditions are present, according to Vygotsky, the event occurs within the student's *zone of proximal development* (ZPD), or the learner's route from social to individual understanding (Tharp, Estrada, Dalton, and Yamauchi, 2000; Vygotsky, 1978).

According to Vygotsky (1978), the social context of the individual is worth examining because "any function in the child's cultural development appears twice, or on two planes. First it appears on the social plane, and then on the psychological plane. First it appears between people as an interpsychological category, and then within the child as an intrapsychological category" (p. 163). The ZPD is "the difference between the actual developmental level as determined by independent problem solving and the level of potential development as determined through problem solving under . . . guidance or collaboration with more capable peers" (p. 86).

The ZPD differs from the developmental level where unassisted individual performance is possible. Learning and problem solving do occur at an individual-psychological level when humans are alone. For example, Rogoff (1995) has suggested that the development of human thinking can be examined at three levels: individual-psychological, social-interactional, and community-institutional.

DEFINING TEACHING

Focusing on the ZPD allows us to see where teaching (which is social and interactional) actually occurs. From Vygotsky's analysis, Tharp and Gallimore (1988, p. 31) derived a general definition of teaching: "Teaching consists of assisting performance through the ZPD. Teaching can be said to occur when assistance is offered at points in the [zone] at which performance requires assistance" (italics in original). In this view, teaching *is* assisting.

The five pedagogy standards together provide a framework of support for teachers to offer their students assistance in their ZPD. Dalton (2002) used video-stimulated recall methods and the five pedagogy standards as analytic tools to examine preservice teachers' early classroom teaching practices in their field experiences for evidence that their teaching applied the definition of *assisted performance*. The students' teacher-preparation program taught them the ZPD concept and the definition of teaching as assisted performance, and encouraged the preservice teachers to apply this concept and definition in their interactions with students. In the video-stimulated recall conversations, the preservice teachers interpreted their early teaching efforts, as presented to them in video, in order to develop their teaching to provide assistance in their students' learning zones. Although the preservice teachers reported on the difficult challenges they faced learning to teach in large classes of diverse students, the clear definition of teaching kept them focused and willing to persist until they succeeded.

RESEARCH ON THE FIVE PEDAGOGY STANDARDS

Research on the five pedagogy standards has rigorously examined the application of one or more standards of pedagogy and, more important, the integrated use of all five standards. Although the effects of individual standards need to be explored, classroom implementation of the standards is intended to include all five. The definition of *pedagogy* requires that the standards be applied systematically and together. The effects ascribed to teaching using the five pedagogy standards are strongest with the integrated implementation of all five. The evidence of their joint effectiveness is described in the following studies conducted in elementary classrooms. Studies of the effects of one or more pedagogy standards are also described after the discussion of the individual standards. Anecdotal comments are provided where appropriate.

Pedagogy Standard I: Teachers and Students Working Together

The first standard of the five-standard guidance system for teaching alters the structures of classroom teaching to produce a new architecture that reflects what is now known about teaching that leads to learning (Tharp, Estrada, Dalton, and Yamauchi, 2000; Resnick, 1995; Dalton, 1998). This standard emphasizes the critical association of activity, conversation, and joint participation in developing thinking and the language for expressing it (National Reading Panel, 2000; Tharp and Gallimore, 1988; Vygotsky, 1978). Theorists have explained that when experts and novices work together for a common product or goal and have opportunities to converse about the activity, learning is a likely outcome (Rogoff, 1990; Tharp and Gallimore, 1988; Wertsch, 1985). The presence of an expert participant provides assistance that raises students' participation to more competent levels. Without an expert "other" to assist activity, understanding is less likely to increase (Vygotsky, 1978).

Community   Using a wide variety of activities, teachers can guide a class of students to form a community of learners. Activity characterized by collaboration and outcome, particularly tangible, goal-oriented products, has the power to develop a sense of community among its participants. It is within such communities that norms and values emerge for working together and assessing work (Kirschner and Wopereis, 2003; Tharp, Estrada, Dalton, and Yamauchi, 2000; Lave and Wenger, 1991). When the teacher and the students make the community's shared values explicit, those values can serve as the guidelines for students' participation and performance in instructional activity.

Activity   Activity is central to new understandings of learning. It stimulates students' learning processes that use everyday and prior knowledge to acquire new understanding. Powerful activity engages students' learning processes to reconcile discrepancies between prior knowledge and new information. Students' individual knowledge may include misconceptions and beliefs that can interfere with the learning process (Wang and Wahlberg, 2001). When these discrepancies are large, more activity and assistance may be required to reduce the gap between what students know and what they need to understand. Teachers can design activity to assess and address such gaps and misconceptions in students' everyday understandings. The design of instructional activity must be informed by students' prior knowledge in order to nurture budding understandings and instruct or correct misconceptions.

Activity designs come in an array of formats, including hands-on tasks, problem solving, pencil and paper activities, information communications technology (ICT), joint productive activity (JPA), student-generated activity (SGA) and parent-generated activity (PGA), games, and other varieties (Tharp, Estrada, Dalton, and Yamauchi, 2000; Dalton and Youpa, 1998; Dalton and Cramer, 1985). As media and ICT become increasingly present in students' lives, their application in the classroom will increase. Like any activity, media and ICT are tools for learning when they stimulate students in their learning zones to help them grasp new understandings.

Joint Productive Activity   JPA is collaborative activity. It requires a joint product and includes an assister—the teacher or a competent other, such as a peer.

Student-Generated Activity   Students design SGAs for their classmates, and sometimes parents and grandparents develop activities for use in the classroom. SGA involves students in creating and developing for their peers consumable tasks based on topics and skills that the class is presently studying or has studied in the past. The teacher and students together develop SGA guidelines that must be met before an SGA can be used by the class. By developing and engaging in SGAs, students expand their participation in the classroom community.

In developing an SGA, a student selects a task, decides how it should be performed, and provides a way to evaluate the task. SGAs range from games for building vocabulary, such as crossword puzzles and word finds, to projects on content-related topics, such as mapmaking, scavenger hunts, crafts, and recipes (Dalton and Cramer, 1988; Dalton and Youpa, 1998).

Grouping   Teachers and researchers report that classrooms with an approximately thirty-to-one ratio of students to teacher rarely support extended dialogue among teacher and students without arranging students into small, manageable discussion groups. The large group is less conducive to dialogue because few students are comfortable speaking in front of all of their peers at once, few have the language proficiency to do so, and few are willing to listen for long to those who are competent to interact with the teacher in front of the class. As a result, large-group discussions are often less productive and may result in management problems for those who do not participate (Cohen, 1994; Bransford, Brown, and Cocking, 2000; Tharp and Gallimore, 1988; Vygotsky, 1978). A National Assessment of Educational Progress (NAEP) data report on fourth grade classrooms stated that about one-third of fourth grade teachers used student groups for reading and about one-third did not use groups (Coley and Coleman, 2004). Activities often occurred with the whole class, and only a few of these activities included students and teacher working productively toward a specific goal. Teachers have difficulty focusing the entire group on a particular goal when the range of students' learning and social needs is wide. Finn, Pannozzo, and Achilles (2003) found that teachers of small classes offer higher-quality instruction than teachers of large classes, due mostly to the reduced range of needs that comes with fewer students.

Classroom Organization   Pedagogy supports teaching throughout the school day through classroom activities and task performances that engage students in learning opportunities with the teacher and with peers. The schedule required to operate the classroom system provides students with a predictable activity pattern that fits both the rhythm of individuals and the demands of the tasks (Dalton, 1998; Tharp, Estrada, Dalton, and Yamauchi, 2000).

Pedagogy suggests arrangements for students and teacher to get together for activity and dialogue in order to increase opportunities for teachers to assist students in their ZPDs. This unit of social activity in classrooms "in which collaborative interaction and assisted performance occur" is referred to as an *activity setting* (AS) (Tharp and Gallimore, 1988, p. 72; Tharp, Estrada, Dalton, and Yamauchi, 2000). Activity settings constitute the structure of the classroom community and are essential for academic learning and values development (Tharp and Gallimore, 1988; Tharp, Estrada, Dalton, and Yamauchi, 2000).

In a study of teachers who used the five pedagogy standards in classroom organization, a four-group taxonomy of high and low pedagogy use and whole class versus activity settings was produced. The findings showed that students of teachers who used the standards and the activity settings in their classroom organization had significantly greater achievement gains than students in the comparison groups on all Stanford Achievement Test, Ninth Edition (SAT-9) tests. In fact, students whose teachers had transformed both their pedagogy and their classroom organization were the only group to evidence achievement gains; students in all other groups evidenced declines in achievement from the prior year (Doherty, Hilberg, Pinal, and Tharp, 2003).

Multitasking Classrooms organized in single sessions with students performing lock-step activity are yielding to settings that offer a variety of activities simultaneously (Dalton, 1998; Tharp, Estrada, Dalton, and Yamauchi, 2000). Many students' real-world experiences of ICT and, at the least, media, cell phones, and digital cameras contrast with not only the resources but also the pace of ordinary classrooms. Significantly, students are functioning successfully in their worlds amid a plethora of simultaneous activities. Teachers can replicate students' real-world activity settings in the classroom through multitasking, which means organizing multiple activities to occur in a single unit of time. In other words, the teacher can guide students to work on multiple activities at various settings inside (and outside, when needed) the classroom, with and without direct supervision. Multitasking is a classroom organization pattern to increase time for teaching and skill practice (Dalton, 1998; Tharp, Estrada, Dalton, and Yamauchi, 2000).

An NAEP study of fourth grade classrooms reported how much time was spent on reading instruction (Coley and Coleman, 2004). The largest group of students, 39 percent, received sixty to ninety minutes of reading instruction per day. Teachers of 11 percent of the students reported spending more than ninety minutes per day on reading instruction. Less than 40 percent of the students studied did not receive daily reading instruction, and slightly more than a tenth of these fourth graders received such instruction for more than an hour and a half per day. Students who are still learning to decode or to acquire basic mathematics skills are usually left behind when curriculum resources no longer target their learning challenges. Organizing the classroom for multitasking provides time and space for simultaneous activities that can increase basic skill practice time within a common format for those who need it. Multitasking maximizes classroom time, increases practice opportunities at every level, and establishes a schedule for work to match the rhythms of students' worlds (Dalton, 1998; Tharp, Estrada, Dalton, and Yamauchi, 2000).

Management Teachers observe that students from varying backgrounds and cultural traditions differ in the ways they relate to authority figures, ask and answer questions, analyze text, receive praise, observe activity, work independently and with peers, and offer to perform. As repertoires, these approaches reflect students' cultural practices, which are familiar ways for them to participate. When the students' repertoires differ from those of the teachers and the school, the teachers must decide how to relate and respond to the students in productive ways. Within the values of a classroom community, students can be assisted to understand how to match a repertoire with a situation, and they can be supported to build new approaches on their known repertoires (Gutierrez and Rogoff, 2003).

Doyle (1997) explains management as teachers' competence in guiding complex systems of activity settings and establishing structures, rhythms, and patterns of participation and productivity. When interruptions or irregularities occur, the restoration of order depends on preexisting structures of orderliness. In Doyle's view, management is what teachers do to structure and monitor classroom activity prior to disruptions or misbehavior. The emphasis in classroom management has thus shifted from the individual to the context and social processes in which the individual engages as a member of a classroom community.

Pedagogy Standard II: Developing Language and Literacy

The second pedagogy standard guides teachers to develop students' competence in language and literacy across the curriculum. For kindergarten through grade eight (K–8) teachers, language development is a continual focus. At every grade level, teachers use JPA to work within Vygotsky's ZPD, discussed earlier, to develop word meaning. Teachers implement this standard in order to meet the challenge of providing assistance for all students to speak, read, and write using academic language. Teachers use the first and second pedagogy standards together to provide systematic instruction that nurtures all students' language and literacy development.

Language Diversity   Students contribute a rich variety of languages, dialects, and cultures to the classroom. Dialects are language varieties that, like other languages, have their own structure and logic. Teachers affirm language diversity when they seek to understand students' diverse language usages, such as code switching and style shifting in response to settings, contexts, and audiences (Ladsen-Billings, 2001; Delpit, 1995). Research shows that teachers who misunderstand language differences may mistake students' unfamiliar language expression for lack of effort or ability. This misconception can lead teachers to underestimate students' ability to perform and to lower their expectations for them. Lee (2006) describes robust learning environments that leverage minority students' everyday knowledge into subject-specific understandings, particularly to promote literacy. Research reports on teachers' success cite the value of recognizing and affirming students' languages and dialects and of encouraging their expression in classroom activities (Godley, Sweetland, Wheeler, Minnici, and Carpenter, 2006).

On the basis of research on educating E-Language Learning System (ELLs), Goldenberg (2006) describes effective teaching as featuring clear goals, appropriate routines, activities, and collaboration by teachers who provide feedback and application opportunities. The design, structure, and predictability of teaching are as beneficial for ELLs as they are for their English-speaking peers. The second pedagogy standard implements specific language-development techniques and urges the implementation of routines that assist all students in improving their speaking and thinking proficiency in both everyday and academic language.

Culture and language differences influence the way ELL teachers think about students' prior knowledge, capacity for learning, and willingness to engage. For example, prevalent classroom discourse patterns (ways of asking and answering questions, challenging claims, and using representations and evidence) are often unfamiliar to ELLs and other at-risk students. Teachers tend to reconcile these differences by limiting ELLs to skill-drill exercises that lack context and a problem-solving focus, on the basis of their assumption that basic skills and proficient English must be acquired before problem solving or comprehension occurs (Resnick, 1995). However, when teachers adapt classroom participation to allow students to use familiar forms of conversation such as their own dialect, vocabulary, grammar, and speech preferences, unfamiliar forms such as hand raising and eye contact drop out of use. This adaptation can increase students' comfort and their willingness to engage in ways that lead to learning (Dalton and Youpa, 1998).

Researchers have documented the effectiveness of the second standard when supported by the other four pedagogy standards using the Sheltered Instruction Observational Protocol (SIOP) (Echevarria, Vogt, and Short, 2000). Grounded in two decades of classroom-based research, sheltered instruction is an approach to teaching content to ELLs in strategic ways that make the subject matter concepts comprehensible while promoting students' English language development. SIOP has a strong language and literacy development component, like the second pedagogy standard, and incorporates elements of the other four standards. Studies on the effects of sheltered instruction found that ELLs in middle school classes taught by teachers trained in sheltered instruction outperformed control students in overall gains in expository writing, and improved significantly in all areas measured by a writing rubric: language production, focus, support and elaboration, organization, and mechanics (Echevarria, Short, and Powers, 2002).

Language Development   Hart and Risley's longitudinal study of language development (1995) revealed how students' thinking is manifested in their speech. Students' language ability enables or limits their participation in the learning activities of school. Less language ability means less capacity to be precise in describing experience and expressing meaning. It also means less ability to generalize or form abstractions. Abstract thinking characterizes learning and is important in all learning activity from the earliest experiences of school. As a result, different experiences of language development have major consequences for thinking and learning.

Interest in the most effective approach to teaching vocabulary led the National Reading Panel (NRP) (2000) to examine numerous studies that met their criteria for scientifically based evidence. The panel found that students do learn vocabulary incidentally from reading and from listening to read-alouds, and in some studies computer use was proved to be more effective than traditional methods. The panel found that teaching vocabulary before reading proved helpful, as did replacing difficult words with simple words to assist at-risk students. They also found that intentionally involving students in tasks requiring use of the same word in multiple situations nurtured vocabulary growth.

Reading   The National Research Council (1998) concluded that effective teaching in kindergarten through third grade is critical for preventing reading failure. NRP (2000) reported on approaches to reading instruction based on scientific evidence. It pointed to the need for teachers to have knowledge of pedagogy in order to teach reading and other content, and to be able to use that pedagogy in instruction. For teaching decoding skills, the NRP identified the following effective instructional approaches for beginning readers: phonemic awareness, systematic synthetic phonics, fluency, vocabulary, and comprehension. They also found that guided oral reading benefits all aspects of reading, and independent silent reading has no beneficial effects on reading skill development. ELL students benefit as much as language majority students from the application of the five instructional approaches. Writing instruction and vocabulary development contribute to ELL literacy development, especially as the curriculum increases the vocabulary load and when content knowledge is the instructional goal (Goldenberg, 2006).

To understand what students can do after the first four years of primary school, Coley and Coleman (2004) took a snapshot of fourth grade classrooms based on the 2000 NAEP. Fourth grade teachers were asked about the variety of techniques they used in their reading instruction. The teachers of more than 80 percent of the students in the study reported assigning silent reading on a daily basis. Recent studies have found small or no gains in reading achievement as a result of classroom silent reading (National Reading Panel, 2000). Silent or independent reading precludes teachers from evaluating the rate, accuracy, and rhythm of students' reading, and reduces teachers' opportunities to give constructive feedback to students (Shanahan, 2002).

Other studies report that unless students are held responsible for what they read, they may spend silent and independent reading time on nonreading tasks such as daydreaming or talking with peers. Classroom silent reading has also been found ineffective when students are left to choose reading materials that are relatively easy. Students must be engaged in the zone just above their current ability and be provided with assistance to improve their skills in reading for vocabulary and comprehension (Kuhn and Stahl, 2003; Vygotsky, 1978). Use of independent silent reading depends on students' capacity to read unassisted and even to improve their reading on their own, and most struggling readers do not have the ability to perform either task.

Reading and Writing   In the Coley and Coleman (2004) study, when fourth grade teachers were asked whether their instructional approaches integrated reading and writing, the teachers of 70 percent of the students reported that they did. When asked if writing about literature was a central part of their instructional approach, the teachers of 43 percent of the students reported that it was, and the teachers of 50 percent of the students reported that it was a supplemental approach. However, teachers infrequently reported having students engage in projects about what they had read, and few teachers reported having their students do extended writing or individual or group projects or presentations.

Pedagogy Standard III: Connecting School to Students' Lives
The third pedagogy standard guides teachers to contextualize teaching by connecting it to students' knowledge and experiences of home and community.

Teaching that makes connections between what is known from home and community with what must be learned in school is now considered essential for students to acquire new knowledge (Wong-Fillmore and Snow, 2000; Resnick, 1995). To contextualize means to link students' life experiences, including those related directly to their community or culture, with what is to be learned. When the connections made are powerful, not only is students' understanding made sturdy but it also provides useful insights that can be applied to other problems and situations. Learning must be conceptually robust and applicable in order to meet both school needs and real-world challenges (Resnick, 1995).

Knowledge Development The behavioral model of teaching based on psychological rules has given way to cognitive psychology models that explore how learners make meaning of real experiences. These models have led to new understandings of how humans learn, such as how students attain understanding and what knowledge is (Kandel and Hawkins, 1992). In addition to identifying effects on thinking, neuroscientists have also found that learning changes the physical features of the human brain (Bransford, Brown, and Cocking, 2000). Such research reports that learners, even very young ones, make sense of their experiences of interacting, using text, and the environment to form their understanding.

These findings and others have shifted understanding of how students develop knowledge to the view that they construct meaning out of new information. This view supports an increasingly active and interactive dynamic in classroom teaching that encourages knowledge sharing and promotes construction of new knowledge (Wilson and Peterson, 2006; Bransford, Brown, and Cocking, 2000; Tharp and Gallimore, 1988).

Prior Knowledge In the constructivist view of learning, students may rely heavily on their own knowledge and experience as a basis for constructing new understandings (Bransford, Brown, and Cocking, 2000; Cobb, 1994). Teachers must monitor students' knowledge foundations to identify what may need to be corrected, developed, or expanded. Teachers need to know their students' prior knowledge and its influence on the formation of new understandings when they design instructional activities, especially instructional conversation (Tharp and Gallimore, 1988). In activity and dialogue, both teachers and students examine their knowledge from home, community, and school for its accuracy and contribution to new knowledge construction (Wilson and Peterson, 2006; Bransford, Brown, and Cocking, 2000; Tharp, Estrada, Dalton and Yamauchi, 2000; Dalton and Sison, 1994).

Although differences are an asset to teaching, not all students' differences are knowable. The third pedagogy standard guides teachers to apprehend and mine the resources of experience and knowledge that students and their families bring to the classroom. It is a way to link new information to what is familiar in students' worlds. For example, the use of context aids students in making meaning of new material. Using a familiar topic as the content theme of an organizing activity during the first weeks of school can provide a context that students know and enjoy. It can also allow teachers to begin developing classroom structures that will support the teaching of content standards for the rest of the year. The third pedagogy standard adds a major component to the guidance system that supports teaching, particularly for culturally and linguistically diverse students.

Funds of Knowledge   To anchor academic learning in students' home and life contexts, teachers must see their students as resources for learning. Families in Mexican American households that are networked by blood and subsistence relationships and other ties have been reported as having developed "funds of knowledge" that are useful, even critical, resources for all the households in the network (Gonzalez, Moll, and Amanti, 2005). Teachers who understand these resources may invite parents and grandparents to take meaningful roles in classroom communities and provide them with simple training on how to participate (Epstein, 2001). When teachers gain more understanding of their students' homes, they can increase their use of the students' experiences in their classrooms. The information that teachers gain about their students' knowledge bases guides them from the start to design instructional activities that are familiar and that respect their students' language proficiencies.

Diversity   Research reports inform teachers about the issues of growing class-room diversity. They also explain the mistakes of the past and they present examples, theories, evidence, and rationales for performing in new ways. In the United States, Valenzuela (1999) studied Mexican American high school students' experiences. He found that differences in diverse students' abilities and interests were ignored or treated as deficits. The deficit approach, labeled *subtractive schooling,* reflected not only teachers' unfamiliarity with their students' cultures and values but also teachers' limited tools for understanding differences, developing knowledge, and assisting second-language acquisition. The misinterpretation of the cultural and language differences of students and their families that characterized teaching in a deficit model permeated the school experience of students of color.

Most people recognize that considerable differences in ability occur across individuals, but different cultures treat these differences in varied ways in school. In most Asian societies, for example, children are placed in mixed-ability classrooms and taught the same curriculum regardless of any differences in ability. Those who require more help in dealing with the lesson materials receive more help rather than an entirely different curriculum (Wong-Fillmore and Snow, 2000). In Japan, teachers espouse the value-added notion of individual differences. Differences are considered natural and advantageous features that increase the range of ideas and problem-solving strategies that are available for student conversation, application, and reflection. Teachers are adept at anticipating students' likely responses, which strengthens their planning and prepares them to be responsive to students' learning needs across a range of levels (Stigler and Hiebert, 1997).

In recent decades, research reports have described classroom models of instruction that reflect the cultural value systems of diverse student populations. The study of how culture and language have influenced the teaching and learning of minority students in the United States has expanded understanding about the processes involved (Au, 1980; Tharp and others, 1984; Tharp, 1989; Tharp and Gallimore, 1988). Examination of diverse students' motivation, organization, speaking, and thinking styles as exercised in classrooms has revealed the close association of those styles with the students' cultures (Gay, 2002; Tharp, Estrada, Dalton, and Yamauchi, 2000; Tharp, 1989). In another example, Moll (1990) described knowledge in Mexican American communities as distributed among the families and individual members. The varied funds of knowledge are shared, when needed, to ensure the welfare of member households.

In other informative discussions of culturally relevant classroom teaching, ethnic and racial awareness is increasingly key to teaching performance that produces student learning outcomes. The challenge of teaching African American students in racially aware ways is leading teachers to refine their teaching repertoires to assist these students' understanding and close the learning gaps between U.S. racial groups (Delpit, 1995; Ladsen-Billings, 2001). In Ferguson's study (2000) of black males' experiences of middle school, the explanation of culture sets aside notions of inherited sets of characteristics. Instead, culture reflects creative and practical activity for enduring and resolving particular historical and social conditions. Cultures accumulate experience resulting in theories, knowledge bases, and empirical explanations that give meaning to daily occurrences. Groups have compiled knowledge for surviving in harsh and inhospitable climates over centuries and developed languages that are complex, defining, and self-protective. Youngsters learn through experience, observation, and practice within their specific cultural context and social stratum. They acquire repertoires and tools for solving practical problems. As understanding about the value of multiculturalism and diversity has grown, deficits have become assets that inform effective teaching rather than the impediments they were originally considered to be.

Information Communications Technology   ICT literacy rivals print literacy for priority as context and content of classroom teaching. If, however, the history of education, particularly education for literacy, is recapitulated in the new domain of technology, teachers will continue to be unprepared to use ICT proactively for learning. Surveys report that teacher preparation and intending teachers are not integrating ICT into their teaching. Less than half of student teachers use ICT frequently or systematically in their teaching (Kirschner and Selinger, 2003). Less proficient teachers may assign word processing and search tasks, which are not synchronized with the world of technology outside of school, to their students who did not get early starts in ICT. Even though students who don't have technology in their homes or previous experience require catch-up skill development, keyboarding, searches, and other basic technology skills must not replace conceptually challenging assignments. Projects that embed skill development in the activities that students design and perform with technology can be assigned to promote learning (Kirschner and Wopereis, 2003).

The technologies that have developed in the twenty-first century are enormously appealing to youth who are used to gaining mastery through hands-on activities, observation, trial and error, and peer assistance. Learning to use software and obtaining information are less important to learn with technology than is students' sharing their technology experiences with one another on the way to solving problems and generating products. This sharing stimulates the interaction of school with home and community, where many resources are available to assist thinking about the learning challenge (Pogrow, 2005). Learners are also inserted into new communities of practice when they play computer games and go to online resources. In these technology communities they find new vocabulary, rules, roles, and ways to express and produce. In an era when technology is expanding knowledge beyond traditional formats and methods, new ways of teaching based on what is known about human learning need to map onto technology's worlds of activity and fast-paced learning (Kirschner and Iwan, 2003).

ICT is best infused into the entire classroom experience as one context for learning. Students need to experience innovative, technology-supported learning through the broadest range of tools available. Work with ICT alters students' performance as do joint participation with peers and practices based on the pedagogy standards, such as instructional conversation (discussed shortly). ICT that goes beyond the application of tools such as e-mail provides clear and specific communication. Other conversation tools, such as databases, are available. These tools assist learners to connect pieces of information to make them more meaningful. The information must be organized, requiring students to identify associations within the data that are relevant to their purposes at a deeper level of analysis than would otherwise be available. The use of search engines has similar potential to expand students' analytic and evaluative thinking in order to meet complex information needs (Davis, 2003; Kirschner and Wopereis, 2003).

Many young students have entered the ICT world, including high-need students who are savvy about what happens in the streets or on television and in movies. Teaching with technology enables teachers to help students display information as it is being transformed into new knowledge. For example, students use digital cameras to record activity or collect data that they then view in different graphing formats and analyze to understand more about such topics as students' heights, allowances, numbers of toys or electronic devices, and observations of nature. Teachers are considered the gatekeepers for technology innovations, but they can be that only if there is support from policymakers and administrators (Kirschner and Davis, 2002). Without system support, applications are difficult, but teachers can still integrate ICT and media into teaching through the use of digital cameras and audio and video technology for example (Entz and Galarza, 2000).

Pedagogy Standard IV: Teaching Complex Thinking

The fourth pedagogy standard supports teachers in guiding students to attain increasingly complex understandings that enhance student achievement. The fourth pedagogy standard builds on the implementation of the first three standards to support teaching that promotes students' complex thinking. Every student can be assisted to think in new ways, even about familiar topics, if they are guided and assisted through appropriately leveled activity and dialogue to perform with increasing independence (Tharp, Estrada, Dalton, and Yamauchi, 2000; Bransford, Brown, and Cocking, 2000; Tharp and Gallimore, 1988; Lave & Wenger, 1991).

For students at risk of educational failure due to cultural or linguistic difference or to poverty, it is especially important to provide instruction that is designed to challenge their abilities (Hilberg, Doherty, Dalton, Youpa, and Tharp, 1998). A study conducted in a school serving predominantly low-income Latino ELLs found that teachers' overall use of the standards predicted achievement gains in comprehension, language, reading, spelling, and vocabulary (Doherty, Hilberg, Pinal, and Tharp, 2003).

Mathematics   In the teaching of constructivist mathematics, students are made active processors of new information and encouraged to reorganize their knowledge in ways that make problems meaningful to them. In a quasi-experimental study in an American Indian middle school, Hilberg, Tharp, and DeGeest (2000) examined the efficacy of applying the five pedagogy standards in mathematics instruction. Two groups of American Indian eighth grade students were randomly assigned to either five standards or traditional conditions for a one-week unit on fractions, decimals, and percentages. Students in the five standards situation outperformed controls on tests of conceptual learning at the end of the study and exhibited better retention of unit content two weeks later.

Reading Comprehension   K–12 students' mediocre and stable academic performance over the last few decades as measured on the NAEP is reason to question current classroom practices based on traditional views of teaching. To maintain and expand students' knowledge, teachers must have many ways to involve them in talking, thinking, reading, and writing about content concepts, using strategies that make a difference for early readers, including well-known directed thinking activities, the language experience approach, and others (Dalton and Dowhower, 1985; Valmont, 1976; Stauffer, 1970). The challenge remains how to provide students with adequate opportunities to talk, think, read, and write about content matters in classrooms of thirty or more students. At the end of the twentieth century, the increased presence of culturally and language-diverse students in U.S. classrooms overwhelmed teaching and schooling capacities across the nation. In the face of changing demographics, teaching defaulted mostly to traditional methods that emphasized control and reception while pedagogy for engaging all students in conceptual learning activities was ignored.

The NRP (2000) recommended two major approaches to reading comprehension instruction. In *direct explanation,* teachers are to view reading as a problem-solving task requiring strategic thinking. They are encouraged to provide students with problem-solving challenges such as finding a theme or main idea and reasoning about it. In *transactional strategy instruction,* teachers provide students with explicit explanations of thinking processes.

Technology   A July 2002 survey by the Pew Internet & American Life Project revealed that three in five children under the age of eighteen and more than 78 percent of children between the ages of twelve and seventeen go online. Students report that there is a substantial disconnect between how they use the Internet at home and how they use it during the school day and under teacher direction (Levin and Arafeh, 2002).

The NRP (2000) described the many successes reported in the literature about the use of computer technology for reading instruction. It considered technology not an instructional method but a delivery system for content. Kirschner and Davis (2003) point to the value of technology for collaborative and cooperative learning that is authentic and supports joint productivity. Computer-based activity nudges students to make connections to the community outside the school and promotes group tasks on real-world problems. Learners use computer applications to represent what they know in new ways and to retrieve information much faster than they can with texts. Computer technology enhances curricular integration and promotes work with and across content at increasingly complex levels (Kamil, Manning, and Walberg, 2002).

When teachers ensure that computer tasks are collaborative, students are assisted in forming a shared setting for interaction and reasoning about content. Shared settings bring together the ways of knowing, talking, and doing that support the conversion of information into knowledge in the community of learners (Shaffer, Squire, Halverson, and Gee, 2005). Research reports measurable, positive impact on scores in the Iowa Test of Basic Skills at the end of fifth grade as the result of integrating technology into instruction on student vocabulary, reading, and writing. Reports on girls in fourth through sixth grade suggest that they may enjoy computers more than boys do (Knezek and Christensen, 2000). At the primary level, a positive impact on students' perceived enjoyment and importance of computers appears to occur within the first three months of exposure to computers in school (Collis and others, 1996).

Pedagogy Standard V: Teaching Through Conversation

The fifth pedagogy standard extends the second standard in order to focus teachers on all the strategies for fully developing students' language and literacy skills. The two standards together reflect research on the interconnectedness of language, literacy, and thinking. They guide teachers to assist K–8 students in understanding the language they speak and read; decoding words; recognizing the layers of meaning in words; comprehending implicit meanings; and grasping large, explicit meanings through regular and systematic instruction using instructional conversation (IC). When interactive occasions occur frequently in a classroom, teachers can assist students to improve their language and comprehension skills through academic conversation (Wong-Fillmore and Snow, 2000; Tharp, Estrada, Dalton, and Yamauchi, 2000; Tharp and Gallimore, 1988).

An IC is most effective when it occurs in a community of learners, and it is by means of such conversation that community is created. Conversation also carries a community's values and emotional shadings. Talking together in natural, informal learning environments not only develops higher order thinking but also socializes children into community values and teaches them the conventions and pleasures of human relationships. Especially in the early grades, students should be immersed in IC experiences routinely throughout the school day.

Dialogic Teaching   Most U.S. public school classrooms infrequently provide occasions for teaching through dialogue instruction or conversation, and they rarely arrange for it to occur on a regular schedule. The consequences are serious, including students' stunted mastery of even their home language, unfamiliarity with conversational conventions, ignorance of the means to express complex thinking, and postponement of or even exclusion from academic content instruction (Au, 1980; Erickson and Mohatt, 1982; Rosebery, Warren, and Conant, 1992). By late elementary or middle school, such restricted opportunities result in language-minority and other at-risk students' limited academic success and low confidence in their own ability to learn (Padron, 1992; Dalton and Youpa, 1998).

In the Coley and Coleman (2004) fourth grade snapshot mentioned earlier, a little more than 50 percent of students had teachers who asked them to make predictions, generalizations, and inferences about what they had read. Less than 50 percent of students had teachers who asked them to explain or write about their understanding of what they had read. Less than 40 percent of students' teachers asked them to talk with other students or write about what they had read. The teachers of only 25 percent of students asked the students to discuss different interpretations and multiple perspectives about what they had read, and the teachers of 15 percent of students reported asking students about the style or structure of what they had read.

Research Reports on Instructional Conversation   ICs are planned, goal-directed conversations between a teacher and a small group of students on an academic topic. The goal is to help ELLs develop reading comprehension ability along with English language proficiency. Teachers facilitate ELLs in discussions about stories, key concepts, and related personal experiences that allow them to appreciate and build on one another's experiences, knowledge, and under-standing. Dalton and Sison (1994) conducted a stimulated recall on video of a mathematics teacher using IC and language levers with Spanish-speaking minority seventh graders. Coding showed that the students increased their use of the targeted mathematics terms and that their contributions in English grew in frequency during the lessons.

Two studies of ICs and literature logs met one level of the evidence standards of the What Works Clearinghouse of the U.S. Department of Education's Institute of Education Sciences, with reservations. These studies included more than two hundred Hispanic ELLs from grades two through five. They reviewed program impacts in two different contexts—the short term (use of the intervention over a few days) and the long term (use of the intervention over a few years)—with the interventions delivered as key components in a broad language arts program. Literature logs require ELLs to keep a log in response to writing prompts or questions related to sections of stories. These responses are then shared in small groups or with a partner. ICs and literature logs were found to have potentially positive effects on reading achievement and English language development.

Several studies have found ICs to be productive in assisting students' literacy development (Saunders, 1999; Saunders and Goldenberg, 1999a, 1999b, 2001; Saunders, O'Brien, Lennon, and McLean, 1998). In an experimental study (Saunders and Goldenberg, 1999a), fourth-grade ELLs were randomly assigned one of two kinds of lessons. The experimental group participated in an IC on a short story while the control group participated in a directed reading lesson on the same story following guidance provided in the teacher's manual for the textbook series used. Both groups of students achieved equivalent levels on posttests of literal comprehension (76 percent), but in the IC group (63 percent) demonstrated comprehension of the story's theme as compared to the control group's 13 percent.

Saunders and Goldenberg's storty (1999a) also found that the third pedagogy standard, making meaning (MM), along with pedagogy standard five, instructional conversation (IC), greatly assisted the reading comprehension and thematic understanding of students with varying levels of English proficiency. This study showed the value of establishing a theme for reading, writing, and conversing about their experience attaining new information and more complex understanding of text. In combination, particularly the third, fourth, and fifth pedagogy standards were demonstrated in a program, Opportunities Through Language Arts (OLA), developed by Center for Research on Education Diversity and Excellence (CREDE) researchers (Saunders and Goldenberg, 2001). In a language arts program for grades 3–5, the five pedagogy standards were tested (Saunders, 1999) and replicated (Saunders and Goldenberg, 1999b) with both longitudinal and short-term quasi-experimental designs. Comparisons of randomly selected matched samples of OLA and non-OLA students indicate that the program produces higher levels of Spanish literacy, significantly higher levels of English literacy, and important literacy-related practices and attitudes for significantly larger numbers of students. By grade five, OLA students, on average, score at least one half of a standard deviation higher than matched controls on standardized tests of English reading and approximately .60 to .75 standard deviations higher on standardized tests of English language expression and mechanics (Saunders, 1999; Saunders & Goldenberg, 1999b; Saunders et al., 1998).

PEDAGOGY STANDARDS INTEGRATED: THE FIVE PEDAGOGY STANDARDS CLASSROOM

As a system, the pedagogy standards provide the means and methods for assisting content achievement by students. For four years Estrada studied the relationship between the five standards and positive outcomes in the first and fourth grades. Greater teacher implementation of the five standards was associated with higher student scores on tests of reading and the language of instruction (English or Spanish). Virtually all students reached grade level in reading in the classes of high implementers, and virtually all students achieved at grade level in reading; less than 70 percent did so in weaker implementers' classrooms (Estrada, 2004, 2005).

SUMMARY

The five pedagogy standards have been studied and tested across multiple classroom settings. They have been validated by research findings on teaching and student achievement. The standards together are a system for supporting teaching that assists student learning through a concentrated implementation of pedagogy. The implementation of the five standards directs pedagogy to support teaching at social and interactive and community levels.

The five standards express the known ways to apply deep social influences to classroom teaching and learning. They communicate through highly practical statements the methods that are supported by consensus as well as by student achievement effects. When implemented in combination, the pedagogy standards offer a system of guidance for teaching that has been demonstrated to make a difference in students' achievement, especially the achievement of at-risk and linguistically and culturally diverse students. Cognitively challenging activity produces learning when it guides students into the zone that is just beyond their current abilities. The main task for teaching, then, is to move students into their learning zones with topics and activities that use what students already know, that have real-world interest, and that respond to individual students' needs. The pedagogy standards support and strengthen processes essential features of teaching that activate students' learning. In this way, pedagogy assists teaching effects in students learning zones.

Findings from implementation models and programs and from controlled and correlation studies consistently demonstrate a systematic relationship between use of the five pedagogy standards and improved student performance across diverse student populations. Taken together, these findings provide strong support for the positive effects of implementing the five pedagogy standards. The effect is reported as the more the five standards are present in a classroom, the more students' scores on standardized tests improve.

PART TWO

Implementing the Standards

Seventh Grade English-Language Learners Discuss Circle Measurement

Teacher:	[What did we do] the last time we were together? [Teacher points to students' chart of pasted strings.]
Adrianna:	*Son hilitos.* [They are strings.]
Adam:	What?
Adrianna:	Ah, shut up.
Teacher:	No, please explain it.
Daniel:	You have like a round thing [jar lid] and then you have to measure around it, and then across.
Adrianna:	You have to measure around and then—
Teacher:	And what was the thing [motioning with finger] around? What was it called?
Luis:	Circumference.
Adrianna:	*Le tienes que dar vueltitas.* [You have to make the string go around in circles.]

Teacher and Students Producing Together

PEDAGOGY STANDARD I

Teacher and Students Producing Together

Facilitate learning through joint productive activity (JPA) among teacher and students using multiple activity settings and student groupings.

Classroom Application Indicators

The teacher

1. Guides students to produce a classroom community agreement.

2. Designs suitable JPAs.

3. Uses an instructional frame to plan and organize instructional activity.

4. Arranges the classroom for interaction and joint activity.

5. Groups students for JPA.

6. Monitors student participation and production in positive ways.

Introduction

Teachers and students are together in classrooms every day, but they rarely collaborate on tasks to completion. In the lesson transcript that opens this chapter, the teacher collaborates with students in a hands-on activity on measuring circles.

Together they measure jar lids with string to determine the relative sizes of two circle features: diameter and circumference. The excerpt, though brief, reveals that the students are English language learners (ELLs) below proficient levels in mathematics. It also shows the teacher probing students' knowledge to involve them in an academic discussion using content terminology. How the teacher designed this collaboration with a small group of students within her class of thirty previews the topic of this book.

Rationale

For novice and even veteran teachers, activity can seem utterly reliable during planning, but be entirely unsuitable when used with students. An activity's unsuitability may be simply a matter of poor timing or inadequate instructions. In other cases, the level of activity may be too difficult or too easy, or the topic may be unfamiliar or even unknown to students. In fact, teachers must have enormous skill to provide activity that attains lesson goals. The design of effective instructional activity, whether it is used for review, instruction, practice, assessment, or other classroom aims such as community building, has rigorous requirements.

Our understanding of how students learn has shifted from a passive, receptive model to an active model. Even when students appear passive during listening, observing, apprehending, and comprehending, they are actively involved in constructing meaning and individual understanding. In an active model of learning, students work together to explore real-world problems in order to develop products and presentations for sharing new knowledge. Collaborative activity design encourages students to talk and think together about the work. The advantages of this approach can be seen in students' increased language use with peers and teacher, and in their involvement with the content of the activity. What may not be immediately obvious is how working together helps students and teachers build their sense of community.

The first pedagogy standard and its indicators introduce a guidance system for organizing instructional activity and arranging classrooms to encourage students' construction of knowledge. The standard and its indicators are foundational for the other four standards and indicators, which are introduced in the following chapters. The guidance system is intended for use in any U.S. classroom of any size on typical school and classroom schedules. This standard is especially useful in large classes, where having more students increases opportunities for collaboration and joint activity.

The first standard's first indicator addresses community building, an essential feature of a collaborative and productive classroom.

INDICATOR 1: THE TEACHER GUIDES STUDENTS TO PRODUCE A CLASSROOM COMMUNITY AGREEMENT

The classroom agreement focuses on student roles and rules for the classroom. It is an expression of values that support teaching and learning. In the early grades, the teacher often emphasizes behavior that may be new to students, such as sharing, taking turns, and helping others. Such values do not just happen; they need to be fostered. A classroom tone of collaboration and valuing of relationships is emphasized in the following kindergarten example:

Kindergarten Classroom Agreement

We promise to help each other play and learn. If someone falls, we will help them up. We will care about each other and share. We will not tattle or fight. We will be friends even when no one is watching and not laugh at each other's mistakes. We will say "good try" and we will not break our promise [Nursery Road Elementary School, Columbia, SC, *Washington Post*, Tuesday, February 21, 2006].

The community agreement is a joint product of teacher and students that should be signed by all. Agreements clarify the value of the roles and rules that each classroom community believes promote every community member's success. In the following example, Mr. Yode involves his fifth grade students in examining what they value and how that value applies in their classroom by developing a classroom agreement:

Fifth Grade Classroom Agreement

From the first day of school, Mr. Yode talks to his fifth graders about his ideas and theirs for working together. He expects everyone to work often in groups as well as on their own. The students say they can work well together even without him. Mr. Yode assigns a task of developing a product together. The product is a document that reflects everyone's views about how to work together. Mr. Yode and the students discuss how they want everyone, including him, to act and move in the classroom and to use classroom furniture, resources, and equipment. Who is responsible for setup and cleanup of work areas? How do they feel about helping one another solve problems? Mr. Yode writes the questions they ask on the board along with their answers. Then the questions are assigned to pairs of students, who are to write and draw. They then present their responses to the class. After more editing, they decide how to produce the document. Should it be a chart, a book, or both? They decide on both. Then they edit, draw, and produce charts and individually illustrated booklets. All of the community's members sign the final version of the agreement. The chart is posted on the classroom wall for ready reference. Students take copies of the booklets home for their parents to review. The teacher also presents them to also parents when they come to Back to School Night.

The community agreement establishes a classroom setting in which teachers can responsively assist students. To perform proficiently, many students require not only multiple practice opportunities, but also high levels of teaching assistance. Teaching is most effective when communities agree to provide everyone opportunity for assistance and achievement. From kindergarten through eighth grade, a community agreement reminds students to participate fully in activities and produce the best outcomes for themselves and their peers, as in the following eighth grade example:

Our community succeeds when we

- Use community voice levels and courtesy in all conversation.
- Are community leaders for classroom setup, cleanup, and supplies.
- Are ready when community activities begin:
  - Have materials, folders, paper, and books ready to use.
  - Have pencils sharpened.
  - Have homework completed.
  - Have an organized portfolio of work.
  - Visit the restroom during passing periods, breaks, and lunch.

- Work together on tasks by helping peers to
  - Participate.
  - Use content vocabulary.
  - Write in academic language.
  - Make corrections.
  - Enjoy membership.
- Follow the class schedule.
- Finish work by the deadline.
- Use extra time to read or do finishing activities.
- Use technology (computers, digital cameras, DVDs) according to directions.
- Use personal technology (cell phones, portable media players, other) only when assigned.
- Share examples of community participation to compliment or problem solve when the community meets.

Teachers may choose to include grading rubrics in the community agreement. Because the agreement focuses on relationship and tone, grading topics are often covered in other ways, especially with younger students. Older students may need information on absences, extra credit, no credit, and the teacher's grading ranges. These topics can be presented at many other points in the classroom activities, such as in association with tests, quizzes, and major projects. Teachers often post the agreement on the school's Web site, which increases the information available to parents.

Joint work on the community agreement usually turns students' attention to questions about rule enforcement and consequences for noncompliance. Students may choose to list consequences for irregular or disruptive community participation that keeps others from their work. They may offer suggestions such as canceling recess or other community rewards for the individual, and calling parents. These and other suggestions can be included in the agreement so that everyone knows what consequences to expect. Any agreement item can be extended to include the privileges lost when the item is ignored, for example, "Turn work in when due or lose two recesses." The teacher must make it abundantly clear, however, that all suggested consequences are useful but will surely be unnecessary in this community. Any infractions need to be discussed with the community as soon as possible to ensure that the agreement fits the needs of the community or to make changes if needed.

To guarantee every student's success, all students must be included in all of the activities associated with community building. From the first day of the school year, Ms. Vent, a fourth grade teacher, involves her students in every aspect of the classroom, especially development of the classroom community agreement. She expects students to assume responsibility for monitoring their peers' compliance with the agreement they prepare:

Drafting a Fourth Grade Classroom Agreement

It is September, the first day of school. The fourth graders have found their seats labeled with their names. They look at Ms. Vent, who welcomes them. She holds a giant marker and stands in front of blank chart paper at the front of the room. On her left is a huge aquarium filled with water but no fish. On her right are several computer stations. Ms. Vent briefs the students about the activity for this first class, which will be to develop an agreement for how to work and produce together. She asks them if it is OK for her or them to talk with friends or leave the room at any time. The students explain how rules are used for these actions. Others suggest how to take a bathroom break, and how to use the pencil sharpener, trash cans, coat closet, personal storage areas, books, materials, and computers. Ms. Vent writes their comments on the chart paper. She asks if they know how to work together on a product. When they hesitate, she points to the fishless aquarium. Seeing their interest, she asks them if it is the way they want it, and if it is not, what do they want? She numbers all of the written comments.

Ms. Vent has the students to form pairs. Each pair copies one of the numbered comments and writes "We agree to" in front of it. Ms. Vent asks for examples. She writes one example on the chart paper. She tells the students that they are good thinkers who need to write down their ideas as she sets her timer for ten minutes. While they are writing she circulates through the room to listen to and guide students. When the timer rings, the student groups exchange their drafts with other pairs and discuss and edit them for ten more minutes. Five minutes are given to the original authors to edit and rewrite. Then Ms. Vent has the authors read their writing aloud and take comments from the class. She closes the discussion saying that this has been one of the best first classes she has ever had. She points to the basket where they should deposit their papers on their way out of the room. For the last ten minutes of the class she leads a debriefing. She asked the students to share what they liked about the activity and if there were problems. They decide together how they could make working together better tomorrow. Then the bell rings and the students drop their papers in the basket on their way out the door.

Community building requires continuous development through activities and talking about accomplishments and improvements. Teachers gather the community on a regular schedule to celebrate, solve problems, and plan for rewards and special group activities. Some classroom communities write about and publish a newsletter to send to parents and others that describes their activities and accomplishments. Students in the upper elementary grades can design a Web page for posting both their community and academic accomplishments.

The next section describes other types of compelling activities that classroom communities can use to learn.

INDICATOR 2: THE TEACHER DESIGNS SUITABLE JOINT PRODUCTIVE ACTIVITIES (JPA)

The second indicator guides teachers in providing students with varied activities designed for the appropriate instructional levels. All classroom activities aim to meet state content standards that can be measured on standardized tests, and students' achievement of these standards requires that they be challenged at appropriate levels and provided with numerous experiences of success. Providing activities that are too hard produces student frustration, even failure. Students who find tasks frustrating may turn their energy to inappropriate activity instead. In contrast, providing tasks that ensure all students' success, especially at the beginning of a school year, builds everyone's confidence in their capacity to learn. Teachers must provide many initial experiences of success to build students' confidence in their capacity to accomplish the challenges they will face in the curriculum. Whole-class hands-on activities that review skills can facilitate such experiences for all students in the beginning of the year.

Appropriate Activity Levels and Duration

Teachers design activities that match students' ability to perform with and without teacher assistance. Students' work with the teacher occurs at an instructional level that requires the teacher's assistance. When students work independently of the teacher, such assistance is unavailable, so students' independent work must be designed at a level they can accomplish on their own, or with peer assistance in the time alotted.

Gauging Level of Difficulty of Text

Research on reading provides all content-area teachers with a useful gauge of the level of challenge provided by a textbook and other narrative or expository material. Text is at a student's *independent* reading level if the student can read it with 95 percent accuracy. It is at the student's *instructional* level if the text contains mostly words that students know or that they can decode easily or at a success rate of 90 percent. When more than one word in ten is too difficult, the challenge is considered *frustration* level [Kuhn and Stahl, 2003; Clay, 1993].

Providing text and tasks at both independent and instructional levels is key to student success in activity-based classrooms. Independent tasks are as important to learning as instructional tasks, although they have different functions. Independent tasks support teachers in multitasking, which means that students regularly work on assignments and tasks away from direct teacher supervision. When the teacher, a proficient peer, parent, or other assister is available, tasks can be set at students' instructional level. However, if students do not have reliable assistance for a task or text, they must be able to accomplish the work on their own or independently.

Tasks and texts that are at students' independent levels encourage effort, motivate, and build confidence for the learning challenges to come. Frustrating tasks erode effort and confidence, and may lead to management problems. The classroom community agreement guides students in independent work, but the teacher must provide tasks at suitable levels and with appropriate timing. Other tools for supporting students in performing independently of the teacher, such as the instructional frame and its components, are described later in the chapter.

Task Cards

To assist students' independent work, directions are included with all activities, unless they are routine. Teachers attach simple instructions on easy-to-find task cards to all work assignments or leave them in the settings in which the tasks are to be completed. The instructions can be written on index cards, chart paper, or colored paper; recorded in a cumulative assignment book that remains in the activity setting; stored in a computer file; or presented in other forms. Teachers and students eventually establish routines for such activities and tasks as journaling, classroom library, and project-based work, so instructions for these tasks will be needed only infrequently.

Task Timing

The challenge of texts and tasks must not only match students' abilities to accomplish them, but also be accomplished within an allotted amount of time. To ensure students' success from the start, teachers must design independent tasks at levels that make it possible for students to accomplish them within the time assigned. Students need to experience success on numerous tasks in order to avoid discouragement and loss of motivation. Until the teacher is familiar with students' work habits and rates, task timing has to be estimated. In the meantime, teachers must ensure that students who finish tasks early know how to spend the rest of the task time reading or in other activities.

Joint Activity Content

A new teacher arranging group work in her third grade classroom grumbled that it would have helped her during her teaching preparation to know that children learn by doing work together and talking about it (Cohen, 1994). Teachers use many levels and functions of activity to assist students in developing new understandings. For example, early content and community building activities provide opportunities for concept review and skill practice. They can also be informal assessments of the levels of students' everyday and school-related knowledge.

Early Content Themes

In the early weeks of the school year, teachers may use an early content theme (ECT) that is interesting and familiar to students as a context for their work together. The ECT becomes the reference for all review and other activities. Teachers often choose the essential task of building classroom community as the ECT. They may relate community building to such topics as the following:

1. My family

2. My neighbors and neighborhood

3. My town or city or country

4. Patterns of color, shape, and size that occur in students' clothing, in people, in the classroom, in mathematics, in the natural world of plants and animals, and so on

5. Popular themes from movies, television, and books such as *Star Wars, Harry Potter,* Disney, *Sesame Street,* and the like

6. Geography of the local area, and familiar science topics such as the cycle of water on the planet through clouds, rain, and so on

7. Historical topics such as explorers, Native Americans, pioneers and the movement west

8. The stock market, weather forecasting, space station and travel, global warming, and others can continue as skill-developing projects throughout the year

Once an ECT is selected, it provides a focus for all of the initial activities of the class, including community building. All activities, bulletin boards, prepared materials, and music support the theme. ECT tasks include games, puzzles, and other paper-and-pencil activities that reflect students' interests. By working with students in ECT tasks, teachers learn about their backgrounds, life outside of school, differing skill levels, language proficiency, and academic needs. They use the information they acquire to design tasks and develop activities, to make decisions about grouping students, and to differentiate their instruction to meet students' particular skill development needs.

For the early grades, themes having to do with family, community, school, and animals are popular. First graders enjoy nature topics such as the seasons, plants, and animal life cycles (butterflies and frogs), and social topics such as different jobs that people do. Young students are particularly interested in themselves and enjoy activities that focus on them. From kindergarten on, students can use information communications technology (ICT) and media resources such as digital cameras for projects requiring communication, data collection, and illustrations. The following ECT activity focusing on where kindergarten and first grade students were born requires a digital camera and a U.S. map.

Kindergarten First Grade Geography

Students take headshots of each other by turns, including one of the teacher. The photographs are placed into wallpaper format to obtain multiple copies of the photographs. [They c]ut out the small wallpaper portraits to use as stickers or with tape on a large U.S. map attached to a wall. Students stick their photo onto the map at the place where they were born. The class sends a note home asking parents, other family members, and friends who have traveled within the U.S. to share their souvenirs or mementos of their travels with the student and to label the items they send by their city and state of origin. Students take digital photographs of each of the souvenirs as they come in. The teacher imports each photo into a page layout program, labels it with the city and state of origin, and prints it. For each photo, the student explains who sent in the item, attaches it to the map and tells what they know about it [Entz and Galarza, 2000, pp. 84–85].

From third grade on, school, community, and natural science themes are interesting to students. Life in the forests, rivers, and oceans is also a popular theme, as are rocks, ancient myths, and early history (see list on page 60).

Third Graders Count and Estimate the Size of Mammal Groups

Students identify mammals that live and travel in herds on land and sea, such as buffalo, wolves, whales, and dolphins. They choose one animal and find pictures of the herds or pods on the Internet or in books. They count the number of animals in the herds they see, which challenges them to problem solve how best to make an accurate count. The students discuss accuracy and estimates with the teacher, who assists them using graph paper and sampling. Several squares are selected randomly and the animals within them are counted and averaged, then multiplied by the number of squares covering the herd to obtain an estimate. The count is then compared to the numbers in the herds reported in the resource books. The information is put on a chart that compares the students' counts with the authoritative counts.

For fourth and fifth graders, school, community, and the natural sciences are interesting themes, but their curiosity is excited more by how things in the school work, for example, the cafeteria or heating and cooling systems. The school's engineer can take the students on a tour and explain these systems. The teacher can assign follow-up reading to the students and have them draw what they saw and explain how the systems work. When they have completed their follow-up activities, the class can invite the engineer to the classroom for corrective feedback and further information.

Fourth, fifth, and sixth graders enjoy such themes as history, games, biography, community service, human development, and plant growth. They enjoy problem-solving activities that require them to read narratives about problems, use media resources, and generate ideas for resolving the problems. Topics with large literatures and media representation, such as outer space (including planets and space shuttle life and work) and environmental concerns having to do with animal habitats and survival, provide rich material for ECT and content review.

From sixth to eighth grade, students find social topics motivating as their peers become more important in their lives. They enjoy exploring demographics related to preteen interests. For example, an ECT on patterns can offer startup activities across the curriculum on topics such as the following:

Personal: What do the different clothes and accessories that students wear have in common, from colors to styles? Group students according to the styles and colors they wear. Have them identify other patterns in the features of what students wear.

Math review: What are the patterns in students' birthdays, ages, heights, and numbers of siblings and cousins? Measure the classroom to find perimeter, area, volume, and other features for making a model.

Language arts: Find spelling patterns in students' names, find rhymes in students' names to use in poetry, summarize summer reading plots to identify patterns, and play and compose word games.

Geography: What are the patterns in the city's street numbering or names? What patterns are there in the bus routes to school?

In the following ECT example, the scientific content is made compelling by converting the metrics to more familiar measures. The size and distances of space objects are scaled down to proportions that students can envision and learn to manipulate.

Mathematics in Space at Florida State University Schools, Tallahassee

Patricia Casey teaches a lesson called Algebra in Space to motivate students and provide a meaning base for mathematical concepts. Astronomy is a useful vehicle for heightening interest and enhancing meaning, which makes it an attractive ECT. It can be used to introduce and review new concepts or to forecast topics of study in science, math, reading, and other content areas. For example, to describe the solar system, students learn to scale down size and distance using concepts of ratio, proportion, and estimation. They convert metrics to standard units by computing the sizes of bodies in the solar system in miles and kilometers. They discuss using linear models to examine planetary size, distance, and rotation. They use graphing calculator technology to show tables and data use, because graphs provide multiple representations at many levels of mathematics.

ECT activities provide a context for practicing skills and reviewing concepts in order to establish a foundation for all students to succeed in content standards-based instruction. Teachers use such activities to ensure that students have experience with formats that the class will continue to use, such as writing, journaling, reporting, record keeping, database development, and standardized test taking. The teacher and students also clarify and demonstrate the expectations established in the classroom community agreement.

Throughout the early weeks of the school year, the teacher uses ECT activities to prepare students to shift into content standards-based instruction. The success of this preparation is measured by the students' success in class activities, especially those requiring interacting with peers to develop a joint product. To ensure students' progress, teachers design leveled tasks and provide assistance wherever needed through the supports identified by the first pedagogy standard. One key support offered by the first standard is a strategy for teachers and students to work together.

Joint Productive Activity

Activity that has a joint product is key to high-quality student participation and performance. Every teacher knows that high student interest alone is no guarantee that teaching and learning will succeed. They also know that students may work together on a project only to have its outcome depend on a single student's effort. The design of a JPA ensures that every student participates in the way their peers and the teacher expect in the development of a joint product. JPA has key features that promote participation in and contribution to the learning goal or outcome.

In JPA, students are most likely to participate and assist one another toward creation of a final product when the activity has the following three features:

- It addresses a compelling, real-world topic.
- It is concept-driven.
- It has more than one possible accurate outcome.
- Completing the joint product requires information from all participants.

The following eighth grade JPA on ratios is compelling and of real-world value for all the students. It shows how every student must share their local knowledge and skills to produce a joint product. The product is the outcome of the students' scientifically examining their homeland, a meaningful topic. The outcome must be accurate relative to the facts of local geography. It must also reflect the students' consensus on how to make their world visual and tangible in a model.

Math Map (JPA)

A Native American teacher taught her students to use ratios by dividing a map of their reservation into six rectangles and assigning each portion to a group in the class. Each group enlarged its portion of the map using a scale of 3:1, after which students constructed a plaster relief model of the enlargement. The finished product required that all the pieces be combined correctly to form a table-sized relief map of the reservation. In addition to teaching students to use ratios, this JPA built on their knowledge of topography, geography, and map making, and taught them how to coordinate with peers across groups to ensure the accuracy of the final outcome. [Adapted from Hilberg, Chang, and Epaloose, 2004, p. 27].

When JPA occurs regularly, it offers numerous occasions for teacher assistance, and peer models for language and thinking. The key to successful JPA design is the requirement of creating a joint product. Any compelling problem that students are assigned to do alone can be transformed into a JPA. In the reservation map construction activity, teams of students worked on different parts of the map model, but the final product required that all the pieces fit together to make the whole. For example, the following activities can be performed by individual students, but they are strengthened when they are assigned as JPAs.

JPA Examples

○ Consensus is required for each step in the development of the classroom community agreement. After the class has discussed the basic features of an agreement, students are assigned or choose to produce portions of the document as teams. The joint product must be presented to the teacher and the rest of the class and accepted. In this way, all students contribute their portion to the final product, which must meet the standard for a public document that parents and others will read. Students must also take responsibility for producing the final agreement in a format that can be posted on the classroom wall, carried in their work folders, and taken home to share with their parents.

○ In a unit on pioneers, individual students stock their covered wagons with eighteen hundred pounds of supplies of the sort available in the nineteenth century. When the project is assigned as a JPA, groups of students stock a single wagon, working together to select enough supplies to last through the trip while staying under the weight limits. All of the students involved contribute to the final product. For follow-up they use the wagon stocks to create menus and daily snacks to discover if they stocked enough food to survive for the period it took the pioneers to make the trip to Oregon from wherever they started.

○ Writing uses process models to involve peers in discussing their preparations for writing and for creating their products. Students, in addition to the teacher, are involved in editing one another's papers.

○ In a toothpick tower construction project, each student's contribution makes or breaks the tower's height. This JPA usually promotes peer assistance because students who are more skilled help those who are less skilled in order to achieve the greatest height.

○ Students often find interactive journals more stimulating than diary-type journals. The teacher responds to students' entries regularly. Some students request that and peers respond as well. Teachers and peers write responses to entries in others' journals.

○ Students share the challenge of growing an ice garden of snowflakes and mysterious ice spikes. The product is their icy "flowers," an explanation of how to grow the flowers, and the scientific principles they learned. (See Appendix 4B.)

In each of these JPAs, the joint product requirement shifts students' attention to the challenge of the outcome from the start. The JPAs engage students in tasks that are compelling and real-world, and that stimulate students to be creative and thoughtful. In the example that follows, the students expand a JPA based on their content knowledge:

An Eighth Grade Magna Carta

An eighth grade class studied English King John's thirteenth-century struggle with his barons that resulted in the Magna Carta. This lesson and seeing the Magna Carta on the National Archives Web site got the class interested in the English barons' practices in signing their agreement. The class researched signatures and seals in the period of King John. The thirteenth-century use of seals to secure signatures was compared with today's signature practices. The class made the case that the use of a personalized seal was as acceptable as a signature. The resulting ornate document was posted prominently on the classroom wall, and the students' comparison of thirteenth- and twenty-first-century signature security practices was posted on the class's Web page (http://www.archives.gov/exhibits/featured_documents/magna_carta/index.html).

Rules, formulas, and rote tasks are less useful topics for JPA than concepts. For example, in grades K–4, students may memorize number facts or decoding rules, and in grades 5–9 they may learn grammar rules or the use of algorithms to solve problems. Tasks that build skills and have known answers are more appropriately used in guided and independent practice activities that include games, homework, and worksheets. One way to use JPA for rote skill practice is to embed it in a game. The following JPA game designed by fourth through sixth graders shows how students and teachers can develop JPAs for rote material:

The students needed to recognize fractions, decimals, and percentages and their meanings in a flash. They prepared a list of fractions, decimals, and percentages with values that matched—such as 1/4, .25, and 25%—and values that did not match, such as 1/4, .45, and 14%. They put each number on paper and pasted one paper on each side of a four-by-four-by-four box taped shut. On another box they pasted some matched numbers and some unmatched numbers. They taped over the boxes to make them sturdy so they could be used as dice for practicing math skills. They made up the rules of the dice game and produced directions and a score sheet. They rolled the dice for the class to show how to learn basic skills by counting the matches for a win.

Throughout the school year, teachers as well as students can design and use JPAs for small-group work or, in some cases, for large groups. JPAs succeed with highly diverse groups that include students with varying academic abilities, languages, and other talents. In any JPA, the more heterogeneous the participants are, the more information there is potentially available to influence the accomplishment of a successful joint product.

INDICATOR 3: THE TEACHER USES AN INSTRUCTIONAL FRAME TO PLAN AND ORGANIZE INSTRUCTIONAL ACTIVITY

Indicator 3 presents the instructional frame, an innovative tool used for planning and organizing classroom instruction. The instructional frame supports the use of a variety of group formats to complement teaching activities. It structures teaching in any format but promotes small groups. It encourages teachers to use small groups for dialogue with students on academic topics. It also guides the teacher to plan and arrange activities for students to perform independently. Students work on independent activities without direct teacher supervision in dedicated settings in, and sometimes outside of side the classroom.

Table 3.1
Basic Instructional Frame

Session 1	Session 2	Session 3
Briefing: Teacher describes what will occur. Teacher explains directions.	*Teaching lesson:* Teacher teaches. Students may be asked to apply the lesson topic.	*Debriefing:* Teacher may or may not assign extending activities and homework.

In the frame the teacher provides a predictable instructional routine for students. The group formats and activities in the frame increase student and teacher interaction and encourage high levels of student activity. The frame's design is based on a linear and sequential activity pattern that has characterized classrooms for centuries.

The basic instructional frame brackets activities that occur mostly in the whole group, through teacher and student *monotasking*. In monotasking, the teacher assigns all of the students the same activity at the same time. There have been variations, but the basic instructional frame shown in Table 3.1 is a predominant format for classroom teaching. The sessions are usually untimed and vary according to assignment type, teacher preference, competing events, and interruptions. Students may have little influence on the regularity or timing of instructional events, and may be unable to predict what activities will occur in their classroom. All classroom teaching essentially begins with this design. It is not necessarily a disadvantage at the start, but it becomes a disadvantage when it constitutes the routine for the entire school year.

In the classroom, a transmission teaching model assumes that students who are motivated receive knowledge directly from the teacher, from texts, and from other sources, when it is clearly presented. Teachers secure students' received knowledge through practice applications and testing. According to this logic, students who do not learn are not paying attention or following directions, and they lack motivation. Students who do learn have succeeded in using their individual psychological or learning processes to integrate new information into their knowledge base. In a transformative teaching model, teachers activate students' learning processes by

	Table 3.2A Timed Instructional Frame: Sixty Minutes		
Session 1	**Session 2**	**Session 3**	**Session 4**
Briefing	Teaching lesson	Follow-up activity*	Debriefing
10 minutes*	20 minutes*	20 minutes*	10 minutes*

*Elements added to this version of the instructional frame

discussing and engaging new information in activities. Teachers nurture students' understandings by providing meaningful occasions for students to use the new information. One way to do this is by providing application tasks immediately following teaching. Such follow-up activities are usually presented and explained during teaching so that students can continue to discuss, apply, and think with peers about new information they were taught.

The instructional frame presented in Table 3.2A looks like the basic model shown in Table 3.1, with the addition of a follow-up activity. To ensure that all students participate, the frame also has a timeline, which contributes a pace and rhythm to activity—a pace and rhythm that teachers can plan with and that students can expect. The units of time are selected to match students' attention spans and other needs, such as for movement. The timeline suggested in Table 3.2A is recommended on the basis of the experiences of many teachers at every grade level, and is suggested especially for those who are just beginning to use the frame. Variations in the timeline that teachers have used productively are described later in the chapter. Before the first session begins, the frame and its timeline are displayed in the classroom as a reference to ensure that everyone, including visitors, knows where and when activities will occur.

Instructional Frame Contents

The instructional frame has three essential components: *briefing, teaching and follow-up activity,* and *debriefing.*

Briefing   The instructional frame's first session is always *briefing.* In this session, the teacher introduces the specific tasks that students are to accomplish, and the expectations for participation specified in the classroom community agreement.

Briefing introduces each activity in the frame, the directions for the tasks, the performance expectations, and the materials required. The briefing is conducted with the entire class, with the students as well as the teacher contributing. In the following excerpt from a briefing, the teacher discusses the tasks the students will perform, incorporating student models and instructions into the presentation:

Teacher: I like the way April has her center sheet out so she can check it and make sure what she's doing is right today. I'm going to call back one person to pick up whatever materials your team needs to use. Who knows what Center 1 is today? [Susan raises her hand.] What's happening at Center 1?

Susan: The teacher center.

Teacher: Right, you're meeting with me at the back table. You need your science books and a pencil. Now what's Center 2 today? [Sacchi raises his hand.] Great, what are you going to be doing?

Sacchi: The planet book.

Teacher: The planet book, great. You know that you find your resources in your science book and in your data tables. I'll ask Ken to come and get it. [Ken walks up to get the materials.] Here is also a sample to show you how to put it together. [The teacher hands over the materials.] Center 3 is Stargo. Edwin come up here, please. [She hands him the game.] Center 4, I would like Giovonni to come get your star path materials. [She hands him the materials.] And finally, Center 5 is doing planet reports. You guys have signed up for your planets, so you know what to do.

Because the teacher has planned work to be performed without her direct supervision, she reviews how and where students will do their work successfully. She clarifies how they will work with resources other than herself when she says, "You know that you find your resources in your science book and in your data tables." She provides a model to guide the students' work when she says, "Here is also a sample to show you how to put it together." She also emphasizes where students are to go to work when she says, "Right, you're meeting with me at the back table." She clarifies the arrangements of the classroom that her instructional frame supports.

After the briefing, the teacher gives the students their folders containing the instructional frame. Each student's path or route through the frame is indicated on his or her copy. The students use their frames as a guide that they revise in

Table 3.2B Instructional Frame: Sixty Minutes			
Session 1	**Session 2**	**Session 3**	**Session 4**
Briefing: Build community. Introduce activity. Explain directions. Clarify expectations. Distribute materials.	*Teaching lesson:* Teacher teaches a prepared lesson to the whole class.	*Follow-up activity:* Students apply the lesson's concepts and skills and assist one another. Teacher focuses on students' success with the activity in the time available.	*Debriefing*
10 minutes	20 minutes	20 minutes	10 minutes

conference with the teacher. The folder holds other materials as decided by the teacher, such as unfinished tasks or individualized assignments. The folder is also used for carrying their current work products and handouts. The students proceed to their work areas and the teacher sets a timer to ensure that the instructional frame is implemented on schedule.

Teaching Activities Table 3.2B shows the instructional frame's briefing and teaching and activity sessions. The middle session contains the teaching activity, or lesson. It also includes a follow-up activity session. In the follow-up activity, the students apply and extend what they learned in the teaching session. The pairing of teaching with follow-up sessions extends students' attention to the teaching topic. Students' performance on the follow-up activity also provides the teacher with immediate feedback about the effect of his or her teaching on the level of students' understanding. Teaching and follow-up are always paired in the instructional frame.

The two sessions, teaching and follow-up, have different formats from the start. The teaching lesson is a single session in which the teacher teaches. At the beginning of the school year, teaching usually includes the entire class. In the follow-up activity, the teacher also works initially with the whole class but with the goal of developing students' independence. From the first follow-up session, the teacher assists students in working successfully with peers and without the teacher's direct supervision.

Major factors that contribute to students' successful independence are the level and timing of the tasks they must perform in the frame. If the teacher designs tasks that students can accomplish at their level of skill within the time available, they will complete them independently and to the standard expected. Teachers must also provide the resources that students need for the task in the setting and encourage them to assist one another in task completion. During early follow-up sessions, the teacher focuses on students' successful performance within the time limits of the session. If the students require assistance beyond what they have received from their peers, the teacher reflects on how to design tasks to best match students' skills, and how to write the instructions provided in the briefing session of the frame.

The teaching and follow-up sessions, which last about twenty minutes each, in combination with the briefing and debriefing sessions, produce a four-session instructional frame that takes sixty minutes to execute. Table 3.2B shows the details of a timed basic instructional frame. This frame is an example of classroom *monotasking,* in which the teacher organizes instruction for guiding all of the students to perform the same task together on the same timeline along with the teacher.

Debriefing   Table 3.3 shows the last session of the instructional frame is the debriefing. In debriefing, the students and the teacher discuss their experience of the frame and whether the students' performance meets the expectations, particularly those laid out in the class agreement developed during community building at the start of the school year. The debriefing involves the students and the teacher in an evaluation of the frame's activities. First, the students describe their successes. Then they raise questions, identify problems to solve, and give feedback about the work and about how the class worked together. If needed, the class can briefly address the problems identified. The class agreement is a guide for the debriefing. The students and teacher match their experience to the standard set in the agreement. They review it as a guide for their work and consider amending it if it is not meeting their needs.

Finally, the teacher affirms the students' successes and expresses respect for the feedback they have provided. The teacher ensures the students of the value their participation, especially their productivity toward meeting the goals they set in the briefing and in the agreement. The teacher reminds the students of their progress toward rewards and celebrations. If extended discussion is required, the teacher schedules a class meeting for in-depth discussion, problem solving, and possible revision of the class agreement. Debriefing is the final event in the frame, but it can be used whenever the class needs to reflect and correct, as shown in the descriptions provided in Table 3.3.

Table 3.3
Instructional Frame: Sixty Minutes

Session 1	Session 2	Session 3	Session 4
Briefing: Build community. Introduce activity. Explain directions. Clarify expectations. Distribute materials.	*Teaching lesson:* Teacher teaches a prepared lesson to the whole class.	*Follow-up activity:* Students apply the lesson's concepts and skills and assist one another. Teacher focuses on students' success with the activity in the time available.	*Debriefing:* *The class talks about the activity, highlighting successes, sharing concerns, relating the activity to the community agreement, reflecting and correcting, and promoting and praising one another.
10 minutes	20 minutes	20 minutes	10 minutes

Classroom Activity Settings

Beginning with community building, which will continue throughout the school year, teachers may provide classroom space for projects or other assignments that will be ongoing. Teachers may call such areas centers or stations; they may give them numbers or functional names such as Library, Journaling, Computers, Vocabulary, Games, or Crafts; or they may label them according to selected content areas. If the teacher intends for an activity to occur continually at a designated place in the classroom, that intention is explained during the briefing and the introduction of the activity setting.

Teachers usually prepare activity settings early in the year for teaching, skill development and practice, ICT, and special interests that students will continue to work on throughout the year. The activity settings are sometimes already in place on the first day of class. Once the teacher has arranged the classroom, all that needs to be done is to introduce the students in the briefing to the work they will do in the various settings and to the expectations for performance in those spaces. The spaces that teachers devote to ongoing work are referred to as *continuing activity settings,* and usually have a specific content- or theme-related name.

The ultimate goal of the five pedagogy standards is to facilitate teaching that uses dialogue, or instructional conversation (IC), regularly, even daily. IC requires a small-group setting for student dialogue with the teacher. So that the teacher may concentrate on conversing with some students, the other students must perform productively on their own in other activity settings. To facilitate this, five-standards classrooms are arranged so that teachers have a small-group teaching area. They also often have a library area for student reading related to study topics. Teachers decide where to place the teaching area and the library on the basis of how students are to use the areas. In an independent area such as the library, students must know how to report on their reading activity while they are there. The teaching or IC area and the library are examples of continuing activity settings, which need permanent furniture in devoted arrangements. Following are examples of continuing activity settings that teachers often incorporate into their classrooms:

Library: Teachers set aside an area stocked with books and magazines for students to visit frequently for reading.

Journaling: Students can write in their journals beginning on the first day of school. Teachers usually provide a journaling and writing activity setting for students to use for writing and for reviewing dictionary, thesaurus, and other resources. Teachers assign writing activities in the early large-group activities of the frame.

Computers: Many students are familiar with computers, but some may need peer assistance to store and retrieve information and use new programs. All students must gain proficiency in keyboarding as early as possible.

Sight vocabulary or vocabulary development: Early-grade students need to build extensive sight vocabulary skills, and vocabulary needs continuing focus and development throughout the grades. It thus deserves its own focus area where stimulation from many resources and activities is available.

Writing: Written products in all genres are essential to learning. Students need to learn the mechanics of writing, and to write often. In the early grades, this setting can include activities in basic letter formation, printing, and spelling, and later, cursive writing practice, composition, and grammar.

Observation: Many K–8 classrooms house live animals, fish in aquariums, gardens, and other habitats. Students observe in these settings in order to record and analyze data on living things. This type of activity has power to build community cooperation for nurturing as well as for learning about living things. Guidelines for data collection, routine record keeping, and cleaning and feeding policies need to be discussed during community building and included in the class agreement.

Games: Board and computer games bring real-world value to the classroom. Games energize students and enliven valuable practice.

Content skill practice: Subject-area concepts and skills, such as multiplication tables that include the teens, calculator proficiency, and creative applications such as science, geography, and other concept and skill applications provide experience in acquiring formulaic, mechanical, and rote skills that expedite learning and lead to new understandings.

Assessment: Testing is a regular feature of classroom teaching and a means of accountability at many levels. In an activity setting reserved for assessment, students may take teacher-made quizzes and tests, and practice for standardized testing. The expectations for the assignments and assessments at the setting must match real test-taking circumstances. This activity setting is usually placed in the quietest area of the classroom and has enough room for students to work separately.

Project: Ongoing projects, such as small-plant cultivation, botanical studies, weather tracking and reporting, geodesy using global positioning techniques, stock market portfolio development, and the like require a devoted space with appropriate equipment, resources and materials, and computer accessibility.

Other languages: When students who speak languages other than English are present in the classroom or school, another language and culture can be emphasized and developed in an activity setting, especially if parents, grandparents, or others who speak the students' language volunteer to monitor and support the activities in the classroom.

When continuing activity settings are installed in classrooms, teachers assign each setting a number. The numbers facilitate planning and the routing of individual students through the activity settings. They also ensure that students can easily navigate their way in the classroom.

Multitasking Classrooms

Multitasking classrooms release teachers to teach and students to participate in a variety of high-quality activities. All teachers begin the school year by monotasking in the large group. They start with an instructional frame that contains a single activity session in which all the students perform together. When the teacher and the class are ready, the teacher plans an instructional frame that supports a simultaneous second activity. For example, Table 3.4 shows how the frame can be expanded by adding classroom library time and a journaling activity to sessions two and three. Although additional student activities are now available within the two sessions, the time to perform the frame remains the same. When the teacher makes this adjustment, the activity of the frame shifts from monotasking to multitasking.

The introduction of simultaneous activities within a session of the frame is an enormous advantage for teaching. When the teacher and students work on different activities at the same time, the teacher shares responsibility for the classroom community with the students. Students who work independently release the teacher to work with small groups in targeted lessons and to use

Table 3.4
Instructional Frame with Multitasking: Sixty Minutes

SESSION 1	SESSION 2	SESSION 3	SESSION 4
Briefing: Introduce community building and journaling about it; explain expectations for the group that will work independently while the teacher works with the other group.	*Teaching activity:* The teacher teaches half of the class about community building.	*Follow-up activity:* Half of the students work independently at their homeroom seats on journaling about classroom community. They are to meet writing expectations while problem solving on their own.	
	Follow-up activity: Half of the students work independently at their homeroom seats on journaling about classroom community. They are to meet writing expectations while problem solving on their own.	*Teaching activity:* The teacher teaches half of the class about community building.	*Debriefing:* Did the students meet the expectations of independent work? Discuss concerns. Highlight successes. Praise and promote independence.
9 minutes	19 minutes	19 minutes	10 minutes

Travel time: 3 minutes

IC. In multitasking, the teacher gains the means to diversify from teaching in a large-group format into teaching in other configurations that are more conducive to thoughtful discourse on academic topics.

Introducing Multitasking   To introduce the students to an instructional frame with simultaneous sessions, one a teaching activity and the other an independent activity (the example in Table 3.4 shows a simultaneous teaching session and a follow-up session on journal writing), the teacher carefully briefs the students, explaining that the simultaneous teaching and follow-up activities will require the class to be divided into two groups. The topic of the teaching, community building, is introduced, and the follow-up activity extends the teaching focus to journaling. The students who are in the group that does the follow-up activity first, before the teaching activity, will write out of their prior knowledge as discussed in briefing. The frame can be rearranged to avoid the out-of-sequence follow-up to teaching, or it can be used, for example, to elicit students' prior knowledge and experience on the topic of community building.

Because the simultaneous activities require two groups, the simplest way to divide the class is to have half of the students (for example, those on the right side of the room) journal in their homeroom seats while the other half (on the left side) meet with the teacher on the topic of community building. The class can also be divided into halves by counting off by ones and twos, or alphabetically, or in other ways that produce two groups. The students engaged in journaling are to meet expectations for writing and problem solving on their own, which is made clear in the briefing. The shaded area in Table 3. indicates when the teacher is teaching.

Depending on the students' experience in independent activities and on the school schedule, the teacher may choose to pause the frame after the first simultaneous session (session two) to debrief. The teacher would resume the frame then or at the next meeting of the class, briefing the students again to reorient them to the frame before proceeding with session three. The teacher uses a kitchen timer or other reminder to time the sessions in order to stay on the frame's schedule.

In the multitasking frame, students must learn to respect the teacher's time with other students (unless there is an emergency), and it is important for the teacher to respect students' independent work time as well. To emphasize the importance of the teacher's time with other students, it is recommended that teachers ignore students who approach or address them with questions during the teaching session. Likewise, teachers must not intervene in students' independent activity except in cases of emergency (such as sickness, injury, highly irregular student behavior, fire drills, power failures, an accident that ruins material or breaks equipment needed for a task, and so on). Because the expectations of activity have been discussed in the briefing along with the classroom community agreement, students know what they are to do. If students remain confused about their work in an independent session, the teacher needs to reflect on the quality of the task provided and on the explanation given to students in the briefing session of the frame.

Debriefing occurs again after both the teaching activity and the follow-up session are completed. The students discuss their success in their independent work and the quality of the task they have performed. Experienced teachers and students may choose to perform the entire frame in one class period on one day, across class periods on one day, or across days as originally planned, without pausing. Even though the journaling activity may take place at students' homeroom seats, the teacher is introducing a continuing activity setting. When the teacher groups students by numbers that will fit the seating at the designated space for journaling, the students proceed to the activity setting to write in their journals.

Teachers may choose to repeat the sixty-minute instructional frame to introduce another continuing activity setting, such as the classroom library. The library would be introduced in the same way during briefing, and the independent activity would be performed at students' homeroom seats. Students would select their books and bring them back to their seats to read. Other grouping arrangements for accommodating students at multiple continuing activity settings, such as those for computers, vocabulary, observation, games, and assessment, are discussed later in the chapter. Teachers may choose to introduce these topics early while students do their tasks at their homeroom seats.

It is important to emphasize that teachers design and oversee multitasking classrooms in order to increase opportunities to teach students in manageable numbers. The term *multitasking* applies to the classroom, not to the students, who are not multitasking but rather are focused on each task as they perform it. The multitasking classroom enables student to experience a great variety of tasks and activities in a rhythm suited to their learning levels.

Stocking Activities for Multitasking The task requirements of monotasking frames and multitasking frames are similar, but each frame uses a different schedule. The number of tasks and activities that teachers need to develop for students to perform depends on how many sessions of the instructional frame are to be completed on a particular day. For every activity in a session there must be a task for students to perform. In a monotasking frame, all students perform the task at the same time in a single session. In a multitasking frame, tasks and activities are distributed across the instructional period, which may extend over a week or more.

In the frame, teaching and follow-up activities are led by the teacher and for the most part require tasks and activities to be prepared for every session. These tasks and activities must be designed for the students' capacity level and for the time available in each session. As teachers discover the potential that a teaching session with small groups of students has for assessing their knowledge and skills. Teachers use the information to design suitably leveled tasks.

For the independent sessions, in which students work without direct teacher supervision, teachers design tasks and activities in standard or generic formats. The products of generic tasks are open ended in order to include student creations such as drawings and writing; they are repetitive or automatic, using workbooks, computer files, data-collection forms, journal entry formats, game scores, and so on.

For example a generic task assignment may be a brief report that includes the title, author, date, and subject of the students' reading during a visit to the library; a journal entry written according to the expectations set for the piece (number of words, length, topic, and so on); or a written response to key comprehension questions about character, plot, theme, conflict, and so on or to comparable content questions on the concepts presented in the text or lesson at the writing activity setting. Suggestions and formats proposed by the curriculum or in teacher guides provided by commercial textbook publishers are helpful in getting started on generic task design. Students come to expect a generic format unless the teacher assigns a specific task. Teachers use generic tasks to develop a system for stocking multitasking frames with many quality skill-building tasks.

Like students in monotasking classrooms, students in multitasking classrooms usually perform all of the activities and tasks that are assigned. However, in multitasking classrooms they do so on different schedules with different groups of students, and often on different days. Students need to know where to find their tasks, how to handle their ongoing work, and where to place their completed work products. They also need to know how the products will be returned to them with feedback from the teacher or peers.

It is important to take enough time to implement the first standard's indicators so that everyone—teacher and students—is comfortable with multitasking. Many teachers and students take from six to eight weeks to shift entirely into using a multitasking instructional frame.

Expanding the Multitasking Frame   To expand the instructional frame, an activity is added to each session. This expansion can be designed vertically or horizontally, depending on the time available. In other words, a vertical expansion requires that more simultaneous activities be added to the second and third sessions in the sixty-minute frame. The activities in the frame will increase from six eight, including briefing and debriefing. One advantage of this approach is that including more activities in the frame does not require more time. Another advantage is that the size of the groups decreases. The teaching group thus becomes smaller and more manageable. Adding two more simultaneous groups to sessions two and three produces eight activities and a teaching group that is smaller and thus more appropriate for using dialogue to teach. This kind of instructional frame suits an hourly class schedule and can be adjusted to meet the specific minute requirements.

In horizontal expansion, another session is added, so the frame expands to ninety minutes, as shown in Table 3.5. The advantage offered in both types of expansions is that the teacher may now work with a smaller portion of the class— one third—in each activity setting and students work with one another in smaller groups. This advantage increases in a vertica expansion as more simultaneous activities are added to the sessions in a frame.

The ninety-minute frame in Table 3.5 provides eleven teaching and learning activities sessions within the period. Each student participates in three activities with the teacher and one-third of the student's peers. One third of the class is a large group because a class of thirty or more would have groups with more than seven students. The instructional frame can be expanded vertically with no cost in time in order to serve fewer students in each activity; or it can be expanded horizontally by increasing the frame's timeline. For example, an additional twenty-minute session on ICT can be added to make a 110-minute frame, which is just under two hours, leaving a few minutes for class cleanup. The expanded frame shown in Table 3.6 consists of briefing, debriefing, and four teaching and activity sessions, totaling eighteen activity settings. The teaching activities focus on

Table 3.5
Multitasking Instructional Frame: 90 Minutes

SESSION 1	SESSION 2	SESSION 3	SESSION 4	SESSION 5
Briefing: The goal of this frame is to develop independent work habits with peers and to teach journaling. Students' names are posted in Groups 1, 2, and 3.	*Teaching activity:* Group 1: Journaling practices.	*Follow-up activity:* Group 1: Journaling activity.	*Follow-up activity:* Group 1 visits library setting.	
	Independent activity: Group 2 visits library setting.	*Teaching activity:* Group 2: Journaling practices.	*Follow-up activity:* Group 2: Journaling activity.	
	Independent activity: Group 3 Content area task such as mathematics activity.	*Independent activity:* Group 3 visits library setting.	*Teaching activity:* Group 3	*Debriefing:* Did the students succeed in independent work? Is everyone ready to perform independently?
11 minutes Travel time: 4 minutes	20 minutes	20 minutes	20 minutes	15 minutes

Table 3.6
Multitasking Instructional Frame: 110 Minutes

Session 1	Session 2	Session 3	Session 4	Session 5	Session 6
Briefing: The goal of this frame is to develop independent work habits with peers, and to teach ICT research. Students' names are posted in groups 1, 2, 3, and 4.	Teach ICT research practices to Group 1.	Group 1 follows up with an ICT research activity.	Group 1 visits library.	Group 1 visits journaling activity setting.	Debriefing: Did the students succeed in independent work? How was work shared at computers?
	Group 2 visits journaling activity setting.	Teach ICT research practices to Group 2.	Group 2 follows up with an ICT research activity.	Group 2 visits library.	
	Group 3 visits library.	Group 3 visits journaling activity setting.	Teach ICT research practices to Group 3.	Group 3 follows up with an ICT research activity.	
	Group 4 performs content area task, such as mathematics activity.	Group 4 visits library.	Group 4 visits journaling activity setting.	Teach ICT research practices to Group 3.	
12 minutes	20 minutes	20 minutes	20 minutes	20 minutes	13 minutes

Travel time: 5 minutes

introducing and using continuing activity settings. The class of thirty is divided into four groups of six to eight students each, which is close to the size of a small group.

Multitasking instructional frames offer teachers the opportunity to increase interaction with students on a regular basis. Increasing the number and type of activities that students perform daily in a multitasking classroom provides numerous opportunities for skill mastery and deepe involvement with content topics. There are many options for expanding the instructional frame depending on the curriculum and the teacher's plans for activity settings. Although the organizational possibilities are compelling, all options must be considered in terms of whether they support teaching through dialogue in order to assist student performance in the learning zone. The instructional frame serves effective teaching using dialogue that produces academic learning outcomes.

Developing the Timeline   The timeline of an instructional frame establishes the pedagogy system in the classroom. The timeline ensures that teachers use the time they have with students to teach. The first step in developing a timeline is for the teacher to identify the total period of an instructional frame. In the early grades or in upper grades with block schedules, instructional frames are planned for 90 to 150 minutes or more depending on the classroom and the school schedule. In upper grades on hourly class schedules, the frame is likely to be limited to two sessions per class period. Because vertical frame expansion costs no additional time, teachers can still provide students with the frame's benefits in terms of predictability, rhythm, a pace matched to students' attention spans, a variety of activities, IC, and so on.

Next, the length of the sessions within the frame must be calculated. The frame always includes ten minutes each for briefing and debriefing, and about six minutes total for students to travel between activity settings. For example, to move from briefing to the first activity setting, no more than one minute is allotted. Students are quick to grasp the schedule and routing because they are moving and participating in activities they enjoy. Briefing, debriefing, and travel, then, together total twenty-six minutes. The teacher subtracts those minutes from the overall instructional frame period to find the teaching and activity time (TAT). The TAT is then divided by twenty, which is the number of minutes given to each session in the frame. The quotient is the number of TAT sessions, or content tasks, that can be inserted into the frame. One or more sessions may need to be shortened, when

Table 3.7 Instructional Frame: 40 Minutes			
Session 1	Session 2	Session 3	Next Class Meeting
Briefing	Teaching lesson	Debriefing	Follow-up
10 minutes	20 minutes	10 minutes	20 minutes

necessary, in order to fit the activities into the TAT. Activity sessions are scheduled for eighteen minutes or less only when absolutely necessary. When they teach for less than eighteen minutes, teachers may find it difficult to accomplish their goals. Still, a shortened teaching activity may be useful for catch-up, review, or procedural tasks. Conversely, if the minutes scheduled for travel or other events are not needed, they are often used to extend the ten-minute debriefing schedule. An instructional frame of forty minutes (the briefest recommended) requires one session to roll over into the next meeting time. An example is presented in Table 3.7.

The instructional frame, then, can be used for forty-minute periods to periods lasting many hours, as needed. The frame is vertically and horizontally elastic enough to support a week or more of class work, in the manner of a unit or other large framework of study. Like a train adding passenger cars, the frame can expand to include many activities. More specific formulas for calculating instructional frame timelines are provided in Appendix 3A.

INDICATOR 4: THE TEACHER ARRANGES THE CLASSROOM FOR INTERACTION AND JOINT ACTIVITY

Multitasking classrooms feature a variety of materials, tools, work areas, and settings that support individual activity as well as collaborative work by students and the teacher. Because according to the first pedagogy standard the teacher and students work together frequently, the teacher sets up a meeting space that will accommodate a small group of up to seven students. This space is in addition to teacher-specific furniture or other space that the teacher uses to administer the classroom. In various other spaces, students use technology, textbooks and workbooks, other print resource materials, manipulatives, and arts and crafts supplies to complete tasks. Teachers arrange their classrooms to assist student interaction and productivity, as in the following fourth grade example:

Fourth Grade Classroom Arrangements

In fourth grade, a triad of students feeds the fish in an aquarium and records their observations, a small group reads a story with the teacher, another small group works on a math puzzle, other students make journal entries, two students research a science topic—Arctic habitats—on the Internet, others make maps of the Arctic areas they are studying, and others prepare crossword puzzles using their new vocabulary. The teacher monitors the whole class while reading with her small group by looking up occasionally and praising those who are working and solving problems efficiently. She can view every student's work area from her position. Before class she placed activities organized by folder color that students know hold their work at every work area, and she checked that adequate materials and supplies were in place. She reviewed all of this with the students during the briefing, but when the session is over she will remind students to tidy their work areas before moving to the next one. The seating arrangements she made at the start of the year continue to meet the needs of students at activity settings.

In classrooms, students are close together most of the time. This usually influences students to talk. When the physical arrangements encourage work together students' urge to talk and relate is usually overwhelming. Even in such arrangements, students do not necessarily relate to those who are next to them, and do tend to relate to those they already know. Just being together does not ensure students will talk or share interpretations to improve teaching and learning. That is accomplished by students working together. Classroom arrangements and joint activities must provide for students to talk, work and produce together as shown in the Fourth Grade Classroom Arrangement example.

Classrooms are highly adaptable when tables and chairs are arranged in groupings to accommodate up to seven students at a time. Often as many as a dozen specific activity settings provide space for work and for materials storage for up to seven students each. Students also have their own homeroom seats, and space for storing appropriate personal belongings and school supplies. The homeroom seat is the starting point for the day's work and provides seating for large-group activities. Of course primary-grade students use other areas of the classroom, such as a carpeted area, for convening in the large group.

Because new space arrangements at any level are major changes for everyone, teachers design their classrooms before students have established a routine. However, teachers can comfortably rearrange their classrooms at any time by ensuring that everyone is ready for the change. With the exception of a carpeted gathering place on the floor for early-grade students, most K–8 classroom arrangements need to include the following spaces:

- A homeroom seat for each student
- Mailboxes for cycling students' work, papers, folders, and so on.
- Storage space for personal items
- A whole-group seating area on the floor for early grades
- Six small-group work areas that can accommodate up to seven students
- Small-group gathering places such as a library, a quiet writing space, a crafts and cooking area (that can accommodate messy tasks), and a technology area (access to electricity and space for components)

Multitasking classrooms require furniture arrangements that promote student communication and production. Several activities occur simultaneously in each session of the instructional frame. Each of these activities or tasks requires a place where teacher and students can sit to work. Activity settings house instructional tasks designed for various student groupings. For conversation with the teacher, an identifiable meeting place with table and chairs and space for books, charts, and other materials is required.

In settings where students are to operate independently of the teacher, such as where they write in journals, or in the library, or where they work on crafts and play games, storage space is needed for their notebooks, pens, supplies, and other materials. Activities that require utilities such as water or electricity should be situated near those resources and contain all the preparation, performance, and cleanup materials that may be needed. It is important that technology be placed to maximize access and to ensure easy maintenance of printers and other equipment. In early elementary classrooms, the settings and supplies should be labeled. A checklist for organizing classrooms is provided in Appendix 3B.

INDICATOR 5: THE TEACHER GROUPS STUDENTS FOR JOINT PRODUCTIVE ACTIVITY

To fully participate in classroom activities, ELLs need to hear and understand what peers and teacher say. The brisk rate of exchange in the large-group setting may disadvantage language minority and low-performing students. Their chances for successful participation are increased in small-group arrangements. In small groups, peers may use their first, or "home," language as well as listen to peers model the language of instruction. When groups are involved in JPA, the students explain their ideas and thinking more comfortably (see Appendix 3C).

Group Size

The activities of the first weeks of school are mostly whole-group, especially if students and teacher are new to small-group arrangements. Community building and ECT activities encourage teachers to break away gradually from large-group instruction by assigning students to task pairs or triads. Teachers can observe students working in these arrangements before moving to small groups.

The ideal group size for ensuring student interaction and mutual assistance is from three to seven students. When teachers first form groups, they may be larger than this depending on how the classroom is arranged to accommodate students working away from the teacher. If there are irregularities, such as students interfering with or distracting others or not doing their work, they need to be discussed in the debriefing to ensure that all students understand the responsibilities of membership in the community that were spelled out in the classroom community agreement. Students ordinarily enjoy independent activities with peers, which motivate them to cooperate to continue the experiences.

Teachers who are familiar with their students' characteristics usually stabilize their groups at no more than seven students for a unit of time. As the students learn to enjoy small-group work, teachers typically report immediate benefits from working with students in such groups. For example, they talk to students they had not attended to previously. They discover personalities, senses of humor, and multiple perspectives in five-year-olds through teenagers. The encounter is especially profound when teachers realize the teaching opportunity that dialogue with students in small groups opens for them.

Group Membership

The membership of student groups is important to the quality of collaboration and mutual assistance. Without teacher intervention, student relating occurs on the basis of social background, neighborhoods, language, and status in school activities. Groupings based on friendship or affinity, common language, or interests encourage sharing, but other features can also promote peer collaboration toward instructional goals. Groups can be based on matched ability, mixed ability, project interests, gender, language, and even students' music preferences.

Grouping often connects students who might otherwise never meet or talk to one another. One goal that teachers set in planning group membership changes over the year is to have every student work with every other student in the classroom. Students who rarely relate to one another can do so in a game or other activity that both or several students can perform successfully. Grouping develops students' sense of belonging to the community. Management is less a concern when students use classroom community agreement they made at the beginning of the year. Any breeches can be discussed in debriefing or taken up in classroom meetings.

Teachers experiment with sorting students to discover how to match them on social and academic skills and other strengths. Students can be sorted into groups in the following ways:

- Randomly
  - Assign students to a color or favorite name, or count off by numbers.
  - Divide the class into increasingly smaller proportions: first into halves, then into thirds, then into quarters, and so on.
- By affinity, or student choice, often according to how many seats or materials are available in the workspace
  - Students select a first- and second-choice group.
  - Students choose their first- or second-choice work groups when there are less than seven students.
  - Students join project groups based on common interests such as gardening, weather tracking, model building, geography, math, science, ICT, games, student-generated activities, and so on.
- According to music preferences (or favorite TV programs, sports, games, and so on)
- By neighborhood or street address, joining those from the same area or those from different areas
- By common language and background

- By ability, matching students' proficiency levels in content, such as reading or math

- On the basis of heterogeneity, mixing students of varying abilities and skills

- By teacher assignment

Group membership usually changes on a regular basis, such as at the quarter mark, when students may have developed academically. Changes may be made according to set criteria for proficiency levels, social organization, curricula, or for other reasons.

Routing Student Groups

Teachers discuss groupings and group work during the briefing, which includes guidance on how and where they are to travel in the classroom. They review where students can find their tasks (in folders or clips) and the time they have to complete the activities. When they are ready, the students move into groups for their first activity in the instructional frame. The teacher observes, assists, praises, and promotes specific progress and accomplishments to reinforce successful interaction and performance in the groups.

Students have many talents to contribute to the success of a socially interactive classroom. From the first day of the school year, teachers observe students to identify their strengths and needs as they perform with their peers. Teachers encourage students to use their strengths to assist one another during joint work, especially when it occurs without the direct supervision of the teacher. Students who are recognized for their contributions, including material maintenance, problem-solving logistics, and other interventions, are likely to increase the responsibility they take for the classroom. Students must feel that they are agents of success working with the teacher.

Students Are Agents

In the whole-group instructional area of the classroom, children sat at individual movable tables and chairs that would be grouped in quads or pairs and arranged in a rectangle or horseshoe configuration, depending on the learning activities. During reading time, children could sit on the floor, at their desk, or on the couch in the reading nook. At the computer, children could rearrange seating by adding or removing chairs where they worked individually, in pairs, in larger groups, or with the teacher, depending on the task, students' computer skills, or student preference. Partners were self-selected or teacher-selected [Chisholm, 1995–1996, pp. 166–167].

INDICATOR 6: THE TEACHER MONITORS STUDENT PARTICIPATION AND PRODUCTION IN POSITIVE WAYS

Teaching within the instructional frame establishes a rhythm for the classroom that responds to students' attention spans and energy levels. A regular and predictable schedule provides a structure for students to use to manage their time and complete their assignments. Given the interruptions that are likely to occur in any classroom, teachers can adapt the frame to fit constraints and challenges. Still, teachers use briefings to remind students of their classroom agreements on noise levels, peer assistance, work space setup and cleanup, and travel from one work setting in the classroom to another. Classroom arrangements that allow teachers to see all work areas facilitate monitoring.

Teachers Monitor and Reward Students

Teachers always monitor students when students work independently of them. Teachers identify diligence and successful collaboration, and praise students who demonstrate these as models for others to emulate. Setting goals that carry rewards for the whole group promotes and maintains the community. Short-term awards can include time for games, lunch line privileges, other first positions, healthy treat choices, and the like. Students themselves can catch peers being good and nominate them for awards. Longer-term rewards in the form of fall, winter, and spring fun days can be discussed and planned from the first day of school. Students may want to skate, face paint, rock climb, swim, eat pizza, dance, and go on a field trip, among many other options.

Teachers know that at times it is necessary to deal with irregular, disruptive, or uncooperative behavior. When irregularities occur, teachers remind students to refer to their community agreement; they invite appropriate participation, and they praise it when it is reestablished. The first pedagogy standard guides teachers use a positive classroom management approach. A usefull rubric focuses on simple and clear communication, the community agreement, and positive support for students' appropriate participation and performance. The rubric uses six elements—simplify, clarify, identify, ignore, promote, and praise (SCIIPP)—to help teachers restore participation to normal levels:

S = Simplify:
- Simplify classroom rules by referring to the class agreement.
- Simplify tasks and directions in the briefing to ensure that all students understand.

C = Clarify:
- Clarify expectations for students by referring to the class agreement.
- Clarify rewards for productivity and participation in the briefing and debriefing.

I = Identify:
- Identify every student's activity regularly by scanning and monitoring. ("I see that table T is already working on their task.")
- Identify participation that meets expectations, and praise or promote. ("Thanks for good listening, thinking, helping the community," and so on.)
- Identify what does not meet expectations; monitor and check back. (Write names of uncooperative students on the board, and erase if check-back shows them returning to task.)

I = Ignore:
- Ignore minor irregularities, allowing them to wither from lack of attention. (Do not look at the disruptive student, and distract any student who is attending to that student.)
- Ignore until the irregularity slows or stops, and immediately praise. ("Thanks, Kel, for keeping the chair legs on the floor. That's helpful.")
- Ignore inappropriate behavior until a consequence is judged necessary. (When needed, ask the student to meet with you during recess or immediately.)

P = Promote:
- Promote by complimenting examples of the class agreement in action. ("Very helpful. You or your group are demonstrating our agreement by...")

- Promote by describing examples of appropriate task performance. ("Table X is following directions, using materials as we agreed," and so on.)

P = Praise:

- Praise students often for participation and collaboration. ("This is really community when you support each other to achieve.")
- Praise academic efforts specifically to show how they meet the standard. ("Take a look at group X's product, which has every step listed and labeled.")

The SCIIPP rubric is a positive approach that teachers use to inform students how to participate and perform in a manner that matches the standards set in the community agreement. Praise and promotion in particular have a strong maintenance function. As teachers come to know their students' needs and preferences, they can tailor SCIIPP to match individual circumstances and norms of the community. For example, one student may experience a teacher's smile and praise as reward for his or her effort, while another may find being singled out of the group by praise in front of peers to be an embarrassment. Specific praise refines students' understanding of the standard they set for academic products. In the following example, the teacher rings a bell during an instructional frame to get the attention of all the students. When she has their attention she thanks the students in one activity setting, Table Four, who are acting appropriately. She reminds all of them about the standards they set for performance and appropriate participation.

Teacher: "Thank you, Table Four. I know you all know what to do at your groups, so please work quietly so my group can hear and, if you're talking at your tables, so that that you can hear each other.

SUMMARY

This chapter was opened with an example of a teacher collaborating with a small group within her class of thirty students. As the chapter has discussed, the teacher had organized her classroom for multitasking. The instructional organization provided a schedule for meeting routinely with small groups of students. The advantage of such organization is that it allows students to meet with their teacher for dialogue on academic topics frequently and regularly than they can in the large group or with the teacher wandering from one student activity to another.

The first pedagogy standard guides teachers to organize and arrange classroom instruction as a system. The system supports teaching, or assistance, by enabling it to occur more regularly and effectively through increased use of activity and small-group instruction. The first standard's indicators describe how to transform a classroom into a community with an agreement; how to plan an instructional frame for teaching systematically; and how to design activity that is suitably leveled, timed, varied, and compelling. The indicators implement the first standard's intention to rearrange classrooms to support joint productive activity and multitasking. Implementation of the first pedagogy standard increases teacher and student participation and improves performance and academic production. The outcomes of implementation of the first standard in the classroom are as follows:

- A classroom community agreement is produced for teacher and students to implement together.
- Collaborative tasks are designed that require joint product development by teacher and students.
- Classrooms are arranged to support teacher and students' small-group collaboration and students' independent work.
- Instructional frames are routinely used for all teaching and associated activities.
- Students are organized into small groups for collaboration with the teacher and for independent activities.
- A positive management approach is used.

The chapter has applied the definition of pedagogy discussed in Chapter Two, which describes it as a system of instruction that supports effective teaching. With the help of the five-standards pedagogy described in this book, students can perform more effectively with their peers and with the teacher, and function at higher levels of academic productivity. Teachers who shift from a monotasking classroom organization to multitasking classrooms increase their access to students and their opportunities to teach. Multitasking classrooms more closely reflect the pace of students' participation in real-world experiences. Even the youngest students can succeed in multitasking classrooms, performing JPA with their peers without direct teacher supervision, as they do in their life outside the classroom. Instructional frames make classrooms predictable for all students. The routine use of briefing and debriefing opens a daily feedback loop from students to teacher and peers that is not ordinarily available.

The chapter has shown how teachers using the guidance of the first pedagogy standard can experience more than a few treasured "aha" moments. The five pedagogy standards make effective teaching and its product, learning, a possibility within every session. The remaining four pedagogy standards in the guidance system supporting effective teaching are discussed in the following chapters.

Seventh Grade English Language Learners Discuss Content Term

Teacher:	Up at the top [of the chart] it says, "Other bodies in the solar system."
Luis:	There's bodies in the solar system?
Teacher:	Well, why do you think they're using that word, *bodies*?
Edgar:	Like they mean the planets. What they mean by bodies is the shaping of the planets and what they're made out of.
Teacher:	Do you think that's right? [Looks at other students in the group.]
Luis:	They mean bodies of rock and ice.
Teacher:	Oh, so they mean bodies of rock and ice, right?

Developing Language and Literacy

PEDAGOGY STANDARD II

Developing Language and Literacy

Develop competence in the language and literacy of instruction across the curriculum.

Classroom Application Indicators

The teacher

1. Affirms students' language preferences for all activities.

2. Listens and speaks to students on everyday and academic topics.

3. Uses language development levers in all interactions.

4. Provides phonics and comprehension activities that lead to all students' literacy.

5. Expands students' expression in spoken and written academic language.

Introduction

Teachers who encourage their students to speak help everyone, especially the teacher, learn about one another's language proficiency. Students who are English-language learners (ELLs) and others may be unfamiliar with either their peers' or their teacher's language. The manner and style of expression may be another unknown for some students. Just as teachers need to learn about students' languages, many students also come to school not knowing the teacher's language or style. The teacher's patterns of talk and discussion (such as ways of asking and answering questions, using representations, and analyzing and validating claims) can challenge the majority student but be unfamiliar to ELLs and other students at risk for school failure.

At every grade level, teachers continually listen to and develop students' language because language is fundamental to academic learning. In the example at the opening of the chapter, the teacher spots a word in a classroom chart that she expects some students may find confusing. She uses language development techniques to ensure that all students grasp the connotative meaning of the term *bodies*. She uses questions, repetitions, and models of appropriate language forms, and encourages students to produce more language by welcoming all contributions. The techniques that the teacher models are powerful levers for influencing students' language development. In the example that opens the chapter, the teacher uses these techniques responsively to assist students.

Rationale

In the classroom, students' speech is often controlled, although school hallways, bathrooms, playgrounds, and other gathering places accommodate a wide range of students' written and spoken expression. Some students are highly flexible and fluent in more than one language and style of speaking. Students may use language, engage in literacy activities, interact with testing formats, and reconcile with peers according to highly specific repertoires learned at home and in their community and culture. In the classroom, students often respond to peers or teachers by shifting their style of speech and switching from one language code to another. Teachers, who may be proficient only in the language of instruction, usually English, must listen in order to learn about their students' expression. They need to understand students' language variety and levels in order to assist them.

The guidance of the first pedagogy standard supports organizing and designing all classroom interactions and activities to develop students' language and literacy. The second pedagogy standard guides teachers in leveraging students' language production in interactive classrooms for academic gains in vocabulary, literacy, and comprehension. The second standard expands the instructional system implemented by the first standard, as demonstrated in the following indicators.

INDICATOR 1: THE TEACHER AFFIRMS STUDENTS' LANGUAGE PREFERENCES FOR ALL ACTIVITIES

Language and thinking are deeply connected to values and culture. People talk in ways that reflect their culture's values. Students from varying traditions may use language repertoires that differ considerably from the mainstream in how they permit students to relate to authority figures such as teachers, answer questions, work with peers, and perform. The repertoires are derived from observation of and participation in community and cultural practices from birth. For the students, they are comfortable and acceptable ways to participate. For teachers, they may be highly unfamiliar and uncomfortable.

Every language and dialect that students use has many dimensions that are figurative, metaphoric, and allusive. Teachers must respect and learn about these dimensions of language, especially so they can use them as building blocks for new ways of speaking and thinking. One teacher creatively used students' rap language to help his students grasp challenging concepts. He combined the students' street language with school content to create a math rap:

Rapping It Up in Eighth Grade

An eighth grade algebra teacher, Alex Kajitani, at Grant Middle School in Escondido, California, puts on a pair of sunglasses to perform rap songs in his classroom. His piece on the decimal point, for example, starts like this:

"Now what in the world is that itty-bitty dot? Yo, I just can't remember, and it's making me distraught. I saw it in the price of the item I just bought. It's the decimal point, yeah, now you're gettin' hot!" [Kajitani, 2006]

Respecting Students' Language Preferences

Teachers learn about students' backgrounds in order to relate appropriately to them. Teachers may be unfamiliar with students' ways of interacting just as students may be unfamiliar with the teacher's ways. Teachers who demonstrate awareness of and respect for community-based language patterns increase their understanding of their students. They also improve their ability to anticipate and respond appropriately, which strengthens them as role models for students. This awareness is also a form of negotiation that involves attending to and respecting others so that they will do the same for you.

For example, academic achievement in mathematics is based as much on the ability to "speak mathematics" as on the ability to perform algorithms and know and apply formulas. Teachers can build on students' language to bridge academic terms and understanding. The eighth grade teacher who raps for his students gets rap back—in the following example, as an application of the concept of negative numbers: "I had a student come to me and say, 'Hey, Mr. Kajitani, I went to a taco shop the other day and my friend offered to pay for me. I really had to think, like, OK, do I want to go to negative five?'" (Kajitani, 2006).

Teachers usually accept all forms of student speech to encourage students' language production. The teacher is more concerned with motivating students to talk and to use the content vocabulary, and less with the forms they use or how they take turns, speak to one another, or overlap their speech. For example, in small groups, students usually do not raise their hands to speak. Their exchange is much more conversational than taking turns talking, and the teacher must pay careful attention in order to understand them.

The following excerpt was presented in Chapter Three and is presented again here to demonstrate teacher acceptance of all student talk, including students' first language expression. These students have little experience conversing in English on an academic topic. The teacher intervenes when a student makes an inappropriate remark—"shut up"—that could interfere with the discussion, but she does so by encouraging more talk and by modeling the courtesies and conventions of conversation.

Teacher:	[What did we do] the last time we were together? [Asking students to review.]
Adrianna:	*Son hilitos.* [They are strings.]
Adam:	What?
Adrianna:	Ah, shut up.
Teacher:	No, please explain it.
Daniel:	You have like a round thing [jar lid] and then you have to measure around it, and then across.
Adrianna:	You have to measure around and then—
Teacher:	And what was the thing [motioning with finger] around? What was it called?
Luis:	Circumference.
Adrianna:	*Le tienes que dar vueltitas.* [You have to make the string go around in circles.]

Note that the teacher stimulated students to talk. She intervened only to focus the conversation on the goal, and to avoid an escalation of inappropriate talk. She was persistent in encouraging students to explain on the basis of their experience in joint productive activity (JPA) and to use content vocabulary terms.

As teachers become familiar with their students, they learn their preferences for speaking that differ from the teacher's and from those of the majority students. The second pedagogy standard supports teachers in accommodating student rhythms that are individual and culturally based, such as adjusting the length of time between speaking turns ('*wait time*'), making eye contact, taking turns, and spotlighting individuals. In other words, teachers adapt their classroom participation practices to reflect students' preferred forms of conversation and activity. They drop unfamiliar forms of interaction such as hand raising and round-robin turns and substitute informal or familiar ways of participating that are used in ordinary conversation outside of school. Teachers continuously monitor interaction to ensure that all students are included in ways that the students find comfortable.

Teaching that intends to develop every student's language must provide multitudinous occasions for students to speak, write, and receive feedback from conversation with teacher and peers. Activities can be designed for students and teachers to practice together their preferred and culturally based ways of talking, especially when classrooms are organized for interaction and students are grouped. Initially, student groups that work independently of the teacher on collaborative tasks, especially using manipulatives and hands-on problem solving, are formed by matching students on the basis of their cooperation, sharing, and relating skills. As more is discovered about the students, JPA groups can be re-formed using other criteria.

Supporting Students' Activity Preferences

Students and teacher relate successfully, regardless of language or preferred style, when their activity is focused on manipulatives and other hands-on materials. During the activity, the teacher develops the students' language in a variety of ways. Vocabulary expansion, for example, is at the core of literacy and language development. Teachers begin building sight vocabulary in the early grades and expand vocabulary in every content area in every grade thereafter. Numerous commercial materials for vocabulary development are available, but homegrown approaches also work.

For example, the teacher of a second grade class developed a personal word box for each student to use as a dictionary and thesaurus. It was also a hands-on tool to support systematic vocabulary development through regular use. Each student owned a three-by-five word box and supplies of colored three-by-five cards for collecting and storing vocabulary. They named the box the Dictosaurus, reflecting youngsters' universal fascination with dinosaurs and to refer to its multiple uses. The Dictosaurus developed from a simple filing system into a source of independent activity and games. It became a portable manipulative for the students to carry from one activity setting to another if they chose. The activity was also easily transferred to computer files for those who chose to use information communications technology for this purpose.

Students develop their own Dictosaurus using a simple plastic box and three-by-five file cards. Students make an individualized vocabulary entry on each card. The Dictosaurus card file grows daily as cards are added for each new vocabulary word assigned and acquired. The cards are alphabetized; personalized; and used in activities and games, and for generation of a task. When students prepare a new card, they write the word and their initials on one side. The initials, or some other designation, enable the card to be shared and retrieved easily and quickly by its owner. On the other side of the card the student writes meaning cues, such as a clear definition, synonyms, sentences, and a drawing. Teachers and peers check the cards for spelling and meaning, and indicate that they've checked by snipping a corner off the card or applying a sticker. Each card is alphabetized or otherwise classified within each student's box. Students use the Dictosaurus independently in a variety of ways, from flashing sight-vocabulary cards with a partner to supporting writing activity, spelling bees, and word games. The cards can be swapped, shuffled, shared, and shown, and they can be used to complete and prepare tasks, play games, and sort vocabulary by concepts and topics for content activities.

The Dictosaurus encouraged students to use the dictionary and thesaurus to find out about word context, to learn multiple definitions and uses, and to choose the definition that met the requirements of their specific context of use. ELLs included their first language on the cards and even made separate cards to develop their first-language vocabulary. Students shared their cards with their parents, and the parents contributed first-language and other culturally related vocabulary. The Dictosaurus was used to support labeling activities that students could work on collaboratively or independently as they were assigned or chosen. The Dictosaurus could also become a personal computer dictionary and be used to create other files and games for vocabulary practice and other independent activities.

As noted earlier, teaching that continuously develops language provides extensive opportunities for students to speak and write and to receive feedback from conversation with teacher and peers. Importantly, students also need opportunities to practice language on their own. The Dictosaurus provides the instructional system with a major vocabulary development focus. It must be continuously fed new words taken from reading and classroom content. The numerous activities that use vocabulary to learn new skills, such as spelling and phonics, include the following:

- *Word Crosses:* Students select several sight or vocabulary words that have a letter in common. They write the words on graph paper, crossing them at the common letter. The borders of the words are then highlighted and the letters erased. For two words, a cross area remains. The paper is decorated with hints, including the missing words. The Word Crosses are used as vocabulary games by the rest of the class. To increase the difficulty, the words in the cross must relate to a topic the student can explain or draw.

- *Word Finds:* Students write their vocabulary words horizontally, vertically, diagonally, upside down, and backwards in the boxes on graph paper. Any remaining boxes are filled in with random letters. A key that shows the location of all the words is prepared. The Word Finds are then used as games by the rest of the class. Other students locate and circle the words. Students in the early grades list the words at the bottom of the page.

The Dictosaurus is the basis for a continuing activity setting that students visit at least one session per week, if not more often. At the setting, students maintain and care for their Dictosauruses and perform the assigned activities. Resource books, dictionaries, picture dictionaries, and thesauruses are provided at the activity setting. Students go to the setting in groups of three to seven within the system of an instructional frame.

INDICATOR 2: THE TEACHER LISTENS AND SPEAKS TO STUDENTS ON EVERYDAY AND ACADEMIC TOPICS

Every morning, teachers serve playground, bus, and hall duty. They greet arriving students and talk to them about their life inside and outside of school. These times of informal conversation with students about familiar topics are valuable opportunities for observation and for assessment of language proficiency. In such conversation, students reveal their language capacities along with information about their previous school experience, prior knowledge, family background, and other aspects of their life—often without the teacher having to ask a single question. Some students may not be so forthcoming, but the teacher's non-judgmental availability for informal conversation may eventually entice the reluctant students as well. In conversation, the teacher continuously models the language of instruction. Although students must engage language themselves in order to acquire it, some may not have attended to language forms, syntax, and vocabulary. By the time the teacher meets students to begin the day's instructional frame, the work of language development is already in progress.

Encouraging Students to Talk

Storytelling takes place in homes and communities around the globe. Intriguing fictional or real characters and exciting plot structures in children's literature immerse students in rich language. In school, teachers use narrative, poetry, and drama to involve students in language. Reading stories and other texts has been demonstrated to develop vocabulary, introduce new ideas, and provide models of language. Language models reflect the variety of forms that occur in speech and text, from patterned words and sentences to complex paragraphs and dialogue.

Early-grade teachers read stories to students to develop their listening skills, present new vocabulary, and stimulate conversation and thinking about narrative and expository reading topics. Conversation begins with sharing experiences, and in time builds skills for following story sequences; identifying details; and understanding plots, themes, and new concepts. For young students, stories and teacher-guided conversation about those stories provide JPA from the outset of school experience.

In a first-day kindergarten example, for her first activity a teacher planned to read a story. Her teaching goal in this activity was to develop students' listening comprehension skills. The approach she selected was a Directed Listening Activity

(DLA). To guide her story reading, she prepared questions to elicit students' language and encouraged their participation by accepting their preferences for responding, which were free of traditional conventions such as hand raising.

It is the opening day of school and Mrs. Won greets each of her kindergartners. She kneels to place a nametag on yarn around each student's neck and asks each child to read it. She helps the students deposit their belongings in bins marked with their names. By school start time, Mrs. Won has chatted with every child, accomplished lineup outside the classroom door, and waved away hesitant parents. She has soothed the discomfited one or two children by holding their hands and keeping them close to her. She has also identified those who can read their own or even others' names and who speak proficiently in both their home language and the language of instruction.

When she has her kindergartners sitting on a rug before her, Mrs. Won explains what they are going to do together. She says, "I'm going to read you a story about a whale family and we are going to talk about it. Afterwards we will draw and color the story topic." She begins by holding up a colorful book about a little whale and its parents swimming together in the ocean. She asks, "What is the story about? Who can tell us where whales live?" She restates the students' comments so everyone can hear them. She asks what they think will happen in the story. They say the baby eats and swims and will get tired. She begins reading the story saying, "Now listen to me read the beginning of the story. Let's find out about what happens to the baby whale."

When she finishes reading the first chunk of the story, she asks them what they heard. After a student comments, she restates the comment in a complete sentence. She asks, "Is that what you predicted would happen to the baby whale?" They say it is not and change their predictions on the basis of what they have heard. She begins reading again so they can find out what happens in the story. When Mrs. Won pauses at the end of another chunk of the story, the students talk excitedly, even simultaneously and overlapping with one another. She selects comments to restate for everyone. Then she focuses discussion on what they heard that supports their predictions. Mrs. Won continues the cycle of reading to find out if students' predictions are confirmed, until the outcome of the story is revealed.

The students are eager to work on the follow-up activity, to draw and color a whale family like the one in the story. They go to easels with crayons around the room. Several students work together to produce a single whale family portrait. After they draw and color for twenty minutes, Mrs. Won asks them to come to the rug and talk about whether they liked reading the story all together and drawing whale families with partners.

Mrs. Won used an instructional frame as guided by the first pedagogy standard. She began with a briefing statement that described the activity. To focus the DTA on listening, she carefully planned the reading portions and pace. She prepared questions for checking students' understanding of each story portion. Following the DTA format, she introduced students to brainstorming about the title and illustrations. Then she guided them to translate their thinking into predictions based on the evidence they had used to brainstorm. After the story-reading activity, she debriefed the students by discussing the quality of the story experience for everyone. The activity was teacher guided and of interest to and at the appropriate level and pace for kindergartners.

Valmont (1976) and Stauffer (1970) introduced the Directed Thinking Activity in the 1970s. The strategy is useful for developing students' thinking in large and small groups and at any grade level. The DTA can be focused on listening, as it was in Mrs. Won's example; on visuals; and on text. In all three instances, teachers lead students to preview text, picture, or stimulus; to examine prior knowledge; to find links; to make predictions; and to find evidence to support or refute predictions. To involve students, teachers question, restate, and require rationales and justifications for their comments in a DTA cycle. Each step of the activity promotes language use as teachers and students model proper language forms such as complete and increasingly complex sentences. The structure of the DTA approach follows; several variations are outlined in Appendix 4A.

Directed Thinking Activity Cycle

1. *Present first evidence:* Have you ever seen or heard anything like this before?

2. *Elicit predictions:* What do you think the outcome could be?

3. *Present additional evidence:* Does the new information support your guesses?

   a. *Review previous predictions:* Which guesses still work and which will not now that you have additional evidence?

   b. *Validate predictions:* What guesses do you want to eliminate? Why can't it be that? Does everyone agree?

   c. *Elicit more predictions:* Now what do you think this will turn out to be?

4. *Review thinking direction:* What finally made your predictions accurate?

Instructional Frame to Foster Language Proficiency

The second standard guides teachers to elicit students' language not only by using a variety of techniques and activities but also by using them routinely. The systematic use of the instructional frame introduced in the previous chapter is one way to establish routines to stimulate student language. The instructional frame for the DTA activity and associated activities is shown in Table 4.1.

On the first day of school, Mrs. Won worked with the entire group of new students. She used the instructional frame's briefing and debriefing sessions to bracket the teaching activity with clear instructions at the start and a review of the experience at the finish. She made the students comfortable and willing to speak in the classroom, and she welcomed all of their contributions.

As explained in the previous chapter on the first pedagogy standard, the instructional frame is routinely implemented as part of the system that supports teaching. The activities offered in the instructional frame develop students' language and other skills when they are frequent, expected, and directed toward academic goals. The number of teaching activities that can be inserted within the elastic instructional frame depends on the schedule and other classroom events.

Using Familiar Topics

Ordinary social talk builds relationships, but it can have other purposes as well. By talking with students, teachers obtain information that supplements and validates the data, test scores, grades, and narratives in students' records.

On the basis of information they gain from discussions with students, teachers decide which language models students need to practice. The information is used to design tasks and activities for both independent work settings away from the teacher and direct instruction with the teacher. For example, in a work setting devoted to language development without teacher assistance, students use tape

Table 4.1
Instructional Frame for Kindergarten DLA

Session 1	Session 2	Session 3	Session 4
Briefing	*Teaching activity*	*Teaching follow-up*	*Debriefing*
"I'm going to read you a story about a whale family and we are going to talk about it. Afterward we will draw and color the story topic. Listen to the story to find out what it is about."	Teaching and modeling language: directed listening-thinking activity (DLTA).	Joint productive activity: several students work together to draw and color a portrait of a whale family like the one in the story. Large sheets of butcher paper are used so that students can work together in groups.	Students are asked to come to the rug to talk together about reading the story. They are asked about the activity of drawing whale families together.
5 minutes	20 minutes	20 minutes	12 minutes

Travel time: 3 minutes

recorders, computers, and other devices to practice language in meaningful contexts such as script writing; storytelling; and collecting, writing, and listening to recordings of plays and other narratives. For students to succeed in such settings, the instructional frame briefing must be specific about work expectations and products.

When students are in conversation with the teacher in a small group, teachers can plan or seize opportunities to provide language development or assess students' knowledge. During a conversation with several students about families, the teacher asked them to discuss signs of age. The teacher realized that she needed to assess her students' knowledge about the aging process to ensure that they would understand the role of a character in the story they were about to read.

Teacher:	What shows signs? How might you know when your grandmother is getting older?
Noelani:	Her hair might get—
Kalani:	No, she gets, face, face—
Makua:	She gets gray hair.
Kalani:	Her face gets, gets wrinkled. And, uh, the way they talk, and they cannot hear so good.

In such conversational exchanges, which require a small-group setting, students explain what they know and express themselves in the grammatical structures and syntax they have acquired. In the large group, language development activities are possible, but sustained conversation that includes everyone and targets specific language development is difficult to manage with more than six students at a time. This is particularly true when teachers are building on students' everyday language to develop academic language that requires new vocabulary understandings.

Teachers shift from everyday language into academic language and back to introduce and develop vocabulary and concepts. This process is modeled in the following dialogue between a Native American teacher and her students about furniture types and styles. The conversation is laden with vocabulary that the teacher models, including *contemporary, romantic, gingerbread,* and *antique,* and the students' preferences for these words.

Teacher:	[Looking at a decorative arts reference book with students] Yeah, this is contemporary.
Sheenan:	All straight and stiff. What if we had a contemporary room?

Teacher:	We do have!
Sheenan:	I don't like it. Ugh.
Teacher:	It's almost. It's a mess, huh? [Turns more pages, then turns book toward Sheenan] Would you like it more like this?
Tanyan:	That would make it romantic.
Sheenan:	Let's look at the last page. What's modern? Like this kind? Or this?
Teacher:	Um-hmm.
Sheenan:	I like this. I like this kind.
Teacher:	Yeah, they, this is, this is modern, this one, this one, and this one.
Sheenan:	This is old one?
Teacher:	Yeah. It's called "gingerbread."
Sheenan:	Yeah, and I like, and I like, um, what is it called? Antiques.
Teacher:	Um-hmm. I like it too. I've been collecting antiques.

In this conversation, the teacher talks with the students to connect everyday terms with concepts that are used to define categories. With the teacher modeling the process, the students classify and label types of furniture. One student identifies a category of furniture she dislikes. The technique focuses on the power of an everyday term to function as a concept that identifies a category. Interactions such as this increase language skills and raise thinking skills to new levels. When these experiences are continuously available in classroom talk, talk pedagogy is working systematically to develop students' language and literacy.

To develop students' language, teachers continuously sample their students' expressions by engaging them in discussion of interesting and familiar topics. Teachers listen to what is said, ignoring or responding as appropriate for their goals. Ignoring is a lack of response, not a failure to gather data on students' needs. As they question and probe, listen actively, ignore, or respond, teachers complete and enrich their students' utterances at any opening in conversation on topics of interest.

INDICATOR 3: THE TEACHER USES LANGUAGE DEVELOPMENT LEVERS IN ALL INTERACTIONS

Spoken language proficiency is key to successful reading and writing. The more students use language, the more their language proficiency increases. For teachers, students' language is the most important instructional resource for developing literacy across the curriculum. Reports establish links between language and thinking in that precise language reflects precise thinking. Conversely, teachers help students develop precise language skills so they will consequently develop the precise thinking abilities they will need for academic success.

The language use that prevails in school, such as ways of asking and answering questions, challenging claims, and using representations, is frequently unfamiliar to ELLs and other at-risk students. In the same way, students' ways of talking may be unfamiliar to teachers. Many opportunities to practice culturally based ways of talking need to be regularly provided throughout the school day for both students and teachers. Teachers can design activities that support first-language and other familiar forms of interaction without requiring students to give up or hide important features of their own lives.

Studies of language reveal that everyday language is the basis for academic language. Research also shows that feedback within ordinary conversation between students and teacher and among peers prompts speakers to modify their usage toward appropriate forms. This outcome strongly suggests that conversation between teacher and students is likely to be more productive of appropriate speech than are drills and applications of rules. The third indicator guides teachers to use language levers routinely in interaction with students. Every opportunity to assist language development is important. When teachers routinize their classroom speech, they provide students with numerous opportunities to hear, see, and practice language in appropriate forms with their peers and the teacher.

Promoting Students' Language Use

Student talk is the raw material that teachers use to develop students' language to proficient levels. Authentic approaches to language use are more productive than practice through drills and worksheets alone. Teachers understand that students increase their language proficiency by using language. They plan ways to stimulate students to use language in the forms and styles they need to practice. For students who may be developing proficiency in everyday language at the same time that they are learning academic language, teachers use the pedagogy standards system of support for instruction. This system provides intensive levels of participation where needed.

In this instructional system, teachers greatly increase students' everyday language use through JPA and independent tasks with peers at activity settings. Teachers must also invite students to express themselves with high-level language about content topics during interaction with students in small groups. The following language levers guide teachers to use language to improve student talk:

- Listen to students.
- Learn and use language from students' communities.
- Make words visible in lists and charts as well as by introducing them verbally.
- Use sight vocabulary and new vocabulary in conversation with students.
- Bridge familiar speech to new vocabulary and concepts.
- Provide labels and labeling activities in content areas often.
- Speak and write sentence patterns often.
- Model new and proper language forms in conversation with students.
- Retell and restate students' utterances.
- Follow up students' efforts with additional chances to perform, especially if they have been unsuccessful.

Teachers help students make connections between everyday talk and academic topics in a bottom-up manner through activity, especially JPA. Learning also takes place in a top-down manner and through a combination of bottom-up and top-down. Teachers use these and other approaches to assist students in acquiring vocabulary and language. In the first line in the following example, the seventh grade teacher reminds the ELLs of their lesson goal and refers to the chart they made in their JPA. Notice how she accepts all of the students' contributions, including one in a student's first language. She also accepts partial responses and overlapping speech when one student finishes another's sentence.

Teacher:	Yeah, we're measuring circles but there's a special word for that, that particular measurement.
Adrianna:	*Ahorita te lo corto.* [I'll cut yours right now.]
Edgar:	Is it—
Luis:	Measuring from one side to the other side?
Teacher:	Yeah, it's measuring from one side to the other side. That's how you would define it. Yes, that word is another big word and it's called [writing *d* on the board]—
Luis:	Degree.

Concha: [Sounding out the word] Dia, diam, dee a meter.

Teacher: Diameter, it's called a diameter.

Here the teacher unsuccessfully cues and questions the students for the mathematical term. In the last line of the excerpt, the teacher restates the vocabulary term and writes it on the board for all the students in the group to hear and see. Many students, especially ELL students, need enormous numbers of repetitions of a word and multiple experiences with its meaning to incorporate it into their vocabulary; others may require few presentations of a word to learn it. The seventh graders in this lesson have not yet received the number of presentations they will need to acquire the mathematical term. The status of their knowledge of the term is important assessment information for deciding next steps in the lesson and in the supporting activity.

Leveraging Students' Language to Increase Proficiency

Teachers at every grade level who learn students' interests and backgrounds gain the means to increase their students' comfort in sharing and using language. Respect and understanding will encourage students to share what they know using the language they have available. Teachers have the opportunity to develop students' language only when students' give it to them. Many teachers develop routines that use speech levers such as the following:

- Invite students to paraphrase and retell in their own words.
- Listen to students.
- Question to ensure that students respond.
- Ask students to describe their feelings.
- Ask students to explain their reasoning and logic.
- Ask students to justify their statements.
- Ask students to evaluate and make judgments about text.
- Guide students toward consensus.
- Assign word games.
- Play with words.
- Praise students for talking.
- Promote language expression for learning and for fun.

In the following excerpt from the measuring planets lesson, not all students consistently participate in the conversation. One student says she is having difficulty, which the teacher does not ignore. For students to participate, the teacher must ensure that they are comfortable. The excerpt shows how the teacher attends to the students' feelings.

Concha: I can't remember anything.

Teacher: You can't remember, that's okay. That's why we are reviewing. Now, do you know what it means when it's that three? What was [your regular classroom teacher] just talking about?

Daniel: Circles.

Concha: Circles and squares, circumference.

Edgar: Circumference.

Daniel: Degrees and all that.

Concha: Radius.

As the excerpt shows, the teacher responds immediately to Concha's statement of frustration. Briefly, the teacher reviews the purpose of the conversation with her. Then she assists Concha's return to the conversation by addressing questions to her. The teacher's attention to Concha is direct and swift, leaving the flow of the conversation undisturbed. The lack of disturbance is evidenced in the way the group continues. Daniel answers questions addressed to Concha as does Edgar. Concha's subsequent appropriate contributions indicate that she has returned to the lesson conversation.

In the excerpt, the teacher is skillful in maintaining the flow of the conversation while dealing with a single student's difficulties. Students' feelings are important to learning. The excerpt shows how a teacher can attend to students' feelings without losing teaching momentum. When students express feelings, they provide feedback to the teacher about the pace of the lesson or about other features that are unsatisfactory. During interaction with students it is critical that teachers make "in-flight" changes that directly relate to their comments. Teachers need to respond to students' statements in ways that are appropriate for the purposes set. These statements may be about feelings, skills, or understanding, and they are important occasions for teachers responsively to assist students.

Teachers who leverage language also model it, elicit it through questions and probes, and assess its proficiency in both social talk and academic discussion. All of the language levers rest on listening as much as on modeling language and responding to students' comments and questions at every opportunity. The same levers that foster facility in everyday language development do so for academic language as well. Most important, students must use language in the forms and style they are expected to learn.

Students Modeling Language

Even though students are usually experts on most task directions and procedures by second grade, they are rarely called on to guide their peers or the teacher. Instead, teachers give students directions on how to perform tasks. Teachers who have students participate by giving directions to their peers in the instructional frame briefings give students an expert role and develop their language skills. If students need more guidance in performing adequately in briefing their peers, the debriefing is another opportunity for peer and teacher feedback. Students can volunteer or be selected to lead their peers through a basic frame.

Within the instructional frame, teachers plan specific occasions and routines for language development. For example, students may brief the class on the community's guidelines for how to work together, what noise level to use, and how to solve problems. Students who have performed JPA previously are capable of presenting their expectations. In fact, beyond third grade there are few formats and activities that students have not previously encountered or performed in some version in some classroom. The briefing presentation is an opportunity for students to present to their peers and to use language that conveys information that everyone can understand. Also, interaction related to routine activities such as morning messages and such administrative tasks as roll call, housekeeping, record keeping, paper filing, and so on can be shared with and assigned to students.

INDICATOR 4: THE TEACHER PROVIDES PHONICS AND COMPREHENSION ACTIVITIES THAT LEAD TO ALL STUDENTS' LITERACY

Information about teaching beginning and content reading is increasingly available. Research reports affirm that teachers must competently teach a number of components of reading, including phonemic awareness, systematic synthetic phonics, vocabulary, fluency, and comprehension. Findings also indicate that inservice professional development produces significantly higher student achievement (National Reading Panel, 2000).

The five pedagogy standards recommend classroom arrangements for providing reading instruction on the basis of these findings. An instructional frame can organize a system for daily teaching in small groups (three to seven students) and follow-up practice activities for reading lessons. The pace of the frame depends on the teaching goals and the classroom schedule. In a first grade classroom of twenty-four students, four reading groups can be organized to meet for daily instruction with the teacher. An instructional frame for first grade reading instruction that includes the research-based reading components and activities described here is presented in Table 4.2.

Phonics, Phonemic Awareness, and Fluency

The pedagogy standards system supports individual phonics, phonemic awareness, and fluency activities as well as comprehensive reading programs that integrate them. Noncommercial and local approaches to reading instruction are also accommodated by the pedagogy standards instructional support system.

In addition to using prepared activities that focus on these components, teachers and students often include activities that they have designed to involve students in learning phonics and phonemic awareness. Students who have developed a Dictosaurus (described earlier in the chapter) continue to develop it, particularly as a resource for many of the following activities designed to help students practice phonics generalizations and phonemic awareness:

- *Crosswords:* The answers to Crosswords can target specific phonic elements and require rhymes and other wordplay to practice phonemic awareness. Students arrange the target vocabulary words to intersect vertically and horizontally on graph paper, and then number them. They then list and number clues for each word. The puzzle is solved when all of the spaces are filled with the letters of the correct words. Depending on the level of difficulty desired, the words can be listed somewhere on the page to help solve the puzzle. The original design is the answer key.

- *Maze Game:* In the Maze Game, sentences are written with some words underlined. The underlined words make little sense in the sentence, which may make for silly reading. The goal is to replace the underlined word with the appropriate vocabulary word. The vocabulary words that work best in the sentences are listed on the page or provided in another list. An answer key is provided.

- *Cloze Game:* Like the Maze Game, the Cloze Game is played using sentences that target specific vocabulary words. The difference is that the sentences develop an idea or narrative for at least a paragraph. Students can use a prewritten paragraph or write one specifically for the cloze. The goal is to systematically omit a word after every five, ten, or other number of words. The player must provide the appropriate word that makes the sentence make sense.

- *Jigsaw Puzzles.* Students can make jigsaw puzzles that are lead-ins to a topic. Students select pictures and paste them on a piece of thin cardboard or construction paper. They cut the cardboard or paper into puzzle pieces. The pieces are put into envelopes and distributed to students, who must work together to complete the puzzles. Writing about the picture they complete can follow the activity.

Fluency activities are a teaching focus for the early grades. Fluency is reading expression that sounds natural. It serves as a bridge from word recognition to comprehension. It develops over time through reading practice. Any reader's fluency is affected when vocabulary is highly technical or the text addresses unknown topics. Practice fluency activities with peer partners take place regularly in the classroom library. Other resources such as information communications technology (ICT), audiotaping, and read-alongs are also useful.

Virtual Reading

Students enrolled at Clement Middle School (California) are using iPods to help them with their reading. Books are recorded onto the portable MP3 players. This enables students to read along in a book while the audio plays on their earphones. While tapes and CDs make it difficult to go back to earlier parts of the story, the iPod makes it easy to repeat dialogue or sections of interest. With the help of the iPod, students learn the pronunciation of new words and read books at their own pace ["Getting Tuned In, . . . " 2005].

Word-processing programs allow teachers and students to revise and edit their written products easily. Database programs allow for the categorization, storage, and orderly retrieval of data collections. Some programs present material in an interactive format, with animated screens offering stories for listening, or individual words from stories, with immediate feedback. Technology facilitates multitasking when computers, graphing calculators, handhelds, interactive boards, iPods, and digital cameras are among other resources in the classroom.

Language Experience Approach

Early reading activities rely on language proficiency. Language development activities precede and promote decoding skills. For students to understand that text is language written down, they require experiences with language that present their very own talk written down. Readers must understand the alphabetic principle that the sounds in spoken words—phonemes—are depicted as letters in written words. All students need experiences linking sounds with letters.

When students listen and talk about objects or activities, their speech provides a source for the text of a story, poem, or fact piece. For example, a group of kindergartners developed their own learning experience approach (LEA) story after they heard a directed listening thinking activity (see Appendix 4A) story about whales:

The Whale

The baby whale is happy. It has a mother. It is black. The whale has a nose on top its head.
The end.
By Red Group
Christy, Deziree, Donald, Karku

The students dictated the story to the teacher. They read it together many times and used it to practice the alphabetic principle, phonics, and phonemic awareness, and to build sight vocabulary. LEA stories allow a focus on fluency and comprehension from the beginning of reading instruction. Teachers use the words that students speak to compose an LEA story, to underscore that reading is talk written down. When the students work on tasks associated with their story, they know they are using their own words. They know that what they said made sense because the teacher wrote it into the story. This activity provides a basis for practicing comprehension skills in early reading activities.

To create the story about whales, the teacher questioned the students about the meaning of the last sentence. A follow-up activity would be for the students to draw and color the whale and paste on labels for *nose, head, top, black,* and *whale* to identify features of the drawing. To make this a JPA, the students would use a large sheet of paper for a joint drawing that they would all color and on which they would all paste labels for specific features.

For additional practice with sight vocabulary, students enter the new sight words into the Dictosaurus described earlier in the chapter. The preparation of the cards is itself a productive practice activity. Using the cards for word recognition tasks has unlimited possibilities; for example, students can use them to practice reading, writing, and alphabetizing, and they can organize them by phonic elements. The cards lend themselves to phonemic awareness tasks that require students to find rhymes and other matches that build facility with word analysis. In combination with other activities of a formal reading program, the Dictosaurus is a versatile manipulative for strengthening sight vocabulary and decoding skills.

Developing Comprehension

Teaching assists readers to understand texts through the use of specific comprehension strategies. These strategies are conscious plans or steps for helping readers make sense out of texts. They aid students in become purposeful, active readers who understand texts. Several strategies have been identified as particularly effective for assisting students' reading comprehension. The guidance system of the five pedagogy standards accommodates these strategies. Routine installment of them in teachers' instructional frames, JPAs, and other collaborative activities, and grounding them in language development techniques, strengthens their effect on students' literacy. The strategies are discussed in the following sections.

Understanding Text   Teachers base reading comprehension instruction on language development techniques. At the outset of conversation about a text, students respond generally and from their experience. As discussion focuses on understanding text on the basis of the reader's experience, teachers use techniques to obtain specific and targeted responses. For example, the *cloze* technique requires students to identify a specific word to demonstrate their language acquisition and understanding. In the following mathematics conversation with ELL seventh graders about measuring circles, the teacher uses an oral cloze technique:

Teacher: And this one around, this is the—? [Traces the string with her finger.]
Luis: Circumference.
Teacher: Yes, and that's the—? [Points to the string on a paper.]
Luis: Diameter
Teacher: All right!

In an oral cloze, students are required to provide a particular word that demonstrates their acquisition of a term and its meaning. In the example, two mathematical terms were provided.

In reading comprehension, the oral cloze technique can be used to check students' understanding of a text. Students are asked to fill in the blanks with terms that show they understand the meaning of the paragraph. To check general and some level of specific content knowledge, every tenth or fifth or other counted word in a cloze can be omitted. The students must fill in the blanks so that the paragraph makes sense, such as in the following paragraphs on electricity:

Your body is mostly water! That means that you _____ a conductor of electricity too! If you touch water _____ has electricity flowing into it, you can become part _____ the circuit and be badly hurt. If you touch _____ that has electric current coming out of it, the _____ can jump to you and you will get a _____.

Cloze tasks can target specific content terms by omitting only those that students are learning. The correct terms can be listed at the bottom of the task sheet, or students can obtain them from their text or from charts in the classroom such as the following:

Everything that exists is made of atoms. The atoms are very _____ [small]. In fact, they are so _____ [small], there are trillions of them on a pinhead. Around each atom are _____ [electrons]. The _____ [electrons] go around atoms like planets go around the sun. Because _____ [electrons] are away from the _____ [center] of the atom, they can take off and jump to other atoms. When electricity flows through a wire, free _____ [electrons] are jumping from one atom to the _____ [next, other] and the _____ [next, other]. _____ [electrons] flow this way along a wire [Spero, 1994].

Teachers can adjust the cloze activity for more or less difficulty by omitting fewer or more words. Any text can become a cloze task. The purpose of cloze is to focus students' attention on understanding the meaning and identifying the correct vocabulary from the context.

Reading comprehension is essential at every level of reading development. For students in the early grades, a cloze task can include pictures with parts missing that students either draw or cut and paste from a source sheet. Cloze tasks provide many practice opportunities for students to use sight vocabulary within familiar and pattern sentences. For example, the story written by beginning readers about whales can be reproduced as a cloze task in which students draw pictures in the blanks or cut and paste words:

The Whale

The baby _____ is happy. It has a _____. It is _____. The whale has a _____ on top its head.
_____ end.
By _____ Group
Christy, _____, Donald, Karku

The cloze task targets basic sight vocabulary such as students' names, colors, and parts of the body; connector words such as *the;* and new words such as *whale* and *mother.* Depending on students' reading level, they can put drawings in the blanks, cut and paste in words listed on the page, or write in the words. The Red Group discussed the final product when they met with the teacher. Cloze tasks are interesting to students when posted on bulletin boards in the classroom, and they may be sent home to parents. Cloze tasks are suitable for homework assignments, especially when they include a list of words to assist fill-in.

Text Analysis   Teachers increase students' understanding of texts by using text analysis to manage the reading challenge. Preparation begins with setting an outcome for the reading that may vary depending on the type of text. The preparation steps for narrative and expository text comprehension are as follows:

Narrative	Expository
State lesson objective.	State lesson objective.
Identify character, setting, main events, resolution.	Identify text structures, themes, key concepts, main ideas.
Preview new vocabulary.	Identify vocabulary to teach.

(Continued)

Narrative	Expository
Select graphic or visual display for narrative structure.	Plan visual display for vocabulary and concepts.
Prepare questions to elicit	Plan study guide to
_____Prior related experience.	_____Recall prior knowledge.
_____Predictions.	_____Review new concepts.
_____Explanations.	_____Apply concepts.
_____Rationalizations.	_____Build knowledge.

When the analysis is used as a reading guide, teachers can include it in any approach to reading comprehension instruction.

Expository Text Comprehension   The first experience of expository text reading for early grades is often the classroom community agreement. Teachers use the community agreement as a text at any level to increase understanding about the classroom community. They develop comprehension questions in a multiple-choice or open-ended format to guide students to discuss and write in small groups. Following is an example of an eighth grade comprehension lesson using the students' own product (their community agreement) with multiple-choice questions that examine explicit and implicit understanding of the text.

Eighth Grade Classroom Agreement

Our community succeeds when we
- Use community voice levels and courtesy in all conversation.

- Act as community leaders for classroom setup, cleanup, and supply monitoring.

- Are ready when community activities begin:

  1. Materials, folders, paper, and books are ready to use.

  2. Pencils are sharpened.

  3. Homework has been completed.

  4. Have an organized portfolio of work.

  5. Visit the restroom during passing periods, breaks, and lunch.

- Work together on tasks by helping peers to
  1. Participate.
  2. Use content vocabulary and language.
  3. Make corrections.
  4. Enjoy membership.
- Follow the class schedule.
- Finish work by the deadline.
- Use extra time to read or do finishing activities.
- Use technology (computers, digital cameras, DVDs) according to directions.
- Use personal technology (cell phones, iPods, other) only when assigned.
- Identify examples of community participation to compliment or problem solve when the community meets.

Comprehension Questions

1. What is a community?
   a. A family.
   b. People with common understandings and shared values.
   c. All students in the classroom.

2. What are community voice levels?
   a. The same as those in the world outside the classroom.
   b. Whatever anyone wants them to be.
   c. Considerate levels of sound that allow concentration.

3. Why is the agreement important?
   a. Parents and principal will be called if it isn't.
   b. Everyone wants to be able to focus on doing interesting work.
   c. Rules need to be written so people can be told what to do.

4. Does the agreement apply to everyone?
   a. No, only those who break the rules will be watched.
   b. Yes, everyone tries to create the best community possible for all to enjoy.

c. Yes, everyone has problems and needs the agreement to learn the rules.

5. List the ways in which community members will know whether they have succeeded.

These five questions lead students to revisit the agreement to deepen their understanding of the document. Good readers make inferences, draw conclusions, and make judgments about a text based on the assumptions and rationales supporting the text. Students need to discuss and write about what is not written in the text but may be implied. A study guide assists students in reading between the lines to understand the meanings that are embedded in the text.

Comic books can help students transition from picture and chapter books to full-length exposition. Graphic forms of material are increasingly available to motivate struggling as well as proficient readers. For example, the *9/11 Commission Report* is sold in a condensed and illustrated format. This makes this government report accessible to many competent readers who would not otherwise read the original report. A list of Web sites that specialize in the use of comic books and graphic novels for literacy development is presented in Appendix 4B.

Directed Reading Activity Directed reading activity (DRA) can be used with any story or content text and is frequently found in published basal series. Most often the DRA begins with an experience-sharing discussion based on or related to the topic of the reading. Language levers discussed earlier in this chapter engage students in the discussion. Then story-reading, either silent or oral, is directed by purpose questions and sometimes a study guide to promote comprehension and factual retention. Usually a skill-building activity is included in the lesson, unless the reading is assigned as an independent activity. In follow-up activity, students often complete workbook exercises on the skills they have learned and on their comprehension of the story. Extension activities sometimes tie the story to related topics and to assigned tasks in those areas.

Directed Reading Thinking Activity The DTA presented earlier in the chapter prepares students to use thinking skills in reading. Directed reading thinking activity (DRTA) activates students' prior knowledge and is an opportunity to expand discussion that develops and clarifies students' new understandings. As in the DTA, students make predictions about what they will read based on title, illustrations, cover remarks and reviews, and their prior knowledge. They then read the first section of text. The teacher guides the students in examining and analyzing the text. The students revise and narrow their predictions in the same manner as in DTA, until they validate their predictions by reading the full text. Preparation for DRTA requires text chunking to support the DTA prediction and validation cycle. In addition, text analysis assists students with vocabulary or other previewing needs in order to develop thinking skills through the activity.

The DRTA strategies for listening, seeing, and reading are examples of JPA for teacher and students. They anticipate the instructional conversation (IC) presented in Chapter Seven and prepare teachers and students for teaching through dialogue. IC is the premier JPA that integrates all five of the pedagogy standards. In IC, teachers routinely use the language levers for developing academic language in combination with the other approaches described in this and other chapters.

Metacognition   Proficient readers use an additional comprehension strategy: *metacognition*. It is defined as thinking about what they are thinking, or managing their thinking during reading and other learning. It represents students' levels of awareness about how they acquire new knowledge. The features of a metacognitive strategy are as follows:

The learner

- Sets a purpose for reading or problem solving.
- Reviews his or her understanding of the text or problem.
- Monitors his or her developing understanding.
- Notices when focus is lost.
- Adjusts reading or work speed to fit the level of the challenge.
- Identifies misreading and confusion.
- Selects and applies a principle or strategy to understand what he or she reads.

Teachers assist students in self-monitoring using metacognition to expand their insight into how they learn. They plan teaching and design follow-up instructional activities to support students' use of metacognition. When students have a clearer sense of the way they learn, they have a greater capacity to see how they can transfer understanding to new problems and situations. To be useful, knowledge must be applied beyond the particular situation in which it was learned. This kind of knowledge capacity is labeled *generative*, which means that students can transfer their learning to other problems, situations, and contexts (Wilson and Peterson, 2006).

INDICATOR 5: THE TEACHER EXPANDS STUDENTS' EXPRESSION IN SPOKEN AND WRITTEN ACADEMIC LANGUAGE

The final indicator for the second pedagogy standard guides teachers to help students develop everyday talk into forms of language that can express their increasing academic understanding.

Written Questions

Structured written questions can be used to encourage students' language use and teachers' opportunity to assess it. Written questions should have the same characteristics as oral questions. For language and literacy development, what is important is the vocabulary used and the fullness of explanation given for a particular choice rather than whether the choice itself is exactly correct. For example:

Brown bears are found in mountains in Canada and white bears are found in the Arctic. Try to think of two reasons to explain why we don't find white bears in the mountains and brown bears in the Arctic.

Orcas, also known as killer whales, have a distinctive black and white coloration. What other animals have the coloration and why do you think they have it?

If you look at the water heater where you live, you might see that it is wrapped. What kind of wrapping is on a water heater? Why is it there?

If accuracy is a goal, students should be given time to research a response in addition to providing an initial spontaneous and possibly creative response.

Shared Writing

Teachers who have high expectations for students' literacy demonstrate as early as possible how writing works. In the beginning, writing can be defined as drawing that gradually comes to have labels and then patterned sentences. To develop young students as writers, teachers give them the models and experiences they need, such as shared writing, to develop as writers at the same time as they are becoming readers.

In shared writing, each student is given a word, sentence, or paragraph role in the activity, but the final product is joint, making this approach a JPA. This activity can begin as a game with the goal of passing the paper along before a certain time. The Dictosaurus is a resource for this task that may initially produce a low-quality writing product. The activity develops into a writing and editing process that students use as a routine to produce an outcome that meets high standards. A routine activity that occurs daily or weekly requires its own special work area. Students are scheduled to go to the designated area to work together on writing as partners.

When students write and respond in one another's journals, briefing and debriefing in the instructional frame needs to focus on the expectations for this activity. Peer access to others' written work is a priority activity that needs to be featured in the classroom agreement. Doing so will ensure that everyone understands its sensitive nature, quality requirements, and writing goals.

Journals

Journaling is a literacy activity that provides an authentic context for real communication between student and teacher, and often with peers. A journal is a compilation of pages stapled into a folder or between pieces of construction paper or in an individual notebook. Journals are stored in the area where students spend time writing in their journals.

Journaling Begins in Kindergarten

Students write or draw whatever they wish from the very first day of kindergarten. The teacher talks with young students about "writing" and guides them to "write" through drawing whatever they want. The teacher asks and listens to students state the content of their writing. The teacher then responds to each student's statement by writing in the student's journal. To focus a student's attention on how she performs, the teacher vocalizes slowly as she writes. Often the teacher will write a question for the entry. In addition, the teacher may sound out the letters in a word. The goal is for the student to understand that writing is talk written down on paper.

Many teachers require students to write in their journals daily. When a journal-writing work area has been established in the classroom, resources such as reference books, magazines, and other materials that students find helpful can be placed there to stimulate writing. Students can be assigned writing stems or other starter topics to stimulate their journaling when they visit the work area.

Interactive Journals

From second grade on, interactive journaling is primarily a written communication among students and with the teacher. Sometimes journaling occurs only between the students and the teacher, with regular, nonthreatening opportunities to write about topics of their own choice. The teacher makes entries as soon as possible to provide both emotional support and a contextualized response to the student. The teacher guides the student's writing effort in the direction of the curriculum or for personal expression. Many classrooms have journaling work settings that students visit often. Their activity can vary as they write their own entries and respond to the teacher's entries. Students who share their journals with peers write their responses according to the directions on the task card at the journaling activity setting.

Creative Writing

Providing many opportunities for writing poetry and short stories helps students to vary their language expression. Creative writing exercises vocabulary development as the author seeks the right word to express a thought or sentiment. Formats such as haiku and ballads are useful starters for reluctant writers, and useful as JPAs. For example, acrostic poems have structure but require creative language use. In an acrostic, each letter of a new vocabulary or theme word is used to start a name or another vocabulary word. A student selects the word to use with each letter of the original word. On the worksheet the student writes a few letters of each word or student name. Peers fill in the missing letters. Each entry must relate somehow to the meaning of the initial acrostic word. Students may then draw the meaning of the acrostic.

Reports

Students write reports as assigned and as products of their JPA and other activity. The guidelines for expository text comprehension can be turned around from use as a comprehension guide to use as a report organizer. Guidelines for reports are discussed in briefing and teaching sessions.

DEVELOPING THE SYSTEM

The overall emphasis of the teaching and activities described in this chapter is to develop students' language and literacy. The emphasis of the first standard was on community building. When needed, activities can return to community building, although community values are discussed to some degree in every debriefing. Some of the activities are designed to be used in the large group. Teachers using DTAs can choose to use them in the large group, as Mrs. Won did, or with a smaller group, if preferred.

In the instructional frame in Table 4.1, small-group activities are scheduled for each session in continuing activity settings. A large-group session can override the scheduled group activities, though this should occur infrequently. With the exception of the DTA teaching and follow-up, the activities—Dictosaurus, journaling, games, and classroom library—are individual practices that students can do independently of the teacher. Their frequent use requires them to take place in a designated or continuing activity setting. This means that there are six continuing activity settings that students are scheduled to attend regularly for the rest of the school year: the teaching activity setting, the Dictosaurus setting, the journaling setting, the classroom library, the games setting, and a teaching-activity follow-up setting dedicated to the lesson content application.

The teacher of a class of twenty-four students assigned them to four groups—blue, yellow, orange, and green—for attending four activity settings for a week. The groups of six were selected on the basis of language and friendship to rotate as a whole from one activity setting to the next. The activities were drawn from this chapter's discussion. The routing schedule of the instructional frame and the group membership were posted on the board. The furniture and supplies at the activity settings were checked. The frame for this arrangement and organization of instruction is shown in Table 4.2.

SUMMARY

The second pedagogy standard, on developing language and literacy, builds on the guidance system of the first standard to support teaching with the goal of ensuring all students' academic language proficiency. Teachers provide systematic language development in frequent interactions with students and literacy instruction that promotes reading skills and comprehension. The indicators for this standard insert and increase language and literacy development for all students in all activities. Students' language abilities enable or limit their participation in the learning activities of school. Teachers focus on fostering the foundations of learning by ensuring continuous attention to language development. Students with less language proficiency have less capacity to be precise in

Table 4.2
Multitasking Instructional Frame: 130 Minutes

Session 1	Session 2	Session 3	Session 4	Session 5	Session 6	
Briefing: To develop independent work habits. To introduce continuing activity settings. Post names of students in Groups B, O, Y, G.	Blue Group to follow-up on DTA	Blue Group to journaling	Blue Group to library	Blue Group to Dictosaurus	Teach DTA to Blue Group	
	Orange Group to Dictosaurus	Teach DTA to Orange Group	Orange Group to follow-up on DTA	Orange Group to library	Orange Group to journaling	
	Yellow group to library	Yellow Group to Dictosaurus	Teach DTA to Yellow Group	Yellow Group to follow-up on DTA	Yellow Group to games	
	Green Group to journaling	Green Group to library	Green Group to Dictosaurus	Teach DTA to Green Group	Green Group follow-up on DTA	*Debriefing:* Did the students succeed in their independent work? How did the games go? Provide feedback, correct.
10 minutes	20 minutes	20 minutes	20 minutes	20 minutes	20 minutes	14 minutes

Travel time: 6 minutes.
Students: 24 in 4 groups.
Routing: Groups all activity settings rotate to.
Activity settings: (1) Teaching DLTA; (2) Follow-up DLTA; (3) Journaling; (4) Dictosaurus vocabulary; (5) Library.

describing experience and expressing meaning. In the verbal setting of school, this disadvantage, if not corrected, usually has unfortunate consequences for students.

The instructional support system of the second pedagogy standard routinizes students' language development so that it is a daily experience in classrooms. Teachers use language levers to tailor their own language performance to meet ELL and at-risk students' needs, and student language levers to encourage students to produce language. Students must use language forms to acquire proficiency. What teachers do to develop the language of students is important to their academic progress.

The second standard is based on the implementation of the first standard, which supports teachers in working together frequently with students, and their routine use of the instructional frame. The first standard's guidance in arranging classrooms, designing activity, and managing positively facilitates implementation of the second pedagogy standard to provide language and literacy development, including for the growing population of ELLs, who remain at risk for mastering the language of instruction and, consequently, the content of the curriculum.

When instruction is organized as a system guided by the first pedagogy standard, there are increases in teacher and student participation, performance, and academic production. The outcomes of teachers' classroom implementation of the first and second standards are that the teacher

- Produced a classroom community agreement.
- Designed collaborative tasks that require joint product development.
- Arranged classrooms to support the teacher's and students' small-group collaboration and students' independent work.
- Routinely uses an instructional frame for all teaching and associated activities.
- Organizes students into small groups for collaboration with the teacher and for independent activities.
- Uses a positive management approach.
- Routinely develops students' literacy and academic language expression.

The second standard contributes language and literacy development emphases to the foundational logistics of the first standard. The first and second pedagogy standards establish key components of the five standards system for effective teaching in an interactive, activity-based classroom. The third pedagogy standard, connecting learning to students' lives, discussed in the next chapter, contributes another important component to the foundation of the pedagogy guidance system.

Seventh Grade ELLs Make Math Meaningful

Teacher: When we look up here, do we see any words on our list that we made that have to do with math?

Luis: Yeah.

Teacher: Like what?

Luis: *Star Trek.*

Concha: Saturn.

Teacher: *Star Trek?*

Luis: Like in the movies, like in—

Teacher: What does that have to do with math?

Luis: Uhmmm, on the machines, the computers that they have on the *Enterprise*, like they measure stuff.

Teacher: They measure stuff? With their computers? OK. Yeah, so the computers on a starship would help you measure. Like measure what? What sort of things?

Luis: Planets.

Connecting Learning to Students' Worlds

PEDAGOGY STANDARD III

Connecting School to Students' Lives

Connect teaching and curriculum to students' experiences at home and in the community.

Classroom Application Indicators

The teacher

1. Links learning to students' lives.

2. Includes all students in instructional activities.

3. Contextualizes academic topics.

4. Matches activities to students' varied needs.

Introduction

Most curriculum standards recommend that teachers begin by assessing students' knowledge and experience to find links between what students know and what they must learn. For a classroom of students who come from a variety of backgrounds and speak a number of languages, instructional activities designed according to the first two pedagogy standards can encourage personal sharing, particularly by ELLs in their home language. The more students exchange information with peers and with the teacher, the more information the teacher will gain about students' worlds.

In the lesson excerpt at the opening of the chapter, one student chose the name of a television program familiar to all students from a list of terms produced in their preceding discussion. Note how the teacher turned the discussion from *Star Trek* to mathematics:

Teacher: *Star Trek?*
Luis: Like in the movies, like in—
Teacher: What does that have to do with math?

Because the students were all familiar with *Star Trek,* the discussion to this point had been about what they knew in general. The teacher used the context to probe the students' knowledge for links, or hooks—in this case, *measure*—that she could use to connect to the new knowledge she wanted to teach. More questioning got the students to mention planets, which the teacher used as a bridge to teaching circle measurement.

This mathematics teacher sought a context in which to attract students into participating in conversation. The students' participation was key for the teacher to assess their level of knowledge and assist them into greater understanding. When teachers understand their students' prior knowledge, they can identify contexts that are relevant and interesting for everyone. Familiar contexts that hook students help teachers find starting points they can use to stimulate students' learning.

Rationale

In school, students are expected to grasp new understandings and build abstract knowledge. We know now that learning depends on teachers connecting lessons to students' prior knowledge. Teachers help students to learn new material when they anchor it in what students already know from their experiences in their homes and communities, and from previous schoolwork. The myriad differences that today's students bring to the classroom increase the need for familiar references that everyone, including the teacher, understands. Teachers build classrooms as communities of learners in order to increase common understandings as bases for developing knowledge. In these communities, teachers and students' differences become resources for understanding how teachers can assist students in their learning zones.

The third pedagogy standard and its indicators guide teachers to learn and use their students' language, prior knowledge, and experience to establish familiar starting points for relating and learning. Using the standards system for organizing instruction, teachers work in community with their students to build bridges to common understandings. They use familiar contexts and compelling activities to stimulate peer interaction and shared understanding. The third standard expands the guidance system for teachers and students working together by connecting learning activity to students' lives.

INDICATOR 1: THE TEACHER LINKS LEARNING TO STUDENTS' LIVES

In any classroom, teachers can ask students to remember and consider personal experiences that may be relevant to new instructional goals. Teachers draw on their students' community experience by visiting their homes, talking with their parents, and being active with them in community settings. Students develop language and knowledge primarily in their homes but also in other communities of learning, including their neighborhoods, their tribal and ethnic cultures, their native countries, and their churches, and from the media and other sources. Familiar starting points for helping students tackle the unfamiliar are available in the rich settings of students' lives.

For example, the rapper-teacher mentioned in Chapter Four expresses in song a mathematics problem that uses positive and negative integers to challenge students. In describing his song, the teacher shows how real-world activity, hip language, and meaning involve students in challenging thinking about heavy topics. The teacher's song called "The Number Line Dance" is "about a student who starts borrowing money to buy some tacos and some ice cream. All the sudden he's negative $5 and negative $8, and then he gets a job washing cars and he's back to zero" (Kajitani, 2006).

Context is much more than a welcome mat for students. A familiar context is comfortable for students, and for teachers, who may have a different background and language than the students. Most of us, like students, have had the experience of not being able to solve a problem as an isolated task; but if it is associated with a familiar activity from an out-of-school context, such as using baseball averages to help with basic mathematics, and pizza and cake cutting to help with fractions, we can succeed. John Marshall (2003), for example, points out that an abstract mathematics topic can be made more available to students by using ordinary activities to demonstrate meaning. In fact, this is the charge of a common mathematics standard. He also notes, however, that examples of some concepts, such as square roots, may not be readily apparent in real-life contexts and thus may be harder to identify than others. He explains the square root of 2 using a pasta-measuring device to measure their spaghetti noodles:

Eating Square Roots

The spaghetti-measuring device provides an experience with ratios that reveals the meaning of the square root of 2 in practical terms. In the spaghetti-measuring device, the holes for a single portion and a double portion, measuring 2.2 centimeters and 3.1 centimeters respectively, give an enlargement factor of 1.41 (3.1 divided by 2.2). The ratio of the diameter of the double portion measure to that of the single portion measure is not 2 but is approximately 1.4 [Marshall, 2003, p.196].

This hands-on activity gives meaning not only to the abstract concept of square roots but also to the elements of the measurement process—centimeter, ratio, diameter, and so on. The square root of 2, 1.414, has meaning in association with the measuring device. Marshall also points to cookie cutters, one of which has a diameter of 5.8 centimeters and another a diameter of 8.2 centimeters. One of the cookie cutters produces a cookie twice the size of the other. This is an enlargement factor of 1.41 (8.2 divided by 5.8) and, again, the square root of 2.

When students' competence in solving a problem is minimal, a known context can stimulate them to retrieve and apply their everyday knowledge to the task. Work that a teacher and students do together to puzzle through a problem to find a solution activates students' learning processes. In a fourth grade mathematics lesson, the teacher uses cookies to provide an interesting context for using fractions:

Teacher: I have ten cookies I want to share with you but I'm not exactly sure how to do that. [Teacher has real cookies.] How in the world am I going to equally share these cookies with this group? [There are seven students in the group.]

John: Teacher, I know. We figured out that there are seven people and there will be three left over if everyone gets one. Then if we break it up into two, everyone will get two except for one. And if we break it up into threes, then there will be twenty-one cookies and everyone will get three pieces.

Contexts make meaning that activates students' learning processes. Teachers use contexts as overarching themes of their classrooms or in specific situations to make the abstract concrete and familiar. Contexts connect when they are important to students, especially when they are suggested by students.

Connecting To Students' Worlds

- Reflects students' interests.
- Drives students to apply what they already know.
- Stimulates students to share thinking rationales.
- Encourages students to participate with peers and the teacher.
- Provides teachers with material for hands-on tasks and group discussion.
- Provides teachers with language-development topics that are of high interest to students.
- Allows students to participate at varying skill levels.
- Enables teachers to help students perform at high levels of proficiency.

Teachers may use extravagant connections, such as inviting students to assume roles, costumes, masks, and other devices to enliven understanding. Markers such as lists, posters, statues, photographs, CDs or tape recordings, balloons, and other visual or aural markers can connect students to new knowledge. Teachers contextualize lessons in order to engage students in learning. Once students are engaged, teachers can use context to work with them at levels slightly above their current abilities.

Personal Funds of Knowledge

Students bring to the classroom myriad differences in ability, interests, talents, language, and potential. Teachers' knowledge of students' homes and communities helps them to understand not only the strengths but also the needs and misconceptions that students bring to learning. Many students' informal knowledge is fragmented and inconsistent, even when it is extensive. It is important to assess students' current schemas and concepts to determine their need for development. Teachers who have knowledge of their students' backgrounds are ready to assist students who may have informal or naive explanations and beliefs about how the world works that are not easily altered. Teachers must listen to find out what students already know that can be used as the basis for new knowledge. Engaging students in compelling activities with peers is useful for advancing students' understandings from naive to formal knowledge, and for reconciling disparities between them.

When a teacher has little awareness of students' background knowledge, the teacher provides joint and hands-on activities that build common experience. By engaging in the instructional tasks associated with the activity, students reveal their current knowledge and understandings, which informs the teacher of the students' thinking skills. The teacher then uses this information to build instruction that advances to slightly higher levels the students' understanding and their language for expressing it.

For example, teachers use directed thinking activity (DTA; see Chapter Four) strategies for listening and reading to build exclusively on what students bring to learning. DTAs are useful for teachers in exploring students' language and thinking in a gamelike manner. Directed seeing thinking activity (DSTA; see Appendix 4A), a variation of DTA that uses a simple picture or drawing, intrigues most students at any level and requires only chart paper or a whiteboard and a marker. DSTA first promotes brainstorming, divergent thinking, and pattern recognition, then requires students to focus and integrate in order to discover the picture. DSTA anticipates the thinking skills that are required for productive reading and study of content. It is suitable for both large and small groups.

To prepare a DSTA, the teacher selects a stimulus to draw that relates to content or particular activities—for example, a key, a door, a telephone, or any vehicle; or molecules, atoms, electric circuits, trees, and so on. The teacher breaks this simple picture into pieces to present sequentially during the DSTA. In the following DSTA, the teacher initially drew a peanut. She first showed the students a few dots to represent the peanut's wrinkled skin. She then drew a piece of the outline of the shell, then another unconnected piece of the outline of the shape, then more dots. Finally she connected the shell parts with the distinctive shape of the peanut shell (the number eight on its side). The focus of the DSTA is on the thinking skills. In the upper grades, discussion can include issues related to content in order to rationalize guesses and apply labels to the drawing.

Guessing Game Thinking

It is the beginning of the school year for the second graders. The teacher, Ms. Lui, explains an activity to her students sitting on the rug in front of her, saying, "We are going to play a guessing game. You are going to make some guesses about what a drawing will turn out to be." She turns to her chart paper and draws the first piece of a picture, telling the students, "Here is a clue to what the picture is going to be. It is your first piece of evidence. What do you think this picture could be?" The students raise their hands to make guesses. Ms. Lui calls on them, encouraging the hesitant and helping students finish their sentences. She praises the students for offering guesses. On the chart paper, she writes a list of their guesses beside the evidence. When several students' guesses have been listed, Ms. Lui reads the list aloud to the students, pointing to each guess.

Then she draws the second piece of evidence onto the chart paper. Even though the second piece motivates students to make new predictions about what the picture will be, Ms. Lui channels their energy into thinking about eliminating previous guesses on the basis of new evidence. She asks the students about each guess they have made: "Does this prediction still work for you?" "Who else thinks this outcome is possible?" and "Tell me more about how you can say the drawing will turn out to be this word?"

In the validation sequence, the students decide to reject or keep a prediction on the basis of the visual evidence. She asks the students, "Who else agrees?" "Are you sure it won't work out?" "Why do you think that?" and "Do you agree that we should cross this prediction off of the list?" Ms. Lui crosses out the guess that they agree is not supported by the new evidence. She says, "You think this guess is not supported by the evidence. I'm putting a line through it because it is no longer a prediction, but it is still part of the written record of our activity." Ms. Lui praises the students for explaining their thinking about why they wanted their guesses kept on or crossed off the list.

After the validation sequence, Ms. Lui asks for more predictions based on the second piece of visual evidence she drew. She accepts any prediction that a student can justify. Group consensus is not necessary for students' predictions to be accepted or rejected. Ms. Lui then reads the remaining guesses from the first round and the new second-round guesses. Next she draws a third piece of the picture. Even though the new evidence stimulates the students to spontaneously offer predictions, she focuses on the DSTA process. She asks the students to review the list of predictions aloud. She asks them again why they should keep or eliminate each of the second-round guesses in light of the additional visual evidence. Her purpose in summarizing is to have the students use the evidence to validate their predictions. She is also narrowing the focus of the students' thinking about predictions. She asks them, "What happens each time I draw another piece of the picture?" "Did the new evidence make you cross out some guesses?" and "What does that mean is happening in this game?"

After the validation step, Ms. Lui draws an additional piece of the picture. This fourth piece of evidence elicits new guesses from the students. Ms. Lui summarizes the predictions, asks the students to validate them one by one, and follows their directions to either keep or cross out unsupported guesses. She asks the students to notice how their thinking about the picture is narrowing as more evidence is introduced. Ms. Lui repeats the evidence-validation-prediction cycle as often as necessary until the complete picture or presentation is assembled. Once the students see the complete drawing and recognize it, to ensure that they understand the process of using an evidence base for making decisions Ms. Lui asks the students to explain how they used the evidence to make accurate guesses about the picture.

Mrs. Lui used the DSTA to engage students in an activity that captured their language for expressing their broadest thinking on the basis of their previously held knowledge. The DSTA discussion led them to narrow the focus of their thinking on the basis of sequential additions of new evidence, and to explain how they did it. This approach is useful at every grade level as an introduction to a unit, or for developing thinking skills. If the stimulus is motivating and the DSTA cycle is routinely implemented within an instructional frame, this thinking practice prepares the students for content area challenges.

In the upper elementary grades, the stimulus material of a DSTA can be readily upgraded to a molecule, a geographic element such as a state or continent, or something as simple as a window or lock, which are metaphors for opening the way to new knowledge. The emphasis in all grades is to have students express reasonable explanations in response to a stimulus on the basis of their logical interpretation of the available evidence. Although there may be several plausible explanations, they must work to find the one with the most weight. In a manner similar to the way scientists work, students use the DSTA as a systematic approach to identifying, communicating, and defending their preferred explanation.

DSTA generates a number of follow-up activities for individuals and groups:

- Add vocabulary describing the stimulus to students' Dictosauruses.
- Label vocabulary as sight words, content vocabulary, formal scientific terms, or other types of content.
- Write to express the logic of the explanation for the stimulus.
- Write to explain the irrelevance of the alternative explanations.
- Write creatively about the stimulus.
- Prepare a habitat or other context for the stimulus as an extension joint productive activity (JPA).
- Do research to expand learning about the DSTA topic.
- Develop a student-generated DSTA for later use in the classroom community.

When teachers have little knowledge of their students' backgrounds, an activity like DSTA provides an interactive setting in which students may reveal their language proficiencies and prior knowledge within the interaction of the DSTA. Through follow-up instructional tasks associated with the activity, students may reveal their current understandings, which inform teachers about their thinking levels. Teachers can use this information to design activities that nudge their students' skills and understanding to more complex levels.

Community Funds of Knowledge

Teachers who have knowledge of students' homes, cultures, and communities are more likely than teachers who do not to consider their students rich resources for learning. Research reports how knowledge works in various ways in different communities. For example, in a Mexican American community, knowledge is distributed and shared among the households. Teachers who know about the ways in which their students understand their community funds of knowledge are prepared to assist their students in building bridges to other approaches to learning (Gonzalez, Moll, and Amanti, 2005). This is true for kindergarten as well as for eighth grade students.

Many teachers are adept at incorporating home and community into their teaching. Some have large collections of treasured resources to share with students as stimuli for learning. Superb examples are available of how teachers have applied home and community funds of knowledge. For example, academic units have been developed on salsa making, pinon nut picking and marketing, lei and hula skirt making, bread baking, crafts, and other activities. In these and other rich contexts that all participants enjoy, teachers continue to learn about differences and develop connections, and they adapt their academic teaching accordingly. The joint productive experience must be continuously guided by content standards and academic learning goals. The learning outcomes of these activities must be assessed both informally and formally to ensure that learning outcomes include those that are academic.

Teachers embed accuracy and other checks into activity to assess students' progress, especially in using new knowledge in new situations. When teaching is strong enough to develop students' skills and increase their understanding of the concepts involved in an activity, they can apply these skills and understandings to new contexts. In the following example, students apply their mathematics and botany skills to develop a marketing plan for their garden produce.

Flowers for Sale

A fifth grade class plans to sell flowers from the class garden to raise money for an upcoming field trip. The students work in small groups to define a plan that would be the most profitable for the class. Each group is to research flower prices and marketing strategies via the Internet or by interviewing the owner of the local flower shop. They must decide on the price of the flowers, how they will market them, and how they will sell them and predict their earnings. They will need to estimate the costs and productivity of their garden and protect the flowers until the harvest date. Each group will present its ideas to the class, and the class as a whole will decide which plan will work best. They will then harvest and sell the flowers. Once they have the money, they will discuss how to spend it.

The flower activity spans classroom and local community. Like the activities done at home and in the community, it is characterized by collaboration for planning and problem solving, by inclusion in order to use all available resources, by shared performance in doing the work, and by role-playing to practice interviewing and selling. Alternative forms of participation and performance in classrooms can alter how students think about their learning and how they present themselves as learners.

INDICATOR 2: THE TEACHER INCLUDES ALL STUDENTS IN INSTRUCTIONAL ACTIVITIES

More students enter school today from homes where languages other that English are spoken than ever before. In the past, schools depended on students' home communities to provide students' basic cognitive development, and schools needed to provide only new stimulation in the form of subject matter and fresh activities. But although basic cognitive development that prepares students for success in the nation's schools is presumed to be parents' responsibility, it cannot happen in homes that do not understand schools and that are not understood by teachers. When social contexts are complicated by language, cultural, and other differences, teachers at every level must assume more responsibility for preparing students.

Varied Forms of Participation

The teacher's first challenge is to ensure that every student participates. In today's diverse classrooms, teachers find that some students need encouragement to participate, and they must engage these students in a variety of ways to encourage them to participate. The second pedagogy standard, discussed in Chapter Four, focuses on students' language development. It guides teachers to leverage their own and students' languages through the use of language levers. Though students may learn without speaking or engaging, teachers cannot assist them unless they participate. The third pedagogy standard supports teachers in leveraging every student's participation by

- Offering practical, familiar activities that students can talk about and do.
- Arranging the classroom to encourage students to talk and support one another.
- Learning early to pronounce students' names correctly.
- Using students' names often in games, acrostics, and other tasks, even as sight vocabulary.
- Providing an interpreter (such as a volunteer peer or family member).
- Assigning a peer partner to guide a student (which can be a community duty included in the community agreement).

- Labeling classroom furniture, equipment and materials in as many languages as needed (a useful, inclusive activity for students to do).

The teacher's second challenge is to ensure that students, particularly ELL and disabled students, develop knowledge through participation and perform to standard by

- Incorporating culturally relevant materials and referring to them often.
- Extending students' experienced-based sharing and discussion in lessons.
- Inviting students into conversation in small groups to explain and justify JPA products.
- Reading aloud.
- Assigning peer reading partners to work together routinely.
- Journaling daily.
- Tracking discussions and instructions with word webs and other displays.
- Using debriefing to obtain feedback from ELLs about their experience in the classroom community.

Activity that builds on what students know from home and community can be highly compelling. For instance, nothing is more personal than one's name. In many cases it carries important family history, and often community status or interest. An activity about students' names, such as the following, usually compels them to participate, for they may want peers and the teacher to understand fully the meaning of their names. Students may be motivated to communicate to others about a topic of such importance to them because they want everyone to get it right.

Eighth Graders Discover What's in a Name?

Every student has a name that is special. Students at any grade level are assigned to ask their mothers (if they do not already know) why they were given their first, second, and third or more names. They thus discover the naming conventions or choices that guided their name selection. They also look up their names on the Internet to discover additional information such as the number of people who have the name, trends in use of the name, sources of the name, and other quantitative information. The last name is researched for other connections, such as geographical relationships, ethnic links, and heroic associations, among many others that students can select. The information is compiled using graphics to present the data and text to explain it.

This activity is compelling for students in the early grades as well. Kindergarten through second graders can draw to explain their names. They can research their names by finding others in the class, school, and neighborhood or who are celebrities who have their name. Name acrostics are also useful for early graders to use to think about the meaning or associations of their names.

Varied Activity Designs

The pedagogy standards support a wide range of independent, guided, and innovative activity designs. For example, the name game just discussed can be made interactive by having students work on a peer partner's name rather than on their own; or even more desirable, the level of activity can be raised to make this game a JPA. In this version, students share and research aspects of names, a more objective process that will include negative associations as well as positive ones. The JPA product can be a compilation of the information to share with their peers and families.

As students move through the grades, they consume innumerable activities. Their experience of types and qualities of activity is certainly enormous by the time they reach the middle and upper grades. Conversely, for ELL students, who may have few skills in the language of instruction, the activities and their directions may be incomprehensible. For all students the arrangement of classrooms into activity settings that encourage interaction is different from that of traditional classrooms. Some of the activity settings, such as the library, settings for computer use and journaling, and observation stations, require a particular type of performance, but these activities become routine and predictable, which the pedagogy system supports. In other settings, students can help one another with activities when they are done independently, without assistance from the teacher. (A full discussion of activities is presented in Chapter Three.)

Games Classroom games and gamelike activities are useful for engaging students in early content themes in every content area. Students can play with one another in pairs or other formations, in homogenous or mixed-ability groups.

Games are universally recognized as contexts for learning. They encourage collaboration, individual expression, personalized meaning making, and experimentation at every grade level. Moreover, they require students to play by the rules of the game. As contexts, they provide connections with the world outside of school, where most students have already played and enjoyed them. They have power to influence students' participation in classrooms through role-playing and other personal expression. As contexts for both competition and cooperation, they bring students together in a variety of ways.

Digital games offer high-level thinking challenges; for example, they take students beyond following directions to discovering what the directions and rules are. Students from every kind of background can do this in any language. Role-playing in games provides all students with opportunities to explore new relationships, motives, and strategies.

Student-Generated and Parent-Generated Activity   Another type of activity design is student-generated activity (SGA) or parent-generated activity (PGA). Students share knowledge and make meaning when they and even their families together design instructional activities for the classroom community. Students at every grade level can design SGAs for their peers to complete. SGAs and PGAs can be anything from a familiar format such as a crossword puzzle or a drawing to color and label; to a word or numbers game; to a more complex project such as map or model making, crafts, and using food recipes, among others.

Many SGAs and PGAs can be developed using vocabulary items. When every student maintains a personal dictionary or thesaurus, such as the Dictosaurus described in Chapter Two, a resource is provided for students to design SGAs. Classroom resources such as charts, books, games, posters, and other visuals that represent the common knowledge of the classroom community also stimulate ideas for task development. A Native American parent offered an experience of fry bread making that produced a delicious outcome for everyone. Other parents have used crafts and reading to engage students, but SGAs and PGAs can be simple paper-and-pencil games and tasks as well. Parents and grandparents usually offer activities related to the family's fund of knowledge. If parents request to be more involved, teachers can work with them on activity designs that relate familiar knowledge to the content that students are studying.

Students quickly learn how their tasks are valuable to the community by how their peers respond to those tasks. Peer feedback informs students about the suitability of the activity and its level of difficulty. The teacher always reviews each SGA to ensure that the task has a goal, is legible, and accurate. The teacher and students decide how to check and edit the task before it is offered to the class. Completed SGAs are usually reviewed by their authors. With experience, students improve their task designs and take on the responsibilities of marking and recording their peers' completed SGAs. With PGAs, the parent reviews, grades, and provides feedback to the teacher and students. When students can produce tasks using newly acquired concepts and skills, they demonstrate a level of understanding that transfers knowledge from the situation in which it was learned.

Most SGAs can be completed at any grade level. Kindergarten and first grade students may require assistance. They can take digital pictures to make collages and class books, and they can play games. Teachers often use SGAs as early finishing activities, and for homework. SGAs are also useful resources for rainy-day indoor perk-ups. Following are examples of SGA tasks and activities that students can prepare for their peers to do individually and as groups:

1. *Learning extensions:* SGAs can require students to apply what they have learned in several situations. The students choose how they will demonstrate their new competency.

2. *Quizzes:* Students can prepare vocabulary and other skill-based tests for their peers to use to check their learning. The teacher may provide specific assessment formats that students can prepare for teacher review and editing. All students have the opportunity to prepare quizzes.

3. *Jigsaw puzzles:* Students can make jigsaw puzzles with digital or prepublished pictures that lead into or address a content topic in a particular way. First they print or select a picture to paste onto a piece of thin cardboard or construction paper. They then cut the picture into puzzle pieces. The puzzles are batched into sets of four or five pieces each and put into envelopes to distribute to students. The students must work together to complete the puzzles. The activity can be followed by writing about the picture they have completed.

4. *Sudokus:* Students can use quadrant or grid paper to prepare a puzzle using the numerals 1 through 9. Like a crossword puzzle, the sudoku is completed before the puzzle is developed with many of the numbers omitted. To solve the puzzle, students fill in the blank spaces in the grid so that every vertical column, every horizontal row, and every

three-by-three box contains a complete set of the numbers without repeating any.

5. *Mathematical party plans:* For any party, the costs need to be calculated. Students can generate a worksheet for calculating how much an outing or eat-in will cost. For a pizza party, an SGA can require that fractions or decimals be used to measure the amount of pizza needed for the community. Students can increase the challenge by using only circumference and area formulas to decide what sizes to order. What pizza diameter will provide the size needed? What pizza circumference will provide a dozen adequate pieces? Other liquid- and solid-measurement SGAs can be developed using edible or nonedible materials of interest.

6. *Scavenger hunts:* Students develop a game that requires peers to find ingredients or components related to content or other classroom activity. The game can be simple, such as finding and distributing classroom supplies or seasonal treats. The activity gives written directions to a spot where more directions are found. Eventually the directions lead the students to locate an item. The item and its message provide more instructions for students to follow, and so on.

SGAs and PGAs are also used as follow-up activities to apply a lesson theme or practice a skill. Teachers can also designate an SGA work area or station dedicated to their development. Students may be assigned to visit SGA stations regularly or they may choose to work at them. If SGAs are a recurring assignment, students can not only produce their own but also help other students prepare them. The SGA area can also hold the solutions and answer keys for checking completed SGAs.

Some teachers reserve using SGAs for when students finish their work early in the instructional frame. SGAs increase the options students have when free time occurs, including on a rainy day when no outdoor recess is available. When SGAs go home with students as homework, parents learn about how SGAs contribute to the learning process. Students can then invite their parents to contribute PGA activities.

Information Communications Technology and Media Computers and other forms of information communications technology (ICT) are frequently found in classrooms today. ICT and media are powerful tools for teaching and learning with technology to produce outcomes rather than overusing them for skill practice. For example, in the early elementary grades, teacher and students can use a digital camera to recognize and capture students in a particular kind of activity, such as a JPA. The photos are used to deepen the meaning of the activity for students, to provide material for early readers, to demonstrate tangible products created by the students who perform the activity, and to record information about projects, which is itself a larger product.

Digital Firsts

The [first grade] teacher takes candid photographs as the students work and play during the day, making sure that each photo includes more than one student. On the computer, the teacher or student inserts each digitalized photograph into a page layout program and prints it. The teacher posts the pictures in the writing activity setting. Students select picture sheets that feature ... pictures [of themselves] working with others. They write a description of what they were doing as the pictures were taken using pattern sentences posted for reference. They date the sheet and copy it for the portfolio and to send home [Entz and Garlarza, 2001].

In addition to developing photography skills, students in later grades use digital graphic design; slide shows; and videos, music videos, and travel brochures that include sound. Students can create blogs, do online journaling, and design Web sites. Today's multimedia programs allow students to input text, draw on screen or draw on paper and scan the material into the computer, use predrawn pictures and backgrounds, and use other software features. Students can also publish online. Word-processing programs allow teachers and students to revise and edit their written products easily. Database programs allow for the categorization, storage, and orderly retrieval of data collections. Some programs present material in an interactive format, with animated screens offering stories to be listened to, or individual words from stories to be read and followed by immediate feedback. When computers, graphing calculators, handhelds, interactive boards, iPods, and digital cameras are among the classroom's resources, multitasking is facilitated.

Middle School Students "Swallow" ICT

A teacher at a middle school in Virginia [that was] trying to raise its low standardized test scores said, "These kids have grown up with technology. All they want to do is play on their PlayStations and Game Boys. Anytime you pop in technology like that [referring to an interactive whiteboard], they swallow it up." With the whiteboard, students could see, touch, and analyze the material of their lesson combining current events and physical science to answer the question, "Where do hurricanes come from"[Chandler, 2005]?

ICT is not only an asset to learning within the classroom community but also an aide to extending performance into other communities of practice. Performance within a community is always characterized by the use of common language to develop shared knowledge on a topic. In addition to exchanging information by e-mail, making meaning includes finding other communities that share similar goals and interests, and learning their language conventions. Online information retrieval and research can lead to the development of vast numbers of communities of learners on unending topics. For example, an interest in global positioning may lead students to the Web site of the National Oceanic and Atmospheric Administration (see Appendix 4B), where geodesy (the science concerned with determining the size and shape of the earth and a person's position on it) is defined and explained.

Several other groups are making important contributions to the advancement of media literacy in and outside the classroom. The Web site of the Media Education Foundation (again, see Appendix 4B) offers more than fifty videos as well as free educational materials that foster critical examination of mainstream media and advertising. In the San Francisco Bay Area, Youth Radio conducts after-school programs that offer classes in radio broadcasting skills, including engineering, DJing, journalism, and Web production. Working as interns at area radio stations, students can produce pieces that air on local and national outlets such as National Public Radio.

Just Think offers several classroom programs and curriculum packages such as *Flipping the Script: Critical Thinking in a Hip-Hop World,* which is designed to help educators teach media-literacy concepts and production skills on the theme of hip-hop culture (http://just think.org). "With this curriculum, kids who normally don't show up at all come to class every day," says Just Think founder Elana Yonah Rosen. "They either love hip-hop or they hate it, but they have opinions about it, as opposed to some piece of nineteenth-century literature they get in English class" (Ellis, 2005).

INDICATOR 3: THE TEACHER CONTEXTUALIZES ACADEMIC TOPICS

The teacher makes meaning when she or he explicitly links classroom activities to students' home and community experiences and knowledge. Because students' understanding builds on what they bring to learning as much as it grows from absorbing the new material, teachers who know their students well can best assist them to knit together their prior and new knowledge. New content material does not appear as distant or abstract when teachers identify links between students' existing knowledge and the information they must learn. The teacher often asks students to supply links they recognize and to apply new knowledge to familiar local issues. Asking students to help their classmates make connections draws them into sharing and learning. Teachers learn about students' contexts from the students. They are the best resource for contextualization ideas.

Students will grapple with unfamiliar language and abstract notions about highly integrated theories in science, math, and other content areas when they are motivated by interesting activities and supported by the teacher. When students strive for understanding at levels slightly above their competence level, they are working within their zone of learning. Teachers design activities at increasingly suitable levels as they learn more about their students' capacities and learning zones. They need to build students' rate of success on instructional tasks from the start. They meet the challenge of appropriate activity design, especially in the beginning of the year, by making tasks too easy rather than too hard. Failure on tasks that are inappropriately leveled may have consequences for some students. Teachers must earn students' trust. By encouraging students' success students have adequate confidence to tackle new knowledge and work with the teacher in their learning zones.

Students play with video games, cell phones, digital cameras, and computers to connect to virtual worlds. Many students participate in virtual communities in order to engage in the knowledge and social contexts of their choice. At every grade level, teachers can teach with ICT by incorporating information retrieval and research components into activities. For example, teachers can guide students to use ICT to change the quality of problem analysis and resolution, or to conduct effective and efficient search procedures. Students can use ICT databases to inform their analyses and problem solving efforts. Media and ICT experiences can help extend students' thinking into analyzing complex social networks, including interplanetary networks; tracking subtle narrative intertwinings; recognizing long-term patterns; resolving contradictions; anticipating and predicting outcomes; and many others efforts.

In the following example, a school involves fifth grade students in technology and media production, with all of the associated rigor of news standards and deadlines. The activity increases the language and literacy demands on students to new, more complex levels.

Good Morning, School

Fifth graders in the video club of one elementary school work together each morning to bring the local news and weather as well as school events to the entire school. Expert adults and parents come in each year to teach students how to run the equipment. With teacher guidance, students play a role in every aspect of the production, as anchors, writers, producers, and sound and cameramen. The club meets every day after school to discuss roles and write out the script for the following morning's production. Everyone enjoys watching the daily morning announcements on their classroom televisions. Students also enjoy giving the broadcasters feedback about their performance and role-playing.

These fifth graders provide their school with daily weather and local news in a real-world version of the instructional frame. The activity models the guidance offered by the first, second, and third pedagogy standards. The second standard is reflected in television's requirements for communicative visual displays. In addition, the audience requires use of familiar and proper language forms. The students' treatment of the topic develops their vocabulary and writing skills as they strive to present information accurately and explain it to their audience. Their work within a familiar context also challenges them to grow beyond their current ability levels into more competent performances, reflecting the expectations of the third pedagogy standard. The project also has all the features of a JPA in that it addresses compelling real-world issues and yields multiple solutions and outcomes and a joint product.

When mathematics, science, language arts, and computer skills are applied in a joint project approach, students combine what they already know with what they are learning to produce more meaningful information. Converting temperature from Fahrenheit to Celsius may not make sense to students as an isolated exercise of mathematics mechanics. However, when they must perform the conversion for a project that requires information about temperature on a particular scale to relate to other data, the procedure takes on meaning. As a product of JPA, the conversion documents students' learning. In the following example, all students are involved in the study of weather. They study the topic on a regular schedule using a variety of skills to perform tasks, or they learn the skills in order to perform specific tasks required by the project. All of the students have a special interest in the weather in their agricultural community on the California central coast. Their parents are agricultural workers, including migrant workers. They are from low-income neighborhoods and speak languages other than English at home. The information obtained from this real-life activity is critical to their families' work. The activity provides the students with a familiar context for learning mathematics, science, computer modeling, and language arts activities.

Weather Works

A large table is arranged against a wall covered with U.S. maps to use for weather study. Students listen to weather reports with earplugs in radios and televisions, read newspapers and use computers to understand and track weather. The students' tasks vary depending on their level and goals. Some students learn meteorological vocabulary through preparing cards for their Dictosauruses. Others collect data from newspapers about temperature, humidity, and wind speed, and make computer models of weather to represent its forces, travel, and possible effects in their home area. Others track and compute rates of weather travel to other areas of interest. Students also research the kind of weather that helps or hinders local crops such as strawberries. This information extends their Web page and makes it more interesting to their parents and the local community.

This activity draws from all of the subjects in the curriculum, from geography to math and science. All of the students are expected to learn content vocabulary and concepts and to use them in assignments, reports, and discussions. When the teacher, Mr. Tom, introduced this activity in other classes, he believed that the interesting activities, peer support, and his occasional assistance through brief comments and feedback on the students' written work were adequate to develop their understanding. He would also stop by the activity setting to check on the students' work and answer their questions. The local parent and community audiences for their newsletter and Web page motivated the students to be accurate in preparing content to post. Of course he checked everything before the information was posted. Still, for some of the students, the high-quality activity and multiple practice opportunities were insufficient to achieve the content standards. After disappointing results persisted for a number of students, the teacher was challenged to explore how to bolster his system and strengthen his students' learning. The weather activity worked well, he realized, because several strong students had taken the lead.

Mr. Tom found that many students performed alone and inaccurately. He discovered that students who did not see how their work fit into the larger products such as the Web site and the newsletter were not increasing their understanding. When he talked with them about the products of their work, he heard more understanding from those who had participated in joint products and received help from their peers. Most of the students who worked alone struggled. He was stunned that his system did not meet all of the students' needs, so he decided to develop the activities to serve the students more evenly and to guarantee more success for everyone.

Mr. Tom reviewed his instructional frame. He decided to strengthen the briefing to ensure that all students understood the directions and expectations. He often assigned students, including those who were underperforming, to do the briefing for the activities. He revised his debriefings by increasing the discussion time by five minutes in order to increase students' opportunities to talk about what they had learned at the activity setting. The adjustments helped, but Mr. Tom found himself spending more time at the activity setting with the students to ensure that they were all proceeding productively in the work.

Mr. Tom regrouped the students so that strong students were always at the weather station setting with those who needed assistance. The students were experienced in moving in groups from one activity setting to another.

The same students who worked on journals went to the library together, to the math practice activity setting, and then to the weather station activity setting.

The new arrangements were productive, but Mr. Tom wanted the students to be independent performers at the weather station. He adjusted the activities to ensure that students could succeed in them or use peer resources to help. Still, he found he needed to assist them constantly. He knew that to achieve the desired effects, he could not lecture the students, but he could talk with them individually if he had more time. He decided that he could support each student more closely if they came to him in small groups.

INDICATOR 4: THE TEACHER MATCHES ACTIVITIES TO STUDENTS' VARIED NEEDS

Uniformity in ways of instructing students denies the students' obvious differences. As our understanding of learning has increased, student learning and other differences mean that more resources and multiple perspectives are available in the classroom community. All students are gifted in some ways and need strengthening in others. Better understanding of student learning processes has underscored the importance of different kinds of instruction and activities, and of teaching that offers assistance for every student.

Differentiated Instruction

With knowledge of students' various learning styles, abilities, and preferences, instruction can be pointed toward assisting the unique needs of each student when necessary. In an inclusive system of instruction such as the five pedagogy standards, students must be fully included in all activities and assisted by peers and teacher or expected to work individually when needed. Teachers address the needs of all students by providing opportunities for them to learn in multiple ways that secure and strengthen their understandings. Teachers also expand the ways in which students can document their learning. Students need to identify more performance opportunities and clarify their preferences for demonstrating their learning within JPA and other approaches. One way that teachers expand all students' opportunities to perform is through projects.

Project-Based Approach

In the previous example, Mr. Tom realized that some students were struggling because they needed his assistance on a regular basis to learn the skills for the weather station. If he wanted them to be independent performers at the weather station he had to teach them the concepts and skills they were not able to learn without his assistance. He decided to rearrange the students into matched-ability groups to meet with him for teaching. In the small groups he would teach the concepts and skills they needed. He would develop their understandings about how to track weather, make computations and projections. and carry out other analyses. He planned to group the students so that all of them would have peer resources available when they visited the weather station; but when the students came to him they would be matched on ability. At a later date he would try different ways of grouping students. Later chapters in this book provide more information about grouping students and routing them to activity settings.

SUMMARY

New understandings about students' learning have revealed the influential role that context plays. Teachers facilitate students' knowledge development by anchoring new material in what students already know from their experiences in their homes, communities, and previous schoolwork. In any classroom, teachers can ask students to remember and consider personal experiences that are relevant to the new instructional goals. Teachers can also tap rich sources of community knowledge by visiting students' homes, talking with their parents, and being active with students in community settings.

The challenge for teachers is to uncover the students' personal knowledge and build bridges between it and new understandings. In some situations teachers must expand students' knowledge beyond everyday misunderstandings that may impede conceptual learning. Learning usually takes place in specific situations, which may also limit students' use of new knowledge. A variety of activities increase students' experience with new concepts and lead to new understandings. Students need many opportunities to learn different ways to strengthen their grasp of new knowledge and use it in applications and problem solving across contexts.

Together the first three pedagogy standards support teaching that links activities and interactions with students' personal knowledge from home and community. The classroom is itself a community that ensures students' inclusion and participation in classroom life. It connects students to academic knowledge. The three standards discussed so far offer a pedagogy guidance system that goes beyond linking new knowledge to what students already know, and into a rich context of classroom activity and interaction.

When instruction is organized as a system guided by the first three pedagogy standards, there are increases in teacher and student participation, performance, and academic production. The pedagogy system organizes instruction to support teaching assistance for every student. The outcomes of teachers' implementation of the first, second, and third standards in the classroom are that the teacher

- Produced a classroom community agreement for working together.
- Designed collaborative tasks that require joint product development.
- Organized classrooms to support the teacher and students' working together.
- Used an instructional frame routinely for all teaching and associated activities.
- Developed students' literacy and academic language expression in speaking and writing.
- Connected learning to students' real-world contexts for new understanding.

The third standard guides the way learning occurs in particular situations and contexts. Together the first three pedagogy standards establish the key components of the five-standards system for effective teaching in an interactive, activity-based classroom. The fourth pedagogy standard, teaching complex thinking, discussed in the next chapter, contributes another key teaching component of the pedagogy guidance system.

Daniel:	This is the conconference, or whatever.
Teacher:	So this one's the circumference, and this one is the diameter?
Daniel:	I just remember that the diameter is the smallest, small, smaller than this one [referring to the circumference string].
Teacher:	Well, which string did you measure around the edges with?
Daniel:	This one [pointing to the circumference string].
Teacher:	This one? The circumference?
Daniel:	Yeah, and this one across it.
Teacher:	Across it? So why do you think that this is smaller than this— that the diameter is smaller than the circumference? Why do you think that happens?
Daniel:	Because if this one shrinks, like she said, it will shrink down; this one's still going to be smaller than that one.
Teacher:	Why? What would happen, what would happen to this, the diameter?
Daniel:	That one stays smaller. It will get smaller.

Challenging Students' Thinking

STANDARD IV

Teaching Complex Thinking

Challenge students to think at increasingly complex levels.

Classroom Application Indicators

The teacher

1. Accesses and expands students' current understanding.

2. Sets high standards for all students' performance.

3. Assists student performance at increasingly advanced levels.

4. Teaches challenging content.

Introduction

Students' performance is challenged when they are expected and assisted to think in new ways, even about familiar topics. Teachers succeed when they develop students' thinking from the beginning to be broader and deeper than the mechanical knowledge such as multiplication and other formulas they master. Until recently, standard prescriptions for struggling and at-risk students were to teach through many repetitions of low-level, basic skill activities to mastery. The assumption that low-performing students are deficient in learning ability or must acquire English language proficiency before attempting higher-level challenges has been discredited by research. Students' ability to grasp academic topics at more complex levels is facilitated by fluent mechanics and advanced through conceptual understanding. The fourth pedagogy standard supports teachers in developing and documenting students' deep understanding of content in small learning settings through scheduled activities designed to help all students perform successfully.

In the excerpt from a seventh grade mathematics lesson at the beginning of the chapter, the teacher and English language learners (ELLs) discuss a mathematics activity on circle measurement. The activity, comparing string measures of jar lids, required students to talk about the concepts of diameter and circumference and the relationship between the two. The teacher's goal, to assist the students in understanding the concept pi, was grounded in concrete representations that they could manipulate and discuss. The hands-on activity encouraged their thinking about and use of mathematics terms in English. The teacher assisted the students by working and speaking with them throughout the activity. She elicited their use of the terms to increase their fluency, and she challenged their thinking about the mathematical meaning of their activity to advance their conceptual understanding.

Rationale

The fourth pedagogy standard guides teachers in developing students' existing knowledge and skills to new levels of understandings. Teachers must challenge students at appropriately high levels to assist them to engage in more complex thinking. The previously described three standards guided teachers to reorganize classrooms to provide teaching and learning settings for increasing students' language, literacy, and content knowledge beyond the familiar. The fourth standard guides teachers to expand students' knowledge and document their increasing understanding in academic products.

INDICATOR 1: THE TEACHER ACCESSES AND EXPANDS STUDENTS' CURRENT UNDERSTANDING

Teachers continuously probe students' existing knowledge through informal conversation and focused discussion during joint activities. Activities can be designed that require students to draw on their background knowledge, especially in the opening weeks of school. Activities early in the school year are comfortable occasions for teachers and students to share existing knowledge and prior experience. Observations of Students in independent activity settings show how they use the models they see and hear to solve problems. The following example illustrates the point:

A Kindergartner Uses a New Concept

Today, Toby is on his way to visit the dress-up activity in his kindergarten classroom. He wants to wear the fireman's hat, coat, and even the boots. Then he remembers that another student, Congor, always gets there ahead of him, and gets the fireman clothes first. This memory makes him hurry to the activity setting, but Congor, as usual, is there already reaching for the fireman's hat. Toby feels disappointment again, but remembers how the teacher says for everyone to take turns. She says, "It's her turn to speak" when she shows them how taking turns works. He must wait for his turn to speak. Toby thinks it's his turn to be the fireman. Maybe Congor will wait to be the fireman later. He walks right up to Congor. Toby points to the fireman's hat, saying, "It's my turn." Congor is surprised, hesitates, but says, "Okay." Toby is a courageous fireman for the whole day.

When teachers work with students, they often use familiar tools as a basis for introducing new topics and new ways of thinking about other topics. As the discussion on contextualization in Chapter Five explained, teachers can explore topics that are familiar to students to find hooks to link the new knowledge to previous knowledge. In an example in Chapter Five on how to teach square roots using a real-world context, Marshall (2003) identified a device for measuring spaghetti noodles. In another example that extends the principle, square pizza boxes also represent the principle of square roots. Large pizza delivery boxes are sized to hold one pizza that is two times the amount that the small box holds. The large box measures 14 inches and the small box measures 10 inches, which is an enlargement factor of 1.4 (14 divided by 10). As another concrete example of the square root of 2, it provides students with a real-world application of the abstract concept. The concrete example helps to establish a sense of square roots that the mere recitation of rules, procedures, or algorithms does not allow.

What students already understand is typically fertile ground in which to nurture new and deeper understandings. Teachers recognize and use the enormous learning resource that students' existing knowledge provides. Yet sometimes what students know can impede new knowledge acquisition. For example, it is difficult for some students to understand fractions; because the denominator of the fraction 1/12 is larger than the denominator of the fraction 1/2, some students think that the first fraction cannot possibly be smaller than the second fraction. Students screen new information that comes to them, and for some the screen impedes reception of the information. Teachers must understand both how students screen and how they interpret. Students are no longer expected merely to absorb information, because interpretation is a factor in understanding and building knowledge. Teachers assist students' learning by diagnosing how the students interpret information, and by helping them modify, alter, and enrich their interpretations.

In assessing students' individual and shared knowledge, teachers monitor students' thinking for misconceptions that may be a source of confusion and interfere with the learning process. When teachers recognize misconceptions and the students' need to alter or enrich them, they offer compelling activity such as field trips and visitors to the classroom.

Students may bring to the classroom pseudoscientific understandings and other beliefs that can be charming and must be respected. Other students, in contrast, may have extensive knowledge of a topic, but this broad-based and sometimes tangential knowledge will need focusing. Through compelling activities students can work together to gain new information and focus that teachers can use to leverage what the students already know into new understandings.

Students come to the classroom with different levels of existing knowledge as well as many other differences that challenge the teacher to arrange time and activities to suit these various differences. The instructional frame uses the pedagogy standards to provide assistance in numerous small-group settings that involve every student according to their developmental level. The system of instruction that supports teaching accommodates many different activities in various groupings and time sequences. A frame includes activities teachers assign that may occur with and without the teacher's direction, such as demonstrations; experiments; and a variety of paper-and-pencil, ICT, and other hands-on tasks. Within the frame, the teacher works with students to assist them to think in new ways about a topic, often indirectly through reading and observing, but also directly through field trips to museums and other venues related to the curriculum. Many in-class and ICT simulations and experiences can also be arranged on unlimited topics such as an earthquake, a tsunami, plant growth, human anatomy, and so on.

INDICATOR 2: THE TEACHER SETS HIGH STANDARDS FOR ALL STUDENTS' PERFORMANCE

Teachers know the power of high achievement standards for student learning. In the community agreement written during community building at the start of the school year, the teacher and students together set high expectations for learning from their work together. Students are more likely to work to meet these high expectations if they understand the criteria. Mastery, proficiency, and achievement are goals that all students can set when progress toward them is informed by a set of rubrics.

Rubrics

When students know the quality criteria for the work that is expected of them, they learn how to perform to a standard. Rubrics are descriptions of and criteria for the quality expected of student work products. They calibrate the evaluative measures to be applied to students' work. As in the development of the community agreement that sets the expectations for community, students are informed about expectations when they collaborate with the teacher to develop the rubrics for judging the quality of their work.

Rubrics describe the criterion of quality at each point on the quality scale. When students understand the rubrics they are to use from the beginning of their work, they are guided to achieve them. When they participate in developing the rubrics, they are even more likely to use them to improve their performance. When students codevelop the rubrics with their teacher, they better understand the quality expectations and how they can meet them.

Many teachers include in the classroom a games activity setting where students can use their numeracy and literacy skills and learn to negotiate and compete with other students. Students usually know that they must master the rules of a game in order to play. Sometimes they must also make up their own rules. The following example shows how students can use a familiar game (Scrabble) to begin to develop a set of rubrics for quality play:

Problem Solving With Rubrics

In a sixth grade classroom, three students at the game activity setting played Scrabble and computed scores carefully. They used dictionaries to check spelling and real-word status. Still, they grew restless every time one student took time for a turn. In the debriefing, the students shared their frustration about one student who held up the game whenever he took his turn. The student refused to put down his letters as a word on the board until he was sure he could land one of his letters on a double or triple word square. He wanted the extra points for covering those squares. In the debriefing, the class brainstormed problem solutions. The solution offered was for the students to use a timer. The high-scoring student agreed to the solution along with the others. He said he liked the timer option because it made his standard for himself and the others even higher.

The rubric the students decided to use raised the expectations and quality of the Scrabble game and also solved the problem. When everyone has a similar notion of quality, there is clarity about how to attain that level of performance. Students can practice their rubrics in student-generated activities (SGAs). They can create their own rubrics for these activities so that their peers will understand how to succeed to the highest level on the task designed for them.

It is important to establish rubrics for large projects and units that students will perform for extended periods in the classroom. In the database-building project referred to in the next example, the lesson guidelines are laid out for the students at the teaching activity setting. The levels of analysis required by database building involve students deeply in the information. Their analysis of information can be more complex and insightful using the database than would be possible without the database. First, the teacher and her seventh graders review the requirements of database building. Then together they cocreate a rubric for the work they would do on databases:

Basic and required:

- Select a topic for collecting information.
- Collect information on the topic.
- Organize the information collected on their topic.

Successful:

- Identify the various dimensions or categories in the information.
- Prepare a spreadsheet into which to enter the information.
- Enter the data into the spreadsheet.

Evidence of learning progress:

- Decide the values to use for the information.
- Describe the relationships among the components.

Evidence of advanced learning progress:

- Learn and apply formulas to the database for sums and other functions.
- Generate new rules to organize information.

The rubric provides the students with a clear understanding of the criteria for the joint work product. In small-group discussion, the teacher continues to focus on students' work on the project, providing assistance for next steps. Some groups will need extra teaching assistance from the start while others will be able to perform to the rubric at independent activity settings. The activity becomes the focus of the teacher's activity setting over the period of the project. In the instructional frame for the database-building project, students are presented with the following assignment:

After gathering in small groups of about six students each, the groups selected a topic from the latest U.S. Census to research their state's demographics (that is, population, age, ethnicity, lifespan, county and city data, gross income, and so on). Some groups used the Internet to log onto the U.S. Census Web site, locate their data topic, and collect data for the database to present and explain to the other students. For example, one group collected data on the populations of the cities in their state. Another group developed the database to use for graphic representations. Another group analyzed the data by making comparisons and discovering high and low levels of population, ages, life spans, and other variables. The joint product of the student groups was a single graphic that integrated all the data they collected to provide the most information they could about their city, county, and state. The culminating activity will be to put together the final product: a display in the school hallway by which everyone can view and benefit from the in-depth analysis of the city, county, and state data.

Database development is not only for middle and upper grade students. First and second graders also need to organize information and identify its dimensions. The first grade students in the following example collect images and information about food to develop awareness of how information can be better understood when it is presented in an organized manner, such as in a database.

A first grade class has been learning about different kinds of food. The teacher starts the students out by asking them what types of food they eat. The students have many answers, including cereal, hamburger, chicken, vegetables, peanut butter, fish, bread, and so on. The students find and draw pictures of the food they eat. They sort the food pictures into categories of meat, vegetable, desserts, and other, which they organize for their database. They decide values to assign to the different foods according to what they like, what they know is healthy, where food comes from, color, and any other preferences. They enter the information into a spreadsheet or other display, such as three-by-five cards, which they can later sort and manipulate for sight vocabulary, writing, games, and other tasks. They continue to track the food they eat at school and home to discover new categories they can use to sort the data they collect on what they eat.

The second graders can cocreate rubrics with the teacher to make their work expectations clear. The rubrics would include measures of how the work products were interesting and helpful. The students could establish a rubric for preparing representations of food by finding pictures or making drawings. A rubric for establishing high quality in their work would require presenting their work on the database and what they learned about the food they eat to their peers. Their work products would be documentation of their understanding.

Corrective Feedback

Students require corrective feedback to acquire deep understanding of content. Teachers provide such feedback in relation to a standard or criteria for performance, such as a rubric. Rubrics for academic work provide examples of criteria for high-quality performance as well as a scale with descriptions indicating quality for each criterion. Rubrics typically address the academic features of students' work, but there can also be rubrics for working together, participating, and performing.

The briefing in an instructional frame introduces students to the expectations set for their work products. In the briefing, the teacher and students can generate rubrics, or the rubrics can be a focus of the lesson at the teaching activity setting. The debriefing reviews the students' experiences in meeting the expectations and provides opportunity for feedback and problem solving.

In the following example, the teacher gives a student feedback according to the rubrics for an essay assignment described in the briefing, which included the requirement to provide evidence to support statements. Notice how the teacher points out where the student's writing was good to balance his critical feedback. He finishes with clear instruction on how to improve the writing.

Teacher: "Sometimes she can be mean." But this example is about how she's nice. Where's the example where she's acting mean?

Student: She got mad.

Teacher: Okay, write about when she got mad. You have two ideas here, one where she's nice and one where she's mean. Make them two different paragraphs. Your assignment says when you look back at the reading explain with evidence what you think will happen. You made a good prediction, now show with evidence why you think this would happen. Why do you think she's going to stay with Max?

Student: They need money. She would go to work and he could go to school.

Teacher: Good, now just put that in here.

Teachers establish rubrics that their students can meet, either independently or with teaching assistance. When teachers include students in the creation of rubrics, the students understand the work expectations clearly. Students who cocreate rubrics for work are informed right from the start about the expected quality of performance. When teachers regularly review work products in discussion at the teaching setting in relation to criteria such as rubrics, they provide corrective feedback that students need to succeed academically. But this is not the end of the process.

Corrective feedback is the beginning of a process of reflection and revision in which the work product is reviewed, new approaches are generated, and outcomes are revised with students. The success or failure of a product is an opportunity for students to analyze and evaluate what they need to know. Then they can build on their mistakes by setting out to develop a more effective product with teacher assistance or independently, depending on the level of assistance they may still require. Corrective feedback comes from many sources that support students and are overseen by the teacher. Students, peers, and teacher all work together to provide the feedback that students need to deepen their content knowledge and meet high standards.

INDICATOR 3: THE TEACHER ASSISTS STUDENT PERFORMANCE AT INCREASINGLY ADVANCED LEVELS

The fourth pedagogy standard emphasizes the design of activities that challenge students to engage in increasingly complex levels of thinking. Using the instructional frame and various small groupings, the teacher and the students discuss challenging texts and activities that require complex thinking. From the first day of the school year, the instructional frame guides, structures, and schedules classroom arrangements and activities. The frame groups students in various arrangements and routes them to multiple, simultaneous activities in various activity settings throughout the classroom, including the teaching activity setting. In this complex instructional frame, teachers multitask in order to teach for deep understanding in small groups. Daily the students work closely with the teacher, who assists them in learning and in documenting their learning.

Although corrective feedback is provided on students' work in the teacher's activity setting, the briefing and debriefing components of the frame are built-in feedback mechanisms. The instructional frame is always posted or drawn on the board where everyone can see it. In the briefing, the teacher and the students provide directions and set the standard for an activity or product. In the debriefing, the students discuss how they have accomplished their tasks and abided by the community agreement. In this way, the system supports teaching that prepares students to think more complexly and in academic terms in order to apply their understanding to new situations in different contexts.

Thinking complexly about the core content curriculum is also labeled higher-order thinking. In the following list, higher-order thinking descends from the first level of thinking (recall) to the highest levels (evaluation and judgment):

- Recall
- Pattern recognition and development
- Spontaneous and systematic observation
- Recognizing symbolic representations
- Classification and categorization
- Identification of cause and effect
- Rationalization
- Generalization
- Analysis
- Synthesis
- Evaluation
- Judgment

Complex Thinking

To prepare activities to challenge students' thinking, teachers use a guide to thinking levels. The list, or taxonomy, like Benjamin Bloom's taxonomy of educational objectives (1956), just presented, provides a way to classify interactions and activities according to the thinking levels they require. Bloom's taxonomy, a staple resource, organizes thinking skills into the following levels:

Level I	Knowledge	Remembering previously learned material: observe, define
Level II	Comprehension	Understanding meaning: paraphrase, describe, locate
Level III	Application	Using the material in new and concrete situations: sequence
Level IV	Analysis	Breaking down material into smaller parts: outline, compare
Level V	Synthesis	Putting material together to form a whole: plan, construct
Level VI	Evaluation	Judging value for a purpose: rank, criticize, justify, assess

Bloom's taxonomy identifies the types of thinking required according to the level of the teacher's tasks or questions. Students can increase their awareness of the level of their thinking. Such increased awareness of their own thinking and learning levels has been associated with students' greater ability to transfer knowledge from one situation into new problem situations. Students who understand more about their own thinking and learning have a *metacognitive* awareness.

Bloom's taxonomy can also guide the design of activities for a particular thinking level or it can target various levels. For example, at the beginning of the chapter, an excerpt from a seventh grade lesson on measuring circles with ELLs shows the teacher prompting a student toward understanding through questions and models:

Daniel: This is the conconference, or whatever.

Teacher: So this one's the circumference, and this one is the diameter?

Daniel: I just remember that the diameter is the smallest, small, smaller than this one [referring to the circumference string].

Teacher: Well, which string did you measure around the edges with?

Daniel: This one [pointing to the circumference string].

Teacher: This one? The circumference?

Daniel: Yeah, and this one across it.

Teacher: Across it? So why do you think that this is smaller than this—that the diameter is smaller than the circumference? Why do you think that happens?

Daniel: Because if this one shrinks, like she said, it will shrink down, this one's still going to be smaller than that one.

Teacher: Why? What would happen, what would happen to this, the diameter?

Daniel: That one stays smaller. It will get smaller.

The teacher's questions reflect several levels of Bloom's Taxonomy, as the following classification of the teacher's questions reveals:

Knowledge   The teacher asks the student to recall and retell.

Comprehension   Then she asks, "Which string did you measure around the edges with?" to check on the student's understanding of the two features, circumference and diameter.

Application	The teacher follows up with a sequence question about the steps of the activity, which the student answers by confirming the circumference measure and describing the diameter measure.
Analysis	The next question the teacher asks requires the student to compare the two diameters.
Synthesis	Finally, the teacher asks the student twice to explain the length relationship between the strings that represent diameter and circumference, which the student firmly answers correctly.

In the excerpt, the teacher directed the student's thinking through questions at every level of the taxonomy except the highest level, Level VI, evaluation. The evaluation level is demonstrated when students make judgments about the value of a product and convince others about it. The teacher's goal in the lesson was largely to guide students to understand the mathematics concepts of circle dimensions and measurement. Her high expectations stretched her teaching skills as well as the thinking of her student. She probed in order to nudge the student to increase his level of understanding about the terms and their meaning. The taxonomy is useful for teachers in understanding their students' levels of thinking and in choosing the levels of the questions they use to develop understanding.

Complex Thinking Activity

Troops to Teachers is a U.S. Department of Education and Department of Defense program that helps eligible military personnel begin new careers as teachers in public schools. Information on the program is available at: http://www.ed.gov/programs/troops/index.html. Gregory Powell, a Troops to Teachers teacher, heard one of his fifth grade students say during a discussion of newspapers that she had never read the business section. She wondered what all the small-print numbers and symbols on pages without pictures represented. Powell promised her that the pages were much less complicated than they appeared. Then he promised himself that he would provide his students with an experience of the stock market that would unravel the mystery. He would equip them to understand the business section of any newspaper so they could use the information to benefit their future fortunes.

Mr. Powell developed an interdisciplinary unit, "Our Stock Is Rising," with the primary goal of demonstrating how basic mathematics concepts and operations are used in the business world. His secondary goal was to identify real-world applications of the curriculum content in the stock market. His overall goal was to develop students' understanding of the concept of money in the context of real-world business applications.

He began by identifying the basic knowledge that students needed in order to read and understand stock market fundamentals as they are presented in the newspaper:

• Addition, subtraction, multiplication, and division at the fifth grade level to determine the value of stocks

• Fractions, decimals, and mixed numbers to compare and annotate changes in stock values

• Positive and negative numbers to understand gain and loss in stock value

• Data analysis skills to determine gains and losses to make comparisons among stock values

• Graphic representation to make bar and line graphs that track long-term changes in values

• Calculator skills for applying operational, decimal, percentage, and memory storage and retrieval functions

Mr. Powell also identified the content skills the students would use from across the curriculum:

• Language arts applications for writing business letters and reports

• Social studies applications, including map skills for locating company sites and tracking shipments

• Economics concepts for discussing events affecting the market

• Multiculturalism concepts for understanding international trade and investments

• Technology skills for recognizing computer applications at the center of stock market activity

- Internet research skills for studying companies' histories, policies, and corporate goals

    Other skills needed include the following:
- Oral presentation skills

- Software packages for spreadsheets, data analysis, word processing, and presentation graphics, to facilitate the tracking of stock performance and the management of company portfolios

- Three-dimensional overhead projectors and digital cameras— peripherals for enhancing presentations and historical documentation

Mr. Powell developed the lessons to advance students' use of the lexicon and language of the stock market and their understanding of the concepts that drive its functions. He provided a context that most students knew little about because they were motivated to learn more in general about money. The teacher motivated the students while developing a concept or definition with examples that were of great interest to the students. One example he used distinguished investors from consumers and demonstrated how investing money in companies returns to an investor:

Consumer or Investor?

Mr. Powell and his students know that a famous brand of sneakers costs more than $100. Some students are wearing them now. Mr. Powell asks them if they also know that as soon as the sneakers are worn one time, their value is zero? The students look a little surprised. Instead of a guaranteed loss of value, more value could be added to that $100 consumer price. Mr. Powell explains how the consumer could invest the cost of the sneaker in the company's stock. This would produce profits for the investor from each consumer's purchase. So, do you want to be a consumer or an investor?

Class Activities

Using Bloom's taxonomy as a guide, Powell designed the following higher-order thinking activities to illustrate selected information on the topic. He also designed activities to prod students to think at the highest levels of synthesis and evaluation. Many of the activities are joint productive activities (JPAs).

1. Knowledge: Define terms such as *stock market, stock, investor, consumer, ticker, share, close, volume, change, Wall Street,* and so on.

2. Knowledge: Unlock acronyms such as NYSE, NASDAQ, NAV, DJIA, and so on, and their meaning.

3. Comprehension: Work in triads to find twenty terms and write explanations for how they are used in the business section of the newspaper.

4. Comprehension: Create a record of the class's work on the stock market that tells the story of the students' success in picking companies.

5. Application: Obtain more information about a company (its size, worth, industry, product, status, address, and logo) in the newspaper and on the Internet.

6. Analyze: Track the price of the company's stock, value, price change, value change, number of shares, and so forth on a spreadsheet.

7. Analyze: Using the financial terms, discuss information gained about each company in a small group with the teacher.

8. Analyze: Using the financial terms, combine the findings for all the companies in a line graph with x and y labels that reflects the performance of all stocks to show how they compare and contrast.

9. Synthesis: Devise a way to facilitate and expedite stock analysis and selection.

10. Evaluation: Prepare a list of criteria for judging a company a worthy investment and one likely to grow and perform.

Class Community

Students work in pairs or triads for the first few activities in a lesson and move into teams or small groups for the next activities. The teacher uses five groups in a club format. The membership of the clubs is voluntary as long as the numbers remain in the small group category of three to seven students.

Class Instruction

At independent activity settings, students perform JPAs. They rotate in groups from one activity setting to another, including meeting with the teacher to discuss their specific understandings of the content. The teacher checks on the students' levels of success in the activities. If the students are unable to use the terms to describe the holdings of their portfolios, the teacher intervenes with explicit assistance. He also adjusts tasks for the group or for individuals to levels that guarantee success.

The teacher can use these activities or generate many others to form an instructional frame for the topic. See Appendix 6A.

Instructional Frame

A suggested instructional frame for stock market study requires a period of slightly more than two and a half hours, or 146 minutes (see Appendix 6B). Briefing and debriefing are planned for ten minutes each. Each session of five simultaneous activities for five clubs is scheduled for twenty minutes. One minute is reserved for traveling between each session. The frame sessions can be distributed over several days. A debriefing to wrap up daily work and a briefing at the start of each day are highly recommended to ensure coherence and continuity in the frame. However, once an instructional frame has begun and students are briefed, they often arrive for class every day prepared and eager to resume their work. Teacher monitoring of student participation and quality of student work is the basis for deciding how a frame functions best in a classroom.

INDICATOR 4: THE TEACHER TEACHES CHALLENGING CONTENT

The fourth pedagogy standard guides teachers to elevate the level of challenge for all activities. This focus does not mean that challenge has been missing from all previous classroom activity and teaching. It does mean that, as a routine matter, challenging thinking is to be a priority in all activity. The guidance of the fourth indicator is to maintain high standards and promote students' success through assistance and compelling activities. Teachers are to ensure that students demonstrate and document explicit understanding of concepts and new content information. They can use many approaches to challenge student thinking and develop understanding that students can document. In addition to the strategies presented in previous chapters, such as JPAs (see Chapter Three), language experience approaches (LEAs), directed thinking activities (DTAs), and language development levers, (see Chapter Four), teachers draw on other approaches, especially those that reflect real-world complexity and problem solving.

Problem Solving

New concepts can be introduced and developed in problem solving activities. Practical problems, such as calculating the amount of paint needed for a project at home or school, have correct answers. A problem with a correct answer can challenge students to take their thinking to more complex levels when they are guided to explore dimensions of the problem beyond the answer. Problems that have no correct answer (open-ended problems) resist quick and easy solutions and prompt students to think in novel ways. The fourth standard promotes the use of problem solving to prod students to think in new ways about ordinary topics, about the application of content concepts, and about values related to those concepts.

To succeed academically, students must develop adaptable understandings of content knowledge, efficient use of basic skill sets, and the ability to apply both knowledge and skills critically. In the following problem-solving example, a real-world dilemma with no correct answer poses a complex challenge for students. To begin to resolve the problem, they must examine the facts of the situation, research the circumstances of the community, and probe the values dimension of the problem. They do so as a JPA. They collaborate to address the community's problem as a debating team. Their joint product (their debating statements) documents their learning.

Eighth grade students consider the situation of bears wandering into a neighborhood to rummage for meals. The bears also tear up trash areas, causing damage to some homes on the edge of the community. To avoid the possible consequences of hungry bears for pets and small children, and the repair costs, families and the community as a whole are motivated to identify the most effective way to deter the visiting bears. Some decide that more careful storage and disposal of trash will eliminate the food sources that bears seek, and the bears will return to their natural habitat. Others want to solve the problem permanently with guns. The community is about to vote on a gun ban, and the bear intruders have turned the entire community's attention to the issue. The community in general finds neither solution acceptable, according to their informal polls. A debate is scheduled for the community members to resolve the dilemma one way or another for safety reasons.

To address this problem, students are assigned to role-play family and community members as debaters so they can relate to the real stakes of an individual's family, environment, and safety, and also to other values that people have, as well as to the costs the community may incur. A competent debate performance requires analysis of both the problem situation and community values. Role-players must articulate their ideas and preferences on the basis of their identification with and research on the issues, such as prior examples and solutions, and bear habitats and habits. The students are encouraged to find conversations on the Internet that discuss similar issues. All debate points and material must be based on Internet research. The students select teams and the class selects a date for the debate. School personnel and parents will be invited to the event.

This problem-solving exercise is appropriate for all grades, including the earliest. Children's literature is rife with complex dilemmas and seemingly inescapable threats that students can read and discuss to prepare for challenging problem solving. Examples include *Three Billy Goats Gruff; Jack and the Beanstalk; Hansel and Gretel;* and many other stories, legends, and myths from Native American and international literatures. Some students will recognize the problems more readily than others, but all will have views to share, predictions and solutions to pose in conversation, and drawings, dramatizations, and craft and art applications to suggest, including LEAs and other strategic and extending instructional activities. Problem solving is one of the most powerful learning experiences.

During classroom community building at the start of the school year, even kindergarten and early elementary students must begin practical problem solving to produce a class community agreement. In every instructional frame, briefing and debriefing encourage students to share their feelings about their experiences in the classroom activities and with the problems they had or need to solve with their peers. Teachers often expose students to children's literature in which narratives present problem-solving scenes and reveal characters' solutions. Students are encouraged to talk about their feelings and concerns in the same way that story characters talk about theirs. Teachers can provide occasions for role-playing that enhance this opportunity, such as in the following example:

First and Second Grade Problem Solving

The teacher read the *Three Billy Goats Gruff* story to the students as they sat on the rug before her. The teacher read the troll's parts with such animation that some of the students were afraid. One way the teacher responded was to have the students turn the story into a play. The students made face masks of the goats and the troll. The students wore the masks to act out the characters' parts as they walked across a board on the floor of the classroom. The troll character with a large ugly mask sat close to the board. The students were guided to focus on how the goats solved their problem of getting across the troll's bridge without being eaten. Then they talked about solving problems and how they could use a strategy for their problems.

Having models and hearing others speak about how they solve a problem benefits all students, especially ELLs and those who are at risk. Working jointly on problem-solving approaches is advantageous for everyone, especially because it enables students to hear alternative methods of problem solving that are more efficient than their own. Their advances in thinking also have a values dimension from their classroom and real-world community. Disagreements about how to solve problems provide varied perspectives on situations, and these multiple perspectives spark creative and alternative problem solving that goes beyond convergent thinking and conventional or "right" solutions. Creative solutions can reflect deepening understandings about new concepts and their relationships.

Complex problems in the curriculum present complex skill demands as well as thinking challenges. In solving problems, such as what the NASA shuttle's orbit should be to avoid space debris, or what the distance to other heavenly bodies is, students must be equipped with the required skills. The shuttle's problems require the use of concepts such as ratio, proportion, and estimation, and the ability to conceptualize the magnitudes of measurement in aerospace applications. Teachers need to ensure that students have the skills necessary for complex problem-solving assignments.

Games

Playing games means following rules, but also discovering and understanding what the rules are. Games, whether old-fashioned board or new digitized, are challenging activities that are familiar, compelling, and based on students' real-world experiences. They require students to relate, collaborate, and assist in order to achieve a win or loose outcome. They nudge players into new awareness of their own and others' motives. Assuming roles in games means predicting others' moves and working from their viewpoints as well as one's own. Games also require players to participate in new social arrangements, with others they do not know; to manage imaginary or real resources; and to identify and manipulate complicated patterns. Games related to content goals that exercise computational, logistical, and other planning processes are appropriately challenging activities.

Engage, Explore, Explain, Elaborate, Evaluate

In a gamelike approach for grades five through eight that is similar to the DTA cycle, students must use information, skills, and ICT, if available, to solve a complex problem. The game requires students to identify, analyze, integrate concepts and ideas across disciplines, and communicate effectively both orally and in writing. In a science example, students interpret "fossil footprint" evidence. The teacher asks students to use the evidence to construct defensible hypotheses or explanations for past geological events. The estimated time requirement for this activity is two class periods. The activity works with a large or small group. It is adapted with permission from the Earth Science Curriculum Project (1973). The steps in the activity form a convenient reminder of the required level of thinking:

- Engage
- Explore
- Explain
- Elaborate
- Evaluate

This "E" strategy fosters inquiry, logic, meaning, pattern recognition, and other critical thinking skills that are the basis for successful knowledge acquisition and problem solving. In the following descriptions of each step of the activity, the thinking levels required by the activity are made clear. The footprint puzzle that is the focus of this activity is found in Appendix 6C.

Engage Use an overhead projector to show position one of the footprints, covering the other two positions with a blank piece of paper; or provide each student with a copy of position one. Tell the students that fossilized tracks like these are common in parts of the United States, such as New England and the Southwest. Point out to the students that they will be attempting to reconstruct geological happenings from the past by analyzing a set of fossilized tracks. Their task is similar to that of a detective. They are to form defensible explanations of past events from limited evidence. As more evidence becomes available, their hypotheses must be modified or abandoned. The only clues are the footprints themselves. Ask the students the following questions:

- Can you tell anything about the size or nature of the organisms?
- Were all the tracks made at the same time?
- How many animals were involved?
- Can you reconstruct a series of events represented by this set of fossil tracks?

Discuss each of the questions and write hypotheses on a chart. Accept any reasonable explanations that the students offer. Try consistently to point out the difference between what they observe and what they infer. Ask them to suggest evidence that would support their proposed explanations.

Explore Reveal the second position of the footprints and allow time for the students to consider the new information. Review the first explanation with the students. Ask them to modify the first explanation and add new ones. Then project the complete footprint puzzle or hand it out on a third page. Ask students to interpret what happened. A key point for students to recognize is that any reasonable explanation must be based only on those proposed explanations that still apply when the entire puzzle is visible. Any interpretation that is consistent with all the evidence is acceptable. To challenge the students' thinking and stimulate the discussion, use the following questions (students should give evidence or suggest what they would look for as evidence to support their proposed explanations):

- In what directions did the animals move?
- Did they change their speed and direction?
- What might have changed the footprint pattern?

- Was the land level or irregular?
- Was the soil moist or dry on the day these tracks were made?
- In what kind of rock were the prints made?
- Were the sediments coarse or fine where the tracks were made?

The environment of the track area should also be discussed. If dinosaurs made the tracks, the climate probably was warm and humid. If students propose that some sort of obstruction prevented the animals from seeing each other, this might suggest vegetation; or perhaps the widened pace might suggest a slope. Speculate on the condition of the surface at the time the footprints were made. Also consider what conditions were necessary for their preservation.

Explain   Students will propose several possible explanations. One of the most common is that two animals met and fought. No real reason exists to assume that one animal attacked and ate the other. Ask students who propose this explanation to indicate the evidence. If they could visit the site, what evidence would they look for that would support their explanation? Certain lines of evidence such as the quickened gaits, circular pattern, and disappearance of one set of tracks could support the fight explanation. They might also support, however, an explanation of a mother picking up her baby. The description and temperament of the animals involved are open to question. Indeed, we lack the evidence to say that the tracks were made at the same time. The intermingling shown in the middle section of the puzzle may be evidence that both tracks were made at one time, but it could be only a coincidence. Perhaps one animal passed by and left, and then the other arrived.

Discuss the expected learning outcomes related to scientific inquiry and the nature of science. To answer the questions posed by the set of fossil footprints, the students, like scientists, should construct reasonable explanations based solely on their logical interpretation of the available evidence. They should recognize and analyze alternative explanations by weighing the evidence and examining the logic to decide which explanations seem most reasonable. Although there may be several plausible explanations, they do not all have equal weight. In a manner similar to the way scientists work, students should be able to use scientific criteria to find, communicate, and defend the preferred explanation.

Elaborate   More discussions can take place on interpreting series of events using animal prints that students find outdoors and reproduce for the class. Do not forget to look for human footprints.

Evaluate   Describe a specific event involving two or more people or animals from footprint evidence remains. Ask the students, either in teams or individually, to diagram footprint evidence that could lead to several different yet defensible explanations regarding what took place. They should be able to explain the strengths and weaknesses of each explanation using the footprint puzzle. (Earth Science Curriculum Project, 1973). See Appendix 4B for the Web site.

To extend or follow up on this activity, an SGA can be designed using students' own fossil footprints or another evidence-based puzzle. Choose several different puzzles and have student teams repeat the activity using the same learning goals. The cycle or process of this activity is similar to the DTA cycle. These activities involve students in thinking the way experts do as they solve complex problems using higher order thinking to expand the human knowledge base.

Complex Joint Productive Activities

Teachers may develop ambitious JPAs to challenge students to apply their knowledge to new situations and problems, to use their skills in new combinations, and to meet requirements for accuracy. Kindergarten students perform at high levels and to high standards just as upper grades do. To carry out a map-making activity, students may not yet have a sense of mapping, but finding positions and directions can be learning objectives for the work.

Kindergartners Make Maps for a School Geographic Display

Map making for kindergartners begins with looking at and talking about maps in large and small groups. The groups draw a large composite map of their classroom. Students work together on different pieces of the map to draw and color in details of windows, doors, the floor, and so. The final map is assembled and put on view. It is compared to the real classroom. The features of the colored map are discussed in large and small groups. Items on the map are labeled. The labels are added to students' sight vocabulary. Students think about where the labels belong on the map. They talk about position words such as *up, down, beside, over,* and *under* and what they mean for placing their own names on the map. They decide how to draw themselves into the classroom until all the students are included on the map. Their names are added and included as sight vocabulary. The label words are used for phonics and word-recognition activities. They are also the basis for making another map of the school hallway, the playground, or other area to generate more vocabulary and word-recognition follow-up activities.

In more complex JPAs there is not a single correct answer, and students are challenged to combine their skills to produce an outcome. In the following map-making activity, fourth graders may understand the notion of maps, and those students who do can model for those who are new to cartography. Even those familiar with maps must capture the main outline of the buildings while ignoring irrelevant details. This JPA is open-ended and requires students to collaborate and negotiate to produce the product.

As a content-focused activity, map making requires fourth graders to use cartography to survey the school. First, students in small groups make a composite drawing of the school as they know it. Then they research the science of cartography on the Internet or in texts to learn about scientific techniques for mapping they can use, such as drawing their classroom and the school to scale. Map making becomes a mathematical exercise in measurement, proportion, and perspective. Students will be using their basic mathematics skills or they will estimate what they are not skilled enough to work out. Finished maps are posted for display and further discussion.

In the following JPA, students understand the notion of maps and map making, and they have the mathematical skills to perform the needed measurements. The level of the activity and the expectations for the product have been raised from reliance on everyday knowledge to more scientific approaches. The students will focus on various aspects of the map-making project and will discuss their joint work with the teacher. In this JPA there is not a single correct answer, and the students must collaborate and negotiate to produce the product. This kind of project is an opportunity for students to develop deeper knowledge of the topic and mastery of the basic measuring skills they use to create the maps. Rather than a one-time experience that may be informative for a few, this activity can be repeated by changing the area to be mapped.

By placing this project in a continuing activity setting, teachers provide students with more opportunities to work with new ideas and applications to strengthen their learning. All participants have a chance to improve their products.

As a content-focused activity, map making involves seventh graders in geodesy. Geodesy is the science of finding places on the surface of the earth. The students use the National Oceanic and Atmospheric Administration's National Ocean Service Web site and resources to survey the school. They do research on the Internet or in texts to learn scientific techniques for mapping their school and environs. Map mapping can involve students in using global positioning techniques and other approaches. They may connect with communities of practice in geodesy and geography on the Internet to strengthen their skills and build their knowledge. This is an ongoing activity that can be assigned an activity setting in the classroom where students can continue to work on their map-making projects.

When activity is JPA, students draw on the experience, skills, and models of their peers as well as their own. The knowledge that is distributed among the participants is the greatest resource available for understanding the new concepts and producing an outcome that documents the students' increasing understanding. Working with others stimulates students and contributes to a more robust learning experience. Students' learning is robust when they can apply the knowledge they acquire from one situation in new situations.

Classroom Community

The social organization of the classroom developed in the first three standards is routine at this point. The activities in the instructional frame occur in small-group activity settings around the classroom. The teacher also has a meeting place for small-group discussions with students. Teachers use small groups to discuss and check on students' progress on review and other tasks at independent work activity settings. The teacher prepares students for the shift into curriculum topics that are increasingly challenging.

The teacher forms groups according to ability, interest, language, friendship, or other arrangements. The groups include three to seven students. The teacher arranges to meet with the groups regularly, daily, for lessons, to discuss their work performed without direct supervision, to review their skills, and to provide corrective feedback on their work products. The teaching activity center is the core of the classroom system, which is energized, monitored, and guided by the teacher. The pedagogy standards system of instructional support guides teaching to focus on assisting the performance of all students.

Classroom Activity

To the arsenal of classroom activity the fourth pedagogy standard contributes problem solving at both the practical and academic levels, and to complex JPAs. Problem solving involves students in applying the lesson content in ways that increase the challenge of their experiences of learning new information and concepts. Teachers gradually shift students away from independent activities that implement the first standard of guaranteeing success for every student, toward conceptually complex activities that challenge and deepen students' understanding. The system for organizing instruction presented in this book supports this process, particularly through the instructional frame, and by grouping students in small groups and routing them to activity settings, many of which are continuing or permanent in the classroom. In these settings, the size of the teaching event is reduced in that the teacher meets with no more than seven students on an ongoing basis, preferably every day, especially for ELL and at-risk students. The first three pedagogy standards emphasize JPA, language expression, and contextualization to involve students in numerous hands-on, concrete, and interactive experiences with content topics, vocabulary, and concepts. Teachers participate, monitor, and coordinate students' progress in these tasks in the teaching activity setting.

Abundant Practice Opportunities

One way to ensure students' success is to provide all of them with sufficient application practices to meet their needs. The activity settings, especially those in which activity is independent and continuous, have a fundamental purpose to provide a multitude of practice opportunities in which students can increase their familiarity with and grasp the language and concepts of the curriculum. Activity settings tied closely to content and teaching activities also motivate and encourage students to practice in many formats, including manipulatives and those activities that students design themselves. The teacher assesses students' skill development and provides assistance in small-group discussion. In some activity settings, students practice basic skills independently of the teacher and with peers as resources.

When students perform very well independently, it is partly because they know that the classroom guidance system includes accountability. They also enjoy the system of predictable classroom events—routines of learning that they understand and interesting activities that they are frequently assigned. Students' activities, tasks, and other work away from the teacher are recorded and turned in daily for the teacher to review. In addition, every student returns routinely to small group discussions with the teacher and peers in which their new skill levels are reviewed, used, challenged, and evaluated. In these ways teachers track students' participation and work products in the system.

SUMMARY

This chapter has described implementing the fourth pedagogy standard, which guides teachers to raise the performance challenge for all students in all activities. Even though teachers' expression of the challenge may have a variety of appearances in different classrooms, all of these expressions build on the activity, language and literacy development, and context structures of the first three standards in every implementation.

The four pedagogy standards support making teaching predictable, productive, and challenging to academic performance that meets high standards. The standards system of support reduces teaching that is incidental, inconsistent, and sometimes incoherent. The structure provides a reliable routine for all participants and a system for managing its requirements. It also provides a rhythm and pace for teaching and learning activities that is brisk and stimulating through simple scheduling routines supporting teachers' use of multitasking. It enables teachers to expect students to work together independently without supervision in order to increase not only practice time with peers that leads to skill mastery, but also academic content proficiency. Teachers must claim time to work with some students while others remain constructively engaged in learning activities. Teachers must multitask in order to reflect students' real worlds, particularly their need to self-regulate within it.

The first standard's guidance for teachers and students working together must be broadly interpreted to mean sometimes physically together and sometimes intellectually together though working apart. The organism of the classroom can differentiate in numerous ways to serve the goals of teaching and learning. The instructional frames recommended in this book's discussion are only one way to initiate needed changes. When the foundational system of the four pedagogy standards is implemented in classrooms, the learning opportunities and outcomes for every student are richer. Other models with similar visions will expand the treasury.

Teachers meet the thinking challenge of the fourth pedagogy standard by designing abundant activities that invite students' participation, performance, and productivity in multitasking classrooms. Teachers can increase students' higher-order thinking capacities when they use a system of instructional support that intensifies every teaching and learning activity. Teachers and students document the learning they experience in joint and individual work products. The outcomes of the implementation of the first through fourth pedagogy standards are that the teacher

- Produced a classroom community agreement for working together.
- Designed collaborative tasks that require joint product development.
- Organized the classroom to support teacher's and students' work together.
- Used an instructional frame routinely for all teaching and associated activities.
- Developed students' literacy and academic language expression in speaking and writing.
- Provided meaning and contexts that link students' lives to learning.
- Challenged students in activity to think more complexly at every level.
- Provided prompt, corrective feedback that informed and guided students' content understanding.

The four pedagogy standards together constitute the foundational guidance system for effective teaching in an interactive, activity-based classroom. The fifth and final pedagogy standard, teaching through conversation, discussed in the next chapter, completes the pedagogy guidance system that ensures every student is assisted to attain academic success.

Seventh Grade English Language Learners Plan How to Measure Planets

Teacher: I asked her, I said, how do you know if we measure Saturn and Jupiter? How can we tell which one's bigger and what did you say?

Adrianna: You measure the diameter. [The activity was to measure jar lids with string.]

Teacher: Uh-huh, uh-huh, you measure the diameter of which one?

Adrianna: Of both.

Teacher: Of both, and then what do you do?

Adrianna: You see which one's bigger than which one.

Teacher: So you compare the diameters of the two?

Adrianna: Yeah.

Teacher: And you told me that if you knew the size of the diameter, that you could know the size of the circumference. How did you know? Why is that? Why do you think that?

Adrianna: Well, because the one string's gonna be bigger than the other.

Teacher: Right. OK, so, which one was the diameter? Can you guys tell me which?

All: The smallest one.

Teacher: How do you know it's the smallest one?

Daniel: Because the diameter is always going to be smaller than the, the circumference.

chapter SEVEN

Using Instructional Conversation

PEDAGOGY STANDARD V
Teaching Through Conversation

Engage students in dialogue, especially instructional conversation (IC).

Classroom Application Indicators

The teacher

1. Performs IC routinely within an instructional frame.

2. Guides students to full participation in IC.

3. Achieves academic outcomes in IC.

Introduction

The premier form of teaching assistance is dialogue. In dialogue, ideas are formed, expressed, and exchanged, through both speech and writing. Dialogue often rises to abstract levels. Even common topics are discussed in thoughtful ways in dialogue. The fifth pedagogy standard emphasizes teaching with dialogue using IC.

Teaching through dialogue is as old as and probably older than Socrates, the ancient Greek who introduced it. A form of dialogue, IC is relatively new to modern classroom teaching. Very few students are granted the privilege of sustained conversation on academic topics with their teachers on a regular basis. The major benefit of the five pedagogy standards is that they address this persistent inequity by guiding teachers to design instruction to support the regular use of IC with every student.

IC inserts dialogue, a unique and essential form of teaching assistance, into the five-pedagogy-standards system. The routine use of IC guarantees that regular, privileged, and sustained interaction time with a teacher occurs for all students. The chapter's opening excerpt presents a slice of an IC led by a teacher working with English language learners (ELLs). The students experience instruction through dialogue by participating in it. Their comments demonstrate their need for IC's language models, language production opportunities, and conceptual learning assistance. Regularly scheduled IC within an instructional frame ensures that all students, regardless of ability or background, participate in the premier teaching strategy just as the ELL students do in the excerpt quoted.

Rationale

IC has been demonstrated to be an effective intervention for improving reading comprehension for all students, but particularly ELLs. Scientifically based findings indicate that its use in combination with other approaches, such as literature logs, has a positive effect on ELLs' comprehension (U.S Department of Education, 2006; Saunders, 1999; Saunders and Goldenbert, 1999a, 1999b). In IC, teachers' dialogue with students is characterized by *responsive assistance.* In other words, the teacher guides students to acquire new information on the basis of what they already know. In dialogue about prior knowledge, teachers identify a hook in students' knowledge to which they can connect new information. If students' knowledge is absent or limited, the teacher provides a joint productive activity (JPA) for building common knowledge. For example, students may write a story together or participate in another activity that shows what they know and builds their understanding about a topic. IC is responsive assistance when dialogue is contextualized in students' experience and when it challenges students' thinking to reach new levels. At the same time, dialogue develops students' language and literacy and deepens content understanding. After participating in IC, students apply their new knowledge and ideas in a follow-up activity.

At its most powerful, IC appears as animated conversation on academic topics among students and teacher. In fact, IC has unique features. It is at once assessment and assistance. Students' participation reveals their language and thinking proficiencies, which teachers can assist in improving. Assessment in IC is a basis for teachers to assist students specifically and provide corrective feedback. It is at once conversation and instruction. Conversation includes everyone in the group and accepts their preferred speech forms, which may differ from the language of instruction. Instruction brings meaning making and coherence to teaching and learning goals. IC is at once pedagogy and teaching because it is a process of and approach to teaching that conveys any content. ICs are opportunities for teachers to help students examine their own knowledge and experience, and make connections to new knowledge.

IC is the culmination of the five pedagogy standards. As an integration of pedagogy and teaching, IC is supported by the standards. The first standard lays the classroom foundations for teaching with IC, and the succeeding standards build on that foundation. The fifth standard rests on the implementation of the first four.

INDICATOR 1: THE TEACHER PERFORMS IC ROUTINELY WITHIN AN INSTRUCTIONAL FRAME

IC occurs in small groups of preferably no fewer than three and no more than seven students. The teacher engages the students in conversation about text, related personal experiences, knowledge of themes, and key concepts in order to accomplish lesson goals. The conversation builds on students' participation and succeeds on the basis of their production of language and understanding that meet the teaching goal of the particular IC lesson. The teacher's IC goal may be modified as a conversation develops, depending on what students say. This unique feature of IC emphasizes its responsive format and its student-centered process. On the basis of students' responses, the teacher may decide to reset the goal of a lesson at a lower or higher level that students can easily achieve, or the teacher may strive for a more complex level of understanding that students are ready to grasp.

IC is a JPA of teacher and students. IC products are often the charted progress of the IC. Teachers may diagram the course of an IC using a structured overview or other semantic diagram, such as a web, sequence, logic tracker, or list. In the upper grades, teachers may have students plot the course of an IC as it develops. In content areas, problem solving or other applications of the concepts have been products. The following diagram lists the main features of K–8 IC, including its product—new knowledge. As might be expected, half of the features are those of conversation and the other half are those of instruction. The six separate features integrate into IC.

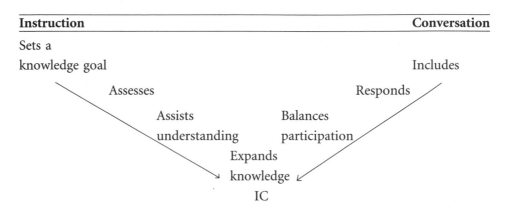

Instruction | **Conversation**

Sets a knowledge goal — Assesses — Assists understanding — Expands knowledge — Balances participation — Responds — Includes

IC

The diagram shows that the IC features for instruction and conversation work together at each level by combining the advantages of direct teaching with those of academic dialogue or conversation to benefit knowledge expansion and development. The first level, which establishes a clear goal and includes everyone, is the most divergent. The IC goal of instruction and the inclusiveness of conversation together produce interaction that neither a goal-oriented nor unstructured (free-for-all) conversation alone can produce. At the second level, the teacher assesses students' prior knowledge. The teacher's response encourages participation and identifies connections between what students know and the unknown. Through assistance, at the third level, the teacher ensures that students make the connection to new knowledge. The teacher also balances the students' participation. Importantly, the teacher's participation is less than the students' participation levels. In IC, students converse at rates equal to or greater than the teacher's rate. Together the features of instruction and conversation develop the conversation to accomplish the lesson goal.

For teachers to assess during IC, they must encourage students to produce language while respecting students' reticence. Teachers encourage students to speak by asking interesting or easy questions that tap feelings as well as knowledge. Even when a teacher nudges a reticent student into conversation, the student may not fully participate. It may take time for a student to learn conversation conventions and language for academic conversation, especially if the student is linguistically or culturally different from the class average. Because learning in IC relies on student participation, students' speaking preferences and conventions are respected. A silent student is not an ignored student but rather spurs the teacher to understand more about students' participation patterns and preferences. Teachers use responsive questioning and comments to increase assessment and to provide assistance. An IC goal is to balance participation across all students.

As a JPA (discussed in Chapter 1), IC is not strictly prescribed or pre-scripted but reflects a plan with a clear academic goal. IC is thoughtful and accountable conversation about content topics. Planning usually anticipates students' contributions of prior and personal knowledge. Teachers prepare questions that they will use to introduce material, to transition from experience to text, and to ensure understanding. The questions might also anticipate surprise contributions and teacher responses. The IC product is the documentation of teacher and students working together.

A teacher begins IC by simply asking students to talk about a selected activity; text; or experience from their point of view, that is, on the basis of their knowledge from home, community, or school. The teacher encourages every student to talk and share experiences that relate to a text and to the concepts the teacher plans to develop in the IC. Students' preferred language forms and styles are accepted, and teacher responds and models appropriate language forms. Students can exercise new vocabulary and concepts, and the teacher assesses their increasing grasp of these. Students share their knowledge and relate it to new information they must acquire. IC reveals gaps in understanding that teachers can assist students to close. This approach dilutes the "sage on the stage" form of instruction and emphasizes the inclusive, informal conversational feature of IC.

IC is planned. It occurs about text, a stimulus, or a learning task and elicits students' language expression. IC features dialogue that is energetic and accomplishes a teaching goal. The goal can be expressed in terms of a product. IC usually begins with discussion of prior knowledge that encourages students' participation for the purpose of scaffolding their understanding and co-constructing knowledge. In a small-group IC, teachers elicit students' talk about a text or narrative reading or other stimulus and expect to receive a large, sometimes loud, and usually joint response from students. Teachers urge students to question and challenge, rationalize and justify, find alternative and insightful solutions to problems, and continuously seek information to produce increasingly complex and higher-order thinking practices.

How Instructional Conversation Works

In a mathematics IC, five seventh grade Spanish-language minority students and their teacher discussed a circle measurement activity. The students had little experience in English conversation on an academic topic. The teacher referred to the product of the activity: a chart with strings that represent circle measurements.

She generated many opportunities for each student to explain the chart and use the concept labels. The teacher's instructional goal was to ensure competence discussing the concepts in English. In IC, the students reveal their language proficiency levels and academic and social skill needs for the teacher to assess.

By the end of the instructional frame, the students were using *circumference* and *diameter* at high rates. The teacher challenged them to understand diameter and circumference and the relationship between the two concepts. The teacher moved the students into the learning zone just beyond what they knew in order to challenge them into more complex thinking about the concepts and the relationship between them. The students understood the concepts as more than a number of facts. The excerpts in the following paragraphs demonstrate the features of the IC.

Instruction Side of IC   The instructional part of IC begins with the goal of assessing students' language proficiencies and levels of content knowledge, and with assisting them to increase their levels of understanding. As the teacher learns more about the students, more information is available to plan for their learning.

IC is the premier teaching occasion on which teachers foster all students' knowledge development through sustained academic dialogue. In IC, teaching assistance is explicit. Teachers guide students to make connections between ideas, facts, and procedures in problems, and to think critically about texts. Teachers monitor students' participation to ensure that each student is assisted more deeply than merely providing procedural applications or an answer. Teachers must assist students in acquiring the thinking and rethinking resources to understand current and subsequent learning challenges. IC is an occasion for teachers to focus on students' content understanding and academic language development. It is the path into students' zones of proximal development (Vygotsky, 1978), where thinking develops and learning occurs.

IC Sets a Clear Goal   In general, a teacher describes the goal of an activity in the briefing session of an instructional frame. The specific goal of an IC can be stated as the IC begins and during the lesson. In the following excerpt, which was also presented in Chapter Four, the teacher states the goal of the lesson:

Teacher: Yeah, we're measuring circles but there's a special word for that, that particular measurement.

In another example, the teacher states the goal at the beginning of the IC:

Teacher: I have ten cookies I want to share with you, but I'm not exactly sure how to do that. How in the world am I going to equally share these cookies with this group?

The teacher can mention the goal of the IC during the lesson whenever it is helpful to students. In the following example, the teacher explains how she is guiding the IC:

Teacher: Now I'm going to help you by relating it back to the Hawaiians.

IC Assesses   IC is an occasion for continuous student assessment. Teachers encourage student participation to obtain language that reflects students' thinking and knowledge, as in this excerpt that is also discussed in Chapter Six:

Daniel: This is the conconference, or whatever.

Teacher: So this one's the circumference, and this one is the diameter?

Daniel: I just remember that the diameter is the smallest, small, smaller than this one [referring to the circumference string].

Teacher: Well, which string did you measure around the edges with?

Daniel: This one [pointing to the circumference string].

Teacher: This one? The circumference?

Daniel: Yeah, and this one across it.

Teacher: Across it? So why do you think that this is smaller than this—that the diameter is smaller than the circumference? Why do you think that happens?

Daniel: Because if this one shrinks, like she said, it will shrink down, this one's still going to be smaller than that one.

Teacher: Why? What would happen, what would happen to this, the diameter?

Daniel: That one stays smaller. It will get smaller.

In this excerpt, the teacher focuses on assessing one student's understanding. The teacher recognizes an ELL student's need for more practice with vocabulary. She models the correct term for him. She checks his performance in the activity and then questions him on his understanding of the concepts and of their relationship to one another.

IC Assists Performance   In an earlier excerpt from the same IC, the teacher modeled the terms *diameter* and *circumference*. She referred to a concrete representation of the terms: a string used to measure the circle elements. In the next excerpt, one student twice uses his everyday language to refer to diameter as "half." In response to the teacher's modeling of the mathematics term, he succeeds in saying it. Even though two students argue over who has the right to answer a question, the teacher ignores the altercation, continuing to assist by modeling the mathematics terms.

Edgar: This is my long, my circle one, and this is my half one

Teacher: OK, this is your circumference line [running a finger up the string].

Edgar: Yeah.

Teacher: The long one? And this is your diameter line?

Edgar: [Nodding] Diameter.

Teacher: How do you know it, how do you know that?

Edgar: 'Cause—

Luis: The, the—

Edgar: Shut up, it's my question, dude.

Luis: This one's bigger and that one's smaller.

Edgar: No, 'cause it's my question, 'cause this is longer [going around the outside of the lid] than half [sliding finger down the middle of the lid and meaning diameter].

Teacher: OK, so you know that the circumference is long, bigger than the diameter.

In addition to modeling language during this exchange, the teacher directed a question at the Bloom taxonomy's level of comprehension (see Chapter Six). She asked, "How do you know it?" to assist the students in describing what they could recognize.

At the beginning of this chapter the students in this IC succeeded in using the content terms to explain how the mathematical concepts of diameter and circumference are related. The teacher's questioning included Bloom's application and analysis levels, which are more complex than the comprehension level. Through the teacher's continual assistance, the students were able to use the mathematics terms. The teacher persistently modeled language. She nudged the students with questions into more complex levels of thinking.

If an IC meanders far from its goal or stalls, the teacher reconsiders questions and prompts, and revises them immediately. The teacher may choose to reassess the level of material under discussion. Teachers often redirect IC by attending to features of the text or stimulus having to do with feelings and effect. The teacher may ask students directly how they feel about the development of the story characters.

Conversation Side of IC

The ideal conversation is inclusive, responsive, and balanced. IC promotes a speaking role for every student. The teacher monitors students' participation, especially to encourage reticent students.

Inclusive   Teachers often begin IC with a topic or stimulus to elicit students' talk about their experiences, feelings, and prior knowledge. To encourage their talk, teachers may use manipulatives, illustrations, semantic webs, overviews, charts, textbooks, trade books, writing, games, student models, and student suggestions and comments. In the following excerpt, the teacher accepts every student's contribution, even irrelevant comments such as Concha's:

Luis: The black hole.
Teacher: Do you know what the black hole is? Can you explain that to everybody in the group?
Luis: It is a round thing, and it has a lot of stars.
Teacher: It is a round thing. [Turns and writes on board] So you're saying that the black hole is something—
Concha: I don't really care.
Teacher: That is round [Luis and Concha laugh] and it has, what else did you say?
Luis: Stars.

In an ideal IC, students do not raise their hands or take round-robin turns. During the early phase of an IC, teacher and students converse about a broad range of topics, but particularly individual experience and background knowledge. In the brief IC excerpt that follows, the teacher uses a photograph from a familiar television series, *Star Trek,* as a stimulus for students to talk about space, an interesting topic previously discussed with the whole class. The teacher selected an opening topic based on general math so she could get to know the students. Her goal was to develop rapport and find out what the students already knew about space. Although five students are participating, one student's responses demonstrate the advantages of IC for sustained dialogue between teacher and student that produces a complete and specific expression of the student's thinking.

Edgar: They have like holes in them. Like— [Moves his hands in a circular motion]
Teacher: They have like holes in the planet. Holes in the planet, does anybody know what else we can call that?
Luis: Pozos. [Holes]
Edgar: Shooting stars.
Teacher: Shooting stars? Is that another name for the holes in the planet? Does anyone know what those—
Edgar: Shooting stars are like stars, but they go shooo [makes sweeping hand gesture] really fast and when you see them you can make a wish.

Responsive   IC assumes that students may have something to say beyond repeating the correct answers from the book. Students often provide correct answers, but IC requires teachers to grasp the intent of students' answers, whether they are correct, incomplete, or irrelevant. Teachers listen to personal and new information from students. They adjust their responses to assist students' communicative efforts to promote the conversation. Teachers continuously monitor the match between their planned IC assistance (such as activity level, questioning, scaffolds, and duration of IC) and the information presented by students' conversational participation, which may change the level or direction of the IC. This approach sounds highly challenging, but it actually involves routine adult conversational skills plus a teacher's insightfulness. For example, the following excerpt shows how a teacher is responsive and provides immediate assistance to a student:

Concha: I can't remember anything!
Teacher: You can't remember, that's OK. That's why we are reviewing. Now, do you know what it means when it's that three? What was [your regular classroom teacher] just talking about?
Daniel: Circles.
Concha: Circles and squares, circumference.
Edgar: Circumference.

Daniel:	Degrees and all that.
Concha:	Radius.

The teacher immediately sensed Concha's feelings of failure. The teacher reviewed the purpose of the conversation with Concha, then directed questions to her. The teacher's attention to Concha did not interrupt the flow of the conversation. The lack of disturbance was evidenced in the way the group continued. Daniel answered questions addressed to Concha, as did Edgar. Concha's subsequent appropriate contribution, "Radius," indicated that she had returned to the conversation.

Certainly the teacher was skillful in maintaining the flow of the conversation while dealing with a single student's difficulties. The students' sustained attention to the content suggests that the group was highly focused and on topic. Later Concha was able to provide assistance to another student. Here the teacher begins to provide assistance again but defers to Concha when she tries to help the other student.

Teacher:	Do you guys want to mark the middle?
Daniel:	Hey, my middle came out crooked.
Teacher:	Did you, when you—
Concha:	Did you fold it twice?
Daniel:	No, I didn't fold it twice.
Concha:	Alright, so that's it.

Daniel accepted Concha's assistance. The course of an IC is open-ended, no matter how well planned. Responsiveness is key to affirming students' input, to exploring its meaning and value for the IC, and to returning the conversation to its goal.

Balanced Participation   Teachers develop IC using students' contributions. In the following IC excerpt about Saturn's rings, the teacher guides but does not dominate. She allows a student to assist the conversation by introducing visual evidence.

Teacher:	Yeah, and we also talked about some other characteristics. We talked about colors, and sometimes some planets have rings around them, right?

Luis:	Just Saturn has it, only Saturn? [He looks up at a poster.]
Teacher:	I don't know. Does only Saturn have a ring around it?
Daniel:	Yeah.
Teacher:	[To Daniel] Yeah?
Luis:	They're all right there. Look. [Points up to poster. Everyone looks up.]
Edgar:	Yeah, I think, huh?
Concha:	Yeah, only Saturn.
Teacher:	[To Concha] Only Saturn? [Concha nods.]

Notice how Luis answers the teacher's question but then returns the question back to the group. Luis then points everyone to the classroom poster. The visual evidence informs everyone, including one student who participates nonverbally with an affirmative nod.

Including IC regularly in the instructional frame of classroom teaching provides discussion and dialogic opportunities that assist learning. IC is an advance, but its occasional or sporadic presence is insufficient. Its full effect is accomplished when it is the culmination of the system of five pedagogy standards.

How to Schedule IC

The system of five pedagogy standards is designed to support IC as the major teaching approach. The instructional frame includes a variety of activities and groupings but schedules IC as a regular, daily activity. IC that is scheduled daily can be devoted to a single lesson on a specific topic, or it can extend over numerous sessions. The seventh grade ELL circle measurement IC was conducted over five classroom sessions of thirty minutes apiece.

Students know what the plan for the day is because the teacher always posts or writes the instructional frame on the board. This happens even before the briefing, when all of the tasks and activities are explained. Every one knows how the frame works and where they are scheduled to be according to their individual schedules with their sequence of numbers indicating the activity setting they are to attend. Or students might have a choice schedule, which contains activity settings they want to attend, which they have worked out with the teacher. On a choice schedule, students still attend the teaching activity setting and follow-up (see Appendix 8C). They understand that the teacher's work with groups in the teaching center is very important and is interrupted only in an emergency.

At the end of a frame's instructional activity session (which usually lasts twenty minutes) the teacher signals for everyone to move on to the next activity. Travel around the classroom is completed within a minute. After another twenty-minute session, the teacher signals the return to a whole-class format to debrief. On the way to the debriefing, the students deposit their papers in their work folders in the places designated to receive the work products. Then the ten-minute briefing begins. Students describe their progress. The classroom agreement is reviewed to check how it matches their experience. The teacher is pleased to inform the students that their progress matches the agreement and they will soon have a pizza party reward. All the students leave the class with smiles and feelings of accomplishment.

INDICATOR 2: THE TEACHER GUIDES STUDENTS TO FULL PARTICIPATION IN IC

Classroom instruction is characterized by the cadences of question-and-answer exchanges. Teachers should not underestimate or disregard the enormous power of questions to divide and deride rather than engage and include. Historically, questions and answers are the customary form of communication from the powerful to the powerless, from the informed to the ignorant, and between adults and the young. Certainly every student learns early about right and wrong answers, and about the feelings associated with them. Teachers' questions may benchmark quality in their classroom instruction, but it is mostly students' questions and comments that signify productive learning outcomes.

IC Participation Rights

Small groups of three to seven students are the most productive settings for student conversation. Larger groups make it difficult to involve all students' equally in IC, increasing the privilege of conversation for some and reducing it for others. Students' participation preferences may be unfamiliar to teachers. When teachers recognize students' preferred forms of participation, they can respond more productively to students' learning needs. Teachers accept and use all forms of student participation in IC. Every student utterance contributes to the developing IC. The forms of participation include the following:

- Students bid to answer.

- Students co-narrate.

- Students respond chorally.

- Students utter incomplete words and sentences.

- Students speak simultaneously.

- Students overlap their speech with that of others.

- Students speak nonroutinely and abruptly.

- Students select the topic of their speech.

- Students select their speaking times.

In the excerpt at the beginning of this chapter, the students did not raise their hands to speak. They spoke as they preferred, or jointly. Notice that the students chorally responded once:

Teacher:	Right. OK, so, which one was the diameter? Can you guys tell me which?
All:	The smallest ones.
Teacher:	How do you know it's the smallest one?
Daniel:	Because the diameter is always going to be smaller than the, the circumference.

The teacher asked the students to explain their choral response to check on their understanding. Throughout IC, the teacher listens to distinguish among the responses, especially when students use overlapping or simultaneous speech. The teacher selects responses to restate, question, or paraphrase for the group. The teacher also selects students' contributions to restate or refine in order to move the conversation toward the academic goal or to stimulate more student conversation. The teacher builds the IC with students' statements, which is different from lectures, which are highly deductive approaches to teaching presentations.

During IC, teachers monitor their own participation to maintain a balanced ratio of student and teacher talk. Student talk should occur at higher levels than teacher talk. Students themselves sometimes negotiate a balance in participation that requires one student to moderate a high level of participation in order to make room for others to contribute. As the following excerpt, presented earlier in the chapter, demonstrates, students value the opportunity to respond:

Teacher:	How do you know it, how do you know that?
Edgar:	'Cause—
Luis:	The, the—
Edgar:	Shut up, it's my question, dude.
Luis:	This one's bigger and that one's smaller
Edgar:	No, 'cause it's my question, 'cause this is longer [going around the outside of the lid] than half [sliding finger down the middle of the lid and meaning diameter].

Students are highly aware of the contributions made by their peers; the offending student uttered barely two syllables. In many ICs, students vie to contribute to get the teacher's attention and approval. In other ICs, students avoid making their contributions just to satisfy the teacher. Teachers monitor for participation equity, especially when dominant students are grouped with reticent students. All students must eventually be brought into full participation in the IC, but teachers will use their judgment to decide how to draw them in. After teachers have formed groups for content instruction, it is recommended the students be regrouped at least quarterly to refresh the participation structures. Regrouping as students develop usually meets the need to change group membership in order to increase social contact among peers.

IC Approaches to Questioning

Recall the directed thinking activities (DTAs) discussed in previous chapters. In DTAs, the approach is to move from highly divergent, broad, and open-ended thinking into convergent, focused thinking based on the evidence. In IC, the same approaches can be used to develop thinking skills. As with DTAs, teachers use structured questions to make conversation open-ended or to narrow it toward more focused outcomes.

At the beginning of IC, teachers use open-ended questions to invite talk in relation to a topic that is divergent, broad, and experience based. Closed-ended questions focus responses in order to converge on particular information. Such questions often request back-up evidence to support an answer. As IC develops, more closed-ended questions are oriented to the goals set for the IC. Teachers use open and closed questions to ensure inclusive talk that progresses toward the IC goal. Following are some examples of such questions:

Closed and Open Questions About Plant Growth

Plants in classrooms provide botanical specimens that students at every level can study. Beginning with seed planting, students learn about plant growth. Through observation, students track plant development as a regular record-keeping task. Records produce data for students to question and analyze and use to form hypotheses about plant growth patterns. The data and hypotheses require students to research more information and continue observation and record keeping. The students and teacher discuss plants and growth in IC. The teacher's goal is to promote predictions about plants based on observational data.

Closed: What do you think a plant needs to start growing?

Open: Can you see a plant moving, growing? Explain what you see.

Closed: What do you think plants need to continue to grow? Is it the same as starting plants?

Open: Explain how you think a plant gets things it needs when not in a garden.

Closed: What is inside of a plant seed?

Open: How much space do you think your plant will need?

Prediction: What size will your plant be in June?

Closed and Open Questions About Water Evaporation

Many water topics and experiments with water provide stimuli for IC. When students care for an aquarium in the classroom, they observe water evaporation when checking the level of the water. If there is no aquarium, students and teacher can place a lamp over a saucer of water to observe evaporation. An IC about water evaporation includes open and closed questions; questions that require students to analyze, synthesize, and infer an explanation based on the evidence of evaporation; and questions that increase focus and conversation.

Closed: What have you observed about the water in the aquarium (or dish)?

Open: What do you think has happened to the water?

Open: What would you do to try to make the water last longer before disappearing?

Closed: Why would your approach work?

Open: What would you do to try to make it disappear more quickly?

Closed: Why does your approach make the water disappear rapidly?

Open: Where would you put a painting you had just done to make it dry quickly?

Closed: Why do you think this would work?

Open: Can you draw a picture to show where you think water goes when a puddle on the road dries up?

Closed: What does evaporation mean? Define evaporation.

DTA techniques are also suitable and enriching for IC. The DLTA, DRTA, and DSTA variations are discussed in the previous chapters (see especially Appendix 4A). In Chapter Six, the 5E approach was presented. It models the scientific inquiry process and is readily applied to solving many problems. It provides a structure for thinking that ascends to the highest level of Bloom's taxonomy of thinking:

- Engage
- Explore
- Explain
- Elaborate
- Evaluate

The conversational face of IC, which is lively, joint, and natural, can mask IC's instructional intent. Teachers' planning, guidance, and deft use of questions to modulate the IC may sometimes be obscure to the casual observer. Questioning techniques to develop students' thinking strengthen IC's rigor and its effects beyond the teaching event. What is evident is the pleasure that participants take in the IC experience, and its progress toward the IC's goals. Students also develop language facility, deepened content knowledge, and confidence to participate.

INDICATOR 3: THE TEACHER ACHIEVES ACADEMIC OUTCOMES IN IC

IC's foundation is the four previous pedagogy standards. In an instructional frame, IC usually spans several daily sessions of about twenty minutes each. Often an IC on a single story or unit of content study continues over a week to two weeks, or more for upper-grade projects and complex problem solving. The teacher decides how to schedule an IC into an instructional frame so that appropriate activities at independent centers support skill, language, and thinking development in the IC.

IC participation is comfortable and familiar for students. They contribute to IC without raising their hands or using other entry bids. They speak as they are motivated to share what they know. Like ordinary conversation, their IC speech may be incomplete and halting, and may overlap other students' contributions, or it may occur in utterances that the teacher may not understand. Teachers often guess a student's meaning and restate what they've said for the student to check their interpretation. The student responds and affirms or clarifies.

When a topic is compelling and students are eager to comment, they may express themselves by overlapping their speaking as they do in their conversations outside of school. This is the basis for developing students' capacity to participate in increasingly sophisticated forms of dialogue. The teacher must leverage what the students bring to the conversation into academic forms through the many approaches described in this chapter.

IC is academic dialogue that expands students' content knowledge. An IC can occur on any topic and be either short or long. Some ICs are single-session events on a specific topic, and when the session is over, the teacher considers the conversation concluded. Mostly, however, ICs extend over several days, particularly when the dialogue is about a text. As already noted, ICs may extend over several sessions spread over weeks. The IC and its schedule are continuously discussed in the briefing of the instructional frame.

IC Teaching

The following excerpt (which continues from the excerpt that opens this chapter) is an example of teaching assistance provided in students' learning zone. The seventh grade students involved in this mathematics IC do not raise their hands but rather speak as they are moved, but if the teacher directs a question to them, they respond. The teacher specifically questions the students to ensure that they grasp the meaning of the terms and the concept. The students present different levels of grasp, and the teacher continues to nudge them to speak and think about the material.

Teacher:	Right. OK, so, which one was the diameter? Can you guys tell me which?
All:	The smallest ones.
Teacher:	How do you know it's the smallest one?
Daniel:	Because the diameter is always going to be smaller than the, the circumference.
Luis:	Well, like this one is three times bigger.
Teacher:	Yes.
Luis:	This is three times smaller.
Teacher:	Yes! Is it exactly three?
Edgar:	No.
Teacher:	No, why? What is it?
Edgar:	This one side will be longer. It could be—
Daniel:	Almost—
Edgar:	It could be two.
Luis:	Like this one. It will always be like this one (pointing to the chart). And this one it will be three times—
Edgar:	This one will be three.
Teacher:	And that one will be three?
Luis:	All of them will be—
Teacher:	So, all of them will be, all of the what will be?
All:	All these diameters will be three times [smaller] than the circumferences.

In the final choral response, the students communicate a level of joint understanding. An interesting feature of this IC is that the teacher's goal is to stretch the students to understand the relationship of the concepts diameter and circumference to another mathematical concept, pi. Her goal was beyond what the students could achieve in this session. The students did demonstrate grasp of the two concepts and their relationship to some degree. The teacher succeeded in working on the mathematics concepts in the students' learning zones for language and thinking development. The string measuring activity that preceded the IC, combined with the dialogue that occurred in the IC, provided circumstances in which the students could practice their new understandings.

Teaching Assistance in IC

In the following IC on Native American identity, the teacher (T:) begins the conversation by asking what students (S:) already know about the topic. She asks an open-ended question to invite the students to share their knowledge of Native Americans. Using a variety of language development levers (see Chapter Four) such as questioning, modeling, summarizing, restating, and focusing, the teacher invites and supports the third grade students' participation. The students are Native Hawaiian.

T: Would an Indian today live and do the same things they did a hundred years ago?

S: No!

S: 'Cause they have all types of new things.

T: Terrific.

S: They have different types of clothes

S: No teepees, feathers.

S: Now they don't have to make things.

S: Yeah, they have money.

T: Why don't they have to make things now?

S: We have stores we can buy things from now.

T: Uhmm. And you said they don't need to use bows and arrows anymore because of—

S: Guns.

T: And you said they don't need to live in teepees anymore because of—

S: Houses.

T:	Would they still have any of these things though?
S:	Yeah.
S:	Corn, turkey.
S:	Bows and arrows, the play kind.
T:	So they might still eat some of the same foods.
S:	[Nods]
T:	You said they still might have bows and arrows.
S:	Yeah.
S:	They can still make crafts.
T:	Uhmm.
S:	Their hairstyle, make-up—

In the first section of this example, the teacher learns about students' prior knowledge of Native Americans. In the next section the teacher shifts her question toward her teaching goal to assist students to understand the value of traditions, even when they are no longer practical and do not serve their original purposes. When the IC stalls on a question about contemporary Indians, the teacher guides the students to consider their own Native Hawaiian culture, asking if they still do some of the same things their ancestors did.

T:	Why would they still have some of these things?
S:	We don't know.
T:	Now I'm going to help you by relating it back to the Hawaiians. You said you don't live the same way that your ancestors did, but you still do some of the same things that they did. For example, you said Hawaiian language. Why are you still doing some of the same things your ancestors did?
S:	So you can learn.
T:	Learn about what?
S:	Your ancestors' history.
T:	So why might the Indians still do some of those things?
S:	To learn more about it.
T:	Sure, by doing some of those things you learn about them. Like in third grade last year, why do you think your teachers made you go through all those things—lei making, Makahiki making— why do you think we did all that?

S: To learn.

T: Exactly. So would Indians today have all the exact same things as these?

S: No.

T: OK. If they had some of those things, they would be doing them to—

S: Learn about their ancestors.

T: Right, to retain their traditions or to learn about their culture.

In this section of the IC, the teacher loops the discussion back to the students' lives. Their response remains at the same level until one student provides a hook. A hook is an understanding or insight, even partial, that a student expresses and a teacher recognizes. A hook or insight from a student can be developed in the IC to scaffold everyone's understanding. The hook the student offers here is "learning about their ancestors." The teacher restates it as tradition and culture. She uses it to assist the students in understanding the meaning of traditional practices in the modern world. This more complex understanding of why contemporary Natives value their history and ancient practices relates directly to the teacher's opening question. In the next section, the teacher again demonstrates her responsiveness.

S: Last night in town I saw someone dressed like an Indian.

T: OK. How were they dressed just like an Indian?

S: They had the leather, the string, and the long pants, the long hair and the feather.

T: Why do you think he was wearing all that in this modern time?

S: That's his tradition.

T: [Nods] That's right, and maybe he just wanted to, what?

S: Dress up like that.

T: Also, do you think he would be proud to be an Indian?

S: Yeah.

T: And wearing the clothes might do what?

S: Help him.

S: Make him more an Indian.

S: Learn to be an Indian.

T: To show that—

> S: He's proud to be an Indian.
>
> T: Sure. In a way say, "I'm proud to be an Indian."

The teacher recognizes another hook when the student tells about recently seeing someone dressed like an Indian on the street. The teacher recognizes this contribution and asks for more information, which the student understands as a value the person had for his tradition. Another student says it would make him more of an Indian and proud. The teacher guided the students through this IC to develop their understanding of tradition at a more abstract level. In follow-up activities the teacher will guide students to apply their new understanding in a variety of ways. In subsequent ICs she will continue to work to refine their understanding at an abstract level that they can relate to personally out of their own cultural heritage.

IC on Text Comprehension

Comprehension strategies are conscious plans or sets of steps that good readers use to make sense of text. IC begins as an experience-based discussion to clarify students' experience base, language proficiency, and prior knowledge. During the following IC opening, third grade students offer many anecdotes that may seem irrelevant, but these contributions often carry valuable cultural, family, and other information. The teacher uses the information to encourage student participation and to build on their experience during IC development.

> T: Where have you seen reptiles before?
>
> S: Behind a shed.
>
> T: Ah, behind a shed, OK. So you think that lizards like to live in dark places?
>
> S: Yeah. And it was kind of cold and slimy.
>
> T: What other kinds of personal experiences have you had with a reptile?
>
> S: I've seen a lizard in a little forest and there was a lizard and me and my cousin, we were going to the forest and we saw one. And it was on a leaf.
>
> T: Oh, it was on a leaf?
>
> S: Yeah.

T:	Oh, wow. What did it look like?
S:	It was green.
S:	I've got two stories about reptiles.
T:	OK.
S:	About when I was four years old, I went to some mall somewhere and we were in the pets area and I was looking at the Dalmatians and it turns out my mom and dad were over there looking at the big fat snake. I saw the snake and this thing was huge and big like this.
T:	Oh.
S:	It was like a boa constrictor.
T:	It was?
S:	It was big and thick.
T:	Oh, wow.
S:	The other one was me and my friends Jan and Dave. We went over there on the side of the track.
T:	Uh huh, nearby then.
S:	Yeah.
T:	There's a snake patch nearby school?
S:	Yeah.

The teacher decides when to shift the IC from a divergent to a convergent focus. This decision is based on the difficulty level of new information and on the teacher's knowledge of the students' preparation and assistance requirement. If the students are not ready for the material, the teacher may shift into an activity that will increase the common understandings the students will need to have before they attempt the new material. The teacher will provide vocabulary development for the story or text. In the shift, the teacher moves from mostly open questions to including closed-ended questions in order to focus on the new information the students must learn. The following excerpt continues the IC, but the focus has shifted to the text phase, in which the teacher questions the students on the knowledge they are expected to obtain from the text.

| T: | What kind of a habitat was the snake living in? |
| S: | It was dry, kind of. |

T: Dry and what else?

S: Dry, hard rock, kind of.

T: Dry, OK.

T: From reading the text, what new things did you learn about reptiles?

S: They're slimy.

T: Now, are they slimy, are reptiles slimy? Were the reptiles you saw slimy?

S: No.

T: What did you learn about reptiles?

S: That they come from eggs.

T: OK, that they're hatched from eggs. What else did it say?

S: And they live in warm places.

S: It says everywhere.

S: They live in warm, wet, tropical rainforest or in a hot, dry desert.

This IC demonstrates an approach that begins with an experience-based discussion and converges on the text content. In the text focus of the last section, the teacher makes repeated efforts to guide the students to draw their information from the text. She questions incorrect student statements to direct them to the text to find the evidence. As they respond, the teacher writes down the answers that are based on the information from the text onto a chart to show reptile habitats and characteristics.

Contextualizing IC in Social Studies

Problems presented within a meaningful context often make material more available to students. For students at risk of school failure, linking the new information to contexts from their world fosters their interest, effort, and eventual grasp of the information. Context can prompt brainstorming and hypothesizing when students are learning new skills and acquiring new understandings. Within the goal of IC, students learn problem solving through joint performance. They share their skills, and learn those they still need from their peers and the teacher as they work toward the goals.

In an IC on Cesar Chavez and the formation of the farm workers union (from Tharp, Hilberg, Dalton, and Teemant, 2002), a teacher dialogues with fifth grade students, some of whose parents currently work in the fields. The teacher maps the key points of their conversation on chart paper. Notice how the teacher asks the students for information but provides them with more than they give her. The teacher begins the IC with a question.

T: What I want to know is why would someone support the union?

S: For their rights.

T: Tell me more. Did the people in general, for example, someone who was not working in the fields—how many of your parents work in the fields? Two out of this group—so for someone who doesn't work in the fields, why would it be important to help protect the people who work in the fields? Why do you think that would be important—let's say for me as a teacher or for you as students or for the cashier at the store or for a businessperson?

S: Maybe they want the person on the farm to live.

T: So they want the people to live and not die—right, from perhaps smelling the pesticides and inhaling pesticides. What would be another reason why you would be interested in protecting other people's rights? Do you want your rights to be protected?

S: Yes.

T: Absolutely. So if you stand up for other people's rights, what do you think is going to happen to you?

S: You'll be safe.

S: They'll have their rights.

S: They'll like how you're treating them.

T: What does that mean?

S: If you treat them with respect then they'll respect you like you treated them.

S: Why didn't they retire so they wouldn't get any pesticides and they could find a job where people would give them protection and give them better wages?

T: That's exactly what Cesar Chavez did. He encouraged them to form groups, form a union, so they could continue to work in safe environments and safe places.

S: Why was the strike successful?

T: Why do you think?

S: They were in large groups.

T:	So one reason was that the protest and strikes would be in large groups, right. What would be another reason why people would want the strike to be successful?
S:	To gain their rights.
T:	To gain their rights, exactly. Because the general public and other farm workers wanted their rights to be respected.
S:	They supported them.
T:	Right, exactly.

During the IC the teacher uses focusing questions, like "What do you mean?" when the students respond in irrelevant ways. When a student directs questions to her, she asks, "What do you think?" to encourage his thinking and speaking on the topic. These questions indicate that the teacher is monitoring the quality of information the students are contributing. This IC is of course just one event in the class's unit on farm workers.

Contextualizing IC in Mathematics

In a fourth grade classroom with at-risk ELL students, the teacher and seven students dialogue to solve a problem using fractions. The teacher draws the problem on the board to provide a visual record of their problem-solving progress (from Tharp, Hilberg, Dalton, and Teemant, 2002).

T:	I have ten cookies I want to share with you, but I'm not exactly sure how to do that. How in the world am I going to equally share these cookies with this group? [There are seven students in the group.]
S:	Teacher, I know. We figured out that there are seven people and there will be three left over if everyone gets one. Then if we break it up into two everyone will get two except for one. And if we break it up into threes then there will be twenty-one cookies and everyone will get three pieces.
T:	I lost you a little bit. You said everyone gets one and there's seven people. [The teacher draws a diagram on the board.] So we have seven cookies split up to each person, so how many do you have left?

S: Three.

T: This is where I lost you a little bit.

S: If we break them into threes then everyone can get three.

T: If we split all of these into thirds [breaks cookies into threes on the diagram], would that work? Would everyone get an equal number of thirds?

S: Yeah, everyone would get three thirds.

T: Prove it to me, why would everyone get three pieces?

S: There's seven people and if you break it into three pieces, then seven times three equals twenty-one pieces.

T: OK, so these seven are taken care of. We can give everyone three thirds or one whole because that's the same thing. But we still have these three cookies to deal with.

S: Break them each up into seven pieces.

T: That's going to be hard for me to do, but I'm going to try. [She divides the cookies on the board into seven pieces.] OK, we broke into seven, so each is a seventh. How many sevenths do you think will each person get from these last three cookies? I'll start you. This one goes to Kieth, Hassana, Scott, Gloria, Isaac, Leslie, and Aaron. [She colors in each seventh on the chart as she gives the cookies away to the students.]

S: Each one gets one more piece.

S: No, three pieces.

T: Everyone gets one seventh there. What does the whole group get right here? [She points at one of the cookies broken up into sevenths.]

S: One seventh.

T: Every one person gets one seventh there. How many do they get here? [She points to the last cookie broken up into sevenths.]

S: One seventh. Everyone gets three pieces.

T: Everyone gets three more what?

S: Pieces.

T: Pieces. How do you say that in fraction words? They get three—

S: More sevenths.

T: So they get three more sevenths. So they're going to get one whole up here and a seventh here, a seventh here and a seventh here.

S: So we each get one whole and three pieces.

T: And three pieces, but we need to label what these pieces are. These pieces are split into—

S: Sevenths.

T: Three sevenths.

In the cookie IC, the teacher is completely responsive to students' approaches for solving the sharing problem. The outcome was a specific and tangible product. The teacher chose to work with the approach the students provided at the start rather than impose an alternate method for solving the problem. Even though an alternate method could have been imposed for efficiency, the teacher was responsive to the IC principle that students' contributions drive the development of the lesson. The outcome was satisfactory to all. The IC process was successful enough to build an experience base for more ICs to target more challenging academic outcomes.

IC Products

ICs have academic outcomes or products. For many ICs, the teacher or a student uses a visual display to track the progress of an IC. Teacher or students chart the IC dialogue as a record of the event and a product to post. Often the display is used as a resource for follow-up activities and to display new vocabulary or concepts. For early grade students, the visual display is the basis for their teaching follow-up activity. The sight vocabulary they need to work with is posted in their IC visual display. The visual display is often the source for additional assignments to use the material. It also becomes a display in the classroom, where student exemplary work is posted for all to see.

For many students, the use of modalities in addition to listening is necessary to understand and learn. When teachers are sensitive to the special needs of students, all students are assisted. Teachers can map stories, provide structured overviews, advance organizers, word webs, lists, and other visual tracking devices as often as possible. The National Reading Panel recommended the following effective strategies for ensuring students' comprehension:

- Comprehension monitoring
- Story structure
- Summarization

- Question generation by readers themselves
- Question answering for immediate feedback
- Use of graphics, semantic organizers, and story maps
- Cooperative learning

These strategies facilitate students' full participation in learning. Some of them are ideal for making a record or product of the event. All students deserve multiple-modality supports for their learning. These supports for students' participation rights are represented in the guidance system of the five pedagogy standards. Use of these strategies in IC strengthens planning and teaching in instructional frames.

SUMMARY

Sustained academic dialogue with a teacher has been limited to very few public school students. The fifth pedagogy standard promotes teaching through dialogue. It is supported by all the standards, which are implemented for the purpose of preparing for the fifth standard and for IC. Participation in IC, with its academic focus in small groups and active student participation, also affirms the students' role in the learning process. Teachers who themselves were never taught in such a manner may see it as a daunting challenge, but it is actually a matter of including everyone, especially the students, in the learning endeavor. Learning is understood to be a much more active process than formerly believed.

In a five-standards classroom, IC is central and routine. Ideally, IC occurs daily for every student. Each excerpt in this chapter presented IC as a single event, but each was usually one of several sessions. IC usually spans several sessions, even weeks, in a large, ongoing unit or interdisciplinary project. The potential of the dialogue experience is evident in each excerpt. When the cumulative effect of these daily experiences is calculated, the value added to teaching and learning is exponential. IC includes all students when it is provided systematically and routinely, and it encourages and supports students to reach for new under-standings. IC fosters student development in dialogue and thinking and has never before been offered to all students in our nation's classrooms.

Together, the five pedagogy standards guide teachers to organize classrooms around academically productive activity and interaction that develop language and literacy; connect learning to students' lives; and challenge students to speak, write, and think more precisely. For most students in the nation's public school classrooms, consistent and routine support for learning and language needs has been insufficient. Installing the five pedagogy standards has the potential to systematize and strengthen effective teaching in the nation's classrooms. When teaching is supported by pedagogy to become more predictable, systematic, and equitable, it has the power to fulfill its potential for assisting every student's academic performance.

Teaching that is explicit, persistent, and personal uses pedagogy to achieve its goals. Teachers can increase their effectiveness in many dimensions when they have a system for teaching, such as the five standards. The outcomes of the implementation of the five pedagogy standards are that the teacher

- Produced a classroom community agreement for working together.
- Designed collaborative tasks that require joint product development.
- Organized classrooms to support teacher's and students' work together.
- Used an instructional frame routinely for all teaching and associated activities.
- Developed students' literacy and academic language expression in speaking and writing.
- Provided meaning and contexts that link students' learning to their lives.
- Challenged students in activity to think more complexly at every level.
- Provided prompt, corrective feedback that informed and guided students' content understanding.
- Used instructional conversation to engage students and teacher daily in sustained academic dialogue.

The fifth standard for effective teaching, teaching Through Instructional Conversation, completes the presentation of the five standards that make up the pedagogy system discussed in this book. The next chapter focuses on the integration and demonstration of the five-standards system in the classroom. The discussion highlights the five standards as they are enacted together.

How to Prepare to Win the Nobel Prize

Jerome Bruner, noted psychologist, offered the advice that one's chances of winning a Nobel Prize increase dramatically by associating with former Nobel winners. He went on to say, "This is obviously not just because the association gives you some 'pull' or makes you more visible. It has to do also with your having entered a community in whose extended intelligence you share. It is that subtle 'sharing' that constitutes distributed intelligence. By entering such a community, you have entered not only upon a set of conventions of praxis but upon a way of exercising intelligence" (Bruner, 1996, p. 154).

The Five Standards Integrated: How to Teach Effectively

In every classroom community there are potential Nobel Prize winners for teachers to assist. Skeptics must note that Einstein was unremarkable as a young student, as were many other eventual Nobel Prize winners and extraordinary achievers. When teachers have such expectations, all their students are winners. To support high achievement, teachers must ensure that students work within a community of learners, as Jerome Bruner explains in the quotation at the beginning of the chapter. The shared knowledge and joint practices of a community expand not only the students' capacity but also the teacher's.

The five pedagogy standards presented in the preceding chapters guide teachers to build classroom community in order to benefit students' language, thinking, and learning, and the teacher's capacity to assist the students. A unique feature of five-standards classrooms is that teachers build community and assist students primarily through dialogue, that is, instructional conversation (IC). IC with the teacher is a regular activity for all students, regardless of academic talent, background, language, or skill level. The classroom community supports students and teacher in working together to produce language and thinking, or in Bruner's words, to exercise their shared intelligence.

Obviously the functioning of schools and classrooms requires the operation and interaction of many systems. This book discusses how employing a system in the classroom strengthens teaching for learning through the use of dialogue with every student. The five pedagogy standards offer teachers a system for organizing instruction into manageable formats and students into manageable groups. This chapter demonstrates an application of the five standards in an ordinary classroom. It discusses how a teacher works with the standards indicators using some of the activities that were presented in earlier chapters. A set of worksheets for planning five standards implementation is also provided in Appendixes 8A, 8B, and 8C.

AN ACCOUNT OF A FIVE STANDARDS CLASSROOM

Five standards classrooms sound and look busy. Visualize thirty students and a teacher working together around a room, instead of a teacher standing at the front of the room or having brief exchanges with students seated at their desks (see Appendix 3C). The following example describes Mr. Yode's five-standards classroom:

A Five Standards Classroom

It is spring. Mr. Yode discusses a story with his group of six fifth grade students at a small table. He uses a chart to track and diagram the students' comments about the story's structure and theme. When he asks the students to return to reading for more information, Mr. Yode looks up to monitor the rest of the class. The other students are talking and working at activity centers around the room. Languages other than English can be heard, along with laughter. Five students in the stock market area use the newspaper to track, record, and compute the progress of their portfolios in their electronic databases. They use the computers when they are available, although they are also scheduled for their own time. In the library area, students read books, magazines, and newspapers alone or with peers. Mr. Yode glances over to the science work area, where six students are planting seeds and making botanical records. He tells them he can see their progress, and makes a note to check on their cleanup when his bell rings for the activity change. Mr. Yode glances over to the assessment setting, where two students are quietly taking tests. He scans other work areas where students write journals, work on vocabulary development, play games, and use the computers for research, writing, and database development assignments. Mr. Yode compliments the class on their community considerate noise levels. He reminds them to be ready to travel to their next activity setting in seven minutes. He returns his attention to his small group and resumes their story discussion. Although he continues monitoring the class, he focuses the remainder of the session on his small group's reading comprehension. He assigns a follow-up activity that will require them to apply their new understanding, which they will perform independently, without his assistance.

Mr. Yode orients the activity in his five standards classroom to support such a classroom's essential feature: teacher-student dialogue, or IC. The following paragraphs describe the supporting features of the five-standards classroom.

Instructional Frame

In Mr. Yode's classroom at this time of the academic year, the frame is a routine for planning and daily teaching. Even though all the students have personalized folders that contain their individual schedules, Mr. Yode draws or posts the frame on the board for easy reference. The frame begins with a briefing to present the activities and their related standards and sequence. Mr. Yode uses IC daily to teach in small groups at his teaching activity setting in the center of the room. Many of his students are far behind in language proficiency and in grasping academic concepts, and he can facilitate their progress most effectively in small-group discussion using language levers and other concept-developing approaches such as directed thinking activity (DTA), joint productive activity (JPA), student-generated activity (SGA), problem solving (PS), and other previously discussed approaches. He also uses his teaching activity setting to guide students' work and review products from independent activity settings, especially those that are cross-content and integrated skills projects.

Students refer to the frame to learn what their activity will be for the day. They rely on the briefing to understand the day's activities, and they use the debriefing to problem solve and share feedback. Students like to be involved in explaining the directions for the day's activities in the briefing, especially if they have assisted Mr. Yode in setting up the daily activity settings. Usually students can find the day's activity assignments in the morning on Mr. Yode's desk in a corner of the room. They know where to place the various tasks and assignments. They also check the supplies in the activity settings, and make copies and other preparations if appropriate and when needed. Whenever Mr. Yode has to be out of school, the students mostly run the classroom for the substitute teacher by continuing to work on their tasks or by placing SGAs in every activity setting. They help the substitute teacher use the timer for their work sessions within the frame.

Community Building

Mr. Yode began the school year working on his first challenge to convert a large group of students into a community of learners. His first classroom product was the written community agreement that described the values they would all use to guide their work together. During the community development stage, Mr. Yode observed the students working together in pairs and triads in order to discover friendship networks, language groups, skill levels, and funds of knowledge. To give the students an objective advantage, Mr. Yode ensured that the early community building activities were at each student's individual level. In other words, each student experienced many assignments that they could complete successfully on their own or with peers. In addition to increasing observing opportunity, this tactic gave the students experiences of repeated success in their work. Mr. Yode made many comments about their successes in order to build their confidence for tackling the demanding curriculum challenges they would later face.

Classroom Management

As successful as Mr. Yode and his students were with community building, the early-year honeymoon of students and teacher gave way to some management problems. The community-building context allowed Mr. Yode to problem solve with the students according to the values that the class had expressed in their agreement. For those with greater needs for intervention, he used the SCIIPP (simplify, clarify, identify, ignore, promote, and praise) management approach (see Chapter Three). Basically, SCIIPP supported Mr. Yode's focus on what was going right in the community. He frequently praised and promoted appropriate participation and performance until he was sure that *every* student had received positive feedback at lease once within the first two days of school. His praise and promotion rate was extraordinarily high, and it had the positive effect he intended. Students understood that his attention would remain only on those who were appropriately participating. Those who were not could expect to be ignored and excluded. They would also have to explain to their parents why they were reluctant to participate in compelling activities with their peers in a happy classroom. Following these steps, Mr. Yode handed out consequences quietly and watched for the first opportunity to begin promoting and praising appropriate participation, even if that meant remarking on something simple like the appropriate use of a chair or pencil. Mr. Yode expected everyone to perform at their level, and he continuously praised and promoted such performance.

Activity

Unlike a new teacher, Mr. Yode has a file of numerous activities and tasks ready to place in his activity settings. Teachers new to five-standards teaching need to be assisted by colleagues who share activities and identify quality, commercially prepared activities, until they have developed their own files. They also need to be encouraged to obtain student- and parent-generated activities (SGAs and PGAs). The use of independent activities at the start of the school year or a challenging unit is key to ensuring students repeatedly succeed in building their confidence in their ability to understand complex topics. Mr. Yode can readily retrieve and use previously successful independent activities and tasks for students to perform without teacher assistance. He can also pull out tasks to assign to individual students for skill practice. When he stocks his activity settings with student work, he provides tasks and activities for student groups. Sometimes groups of students are given JPAs to perform, which they learn about in the briefing.

Teacher Multitasking

Mr. Yode's teaching assistance occurs in many forms, at different levels, and in multiple locations in the classroom. At thirty-five students, his class is large, but he finds that the numbers increase students' opportunities to learn language, thinking skills, and content from one another. His management, like his instruction, is embedded within the activities and routines of the classroom community he has developed. For example, students know to always look to see if they have an individual task to complete at an activity setting before they start on their group assignment. In this way Mr. Yode can monitor students' skill progress on the same day as he assigns practice tasks or prepares students for assessments. The students know that what they do not complete at activity settings becomes homework due the next morning, or they can do it during recess. Any student who is assigned an individual task at an activity setting may find it is possible to finish the task in time to complete the group task as well.

Assessment

Mr. Yode devotes one activity setting to student assessment. There he assigns quizzes and tests to obtain information about students' learning progress that he can use for instructional decision making and planning. The assessment setting is also where students practice for standardized tests. This activity setting is one that requires individual effort in silence. It also requires ethical conduct since students attend the activity setting without direct teacher supervision. Mr. Yode defined and discussed ethics with his students, who added ethics guidelines to their class agreement.

Students' portfolios of work products are stored at this activity setting for easy retrieval and review. Students maintain their portfolios as part of the requirements of the assessment activity center. Mr. Yode guides the process with notes to students about completing their records and organizing and presenting their work. When parents or administrators visit, Mr. Yode uses the portfolios to highlight the accomplishments of his students.

DEVELOPING A FIVE-STANDARDS CLASSROOM

Obviously Mr. Yode's five-standards classroom now looks very different than it did when he first started applying the five standards. A teacher and more than thirty students came together at the beginning of the school year to agree on how to work and converse together for academic purposes. How Mr. Yode went about developing his five standards classroom is portrayed in the following excerpts about his work. For more information on and a full discussion of any of the standards, turn to the previous chapters devoted to each standard and its indicators.

Getting Started in Fifth Grade

Mr. Yode begins by developing his classroom as a community of learners who view the classroom agreement as their joint product. The students interact, problem solve, and perform compelling hands-on activities in large groups pairs, and triads to produce their classroom agreement. Mr. Yode has developed many JPAs and other types of activities over his years of experience. Some of these activities are his or colleagues' creations, some are commercial, and some are student generated. His criteria for activities, whether they are designed for large-group, small-group, pair, or individual activities, have been that they must be compelling and language developing, and they must relate to something the students already know. If the only topic all the students have in common is Mickey Mouse, that's what they will work with to get started. If there is no common context, he and his students create one through a joint activity, such as building an aquarium, mapping the students' backgrounds, putting on a play, or some other project that can involve all of the students.

THE TEACHER IMPLEMENTS STANDARD I: TEACHER AND STUDENTS PRODUCING TOGETHER

The first pedagogy standard builds the foundation for a five-standards classroom through community building and the use of the instructional frame. The frame is a tool for planning a routine that makes teaching and learning predictable for students. JPA increases student interaction and joint work, which require supportive classroom organization. Table 8.1 contains an instructional frame for teaching two activities with two large groups to implement this phase of the five-standards classroom.

Table 8.1
Timed Instructional Frame: 60 Minutes; Standard I: Teacher and Students Producing Together

Session 1	Session 2	Session 3	Session 4
Briefing	Teach Group 1	Group 1, Garden Mural	
	Group 2, Garden Mural	Teach Group 2	Debriefing
8 minutes	20 minutes	20 minutes	9 minutes

Travel time: 3 minutes
Students: 30 fifth graders in two groups
Routing: Two mixed groups rotate
Activity settings: (1) Teaching; (2) Follow-up

Mr. Yode begins the day with a briefing about what the class will do together from the instructional frame for the day. The frame is posted so that all of the students can see that after a large-group session half of the class will work with Mr. Yode while the other half works on another task. They will then switch the groups so that Mr. Yode works with the other half, and the students he has already worked with will perform the independent activity. When everyone understands that sometimes they will have assignments to do without the teacher and on their own, they start the timed cycle of the frame. First Mr. Yode has the students who are sitting in their homeroom seats count off on one and two to form two groups. To rotate the students, Mr. Yode points out where the ones will sit and where the twos will sit. He asks the students how they will progress to their new seats, what they will do with their writing tools, and how long it will take. After they have decided as a community how to move around the room, Mr. Yode gives them thirty seconds to do it. To help them get their ideas, with half of the class Mr. Yode then discusses plant growth, introduces botanical terms, and discusses a mural they will paint. The other students in the class work on a JPA, which is a mural of a garden. Every student selects and draws a plant to place accurately in the garden mural. From a fishbowl they drew a paper slip that tells them which water, cactus, or other plant type they will study. The students work successfully through five sessions of their instructional frame. They have been briefed, have met for instruction in three sessions—one as a whole group and two as two smaller groups, and have been debriefed to provide feedback to the teacher about the experience. Mr. Yode praises them for working well independently on their tasks without his direct oversight.

The first pedagogy standard promotes the use of routines such as the instructional frame, traveling in the classroom, early grouping, and students working together independently. Following are the basic guidelines and recommendations for the first standard:

- Build community.
- Use an instructional frame.
- Provide joint productive activity.
- Build students' independence.
- Group students for joint work.
- Rotate groups to different tasks.
- Use positive classroom management like SCIIP.

THE TEACHER IMPLEMENTS PEDAGOGY STANDARD II: DEVELOPING LANGUAGE AND LITERACY

Mr. Yode and the class review their instructional frame. It shows that the class will be divided into three groups, so two groups at a time will work without Mr. Yode's direct supervision. In those activities, students will assist one another in the activities using both their home language and English. Mr. Yode encourages the students to model language for one another and to translate where needed. In the briefing, the class discusses how they are grouped into thirds. They will perform the botany (planning), teaching, and garden-mural activities by gathering in the areas of the classroom where the respective activities and supplies are kept. Mr. Yode has the students count off by threes. During the briefing, Mr. Yode uses language levers (see Chapter Four) to ensure that everyone understands. Table 8.2 contains the instructional frame for the three groups.

One group of students plants seeds in small containers of soil at a large table spread with newspapers. After they plant the seeds, they draw and label mature versions of the plants (their visions for their seeds) using scientific plant names and terms. Chart paper containing lists of scientific names is posted near the activity setting. The students

Table 8.2
Timed Instructional Frame: 85 Minutes; Developing Language and Literacy

Session 1	Session 2	Session 3	Session 4	Session 5
Briefing	Teach Group 1	Group 1 Mural	Group 1 Botany	
	Group 2 Botany	Teach Group 2	Group 2 Mural	
	Group 3 Mural	Group 3 Botany	Teach Group 3	Debriefing
10 minutes	20 minutes	20 minutes	20 minutes	11 minutes

Travel time: 4 minutes
Students: Thirty fifth graders in three groups
Routing: Three mixed groups rotate
Activity settings: (1) Teaching; (2) Follow-up; (3) Science project

will include their labeled drawings in a botany dictionary. Everyone prepares entries for the dictionary, including pronunciation guides, plant history, a sentence for context, and a labeled drawing. Digital photos of the plants will be added to the dictionary, to compare them to the drawn illustrations. A huge three-ring binder is set out in the activity setting along with the materials and other resources students need.

The second group of students performs to the garden mural activity. The third group meets with Mr. Yode to discuss plant growth using the information from their science textbook. Mr. Yode asks the students how they will find out more through Web site research. He tracks the discussion by writing key words on chart paper taped to the wall. He questions the students and restates their responses, inserting and modeling content vocabulary and grammar where needed. Then the Spanish speakers ask Mr. Yode to add Spanish to the chart. Mr. Yode asks the students to guide him in writing the terms. He invites two students to add English translations to the chart so that everyone can read them. Mr. Yode jokes that soon they will all learn Spanish, English, and Latin from their botany work.

After the class discussion, Mr. Yode extends the activity by adding Spanish-English dictionaries and other Spanish texts to the activity materials. In the next day's briefing, to introduce students to new tasks he asks them to include entries in the dictionary in Spanish as well as English. Everyone is excited to work on botany in three languages. In the debriefing, the students review their quality work in independent activities. The debriefing discussion includes review of how the students are doing with their independent work. They are reminded to hand in their work at the designated time and place.

The basic guidelines and recommendations for the second standard are as follows:

- Use language levers continuously.

- Provide writing activities.

- Promote students' language expression in every activity.

- Use evidence-based reading instruction.

- Make the instruction frame a daily routine.

- Design leveled and timed tasks.

- Increase independent activities.

- Form student groups.

- Increase multitasking.

- Debrief on independent work.

IMPLEMENTING PEDAGOGY STANDARD III: CONNECTING LEARNING TO STUDENTS' LIVES

Mr. Yode lives in and is familiar with the local community. He uses the contexts that students know to introduce them to new learning material. The produce from the fields in which his students' families work are entry points for mathematics and science activities. Students work on problems relating to agricultural work, such as measures and weights of fruit and vegetables, making estimates about produce yields, and tracking weather. These contexts guide the content of the classroom library, academic activities, and special-interest activity settings, such as the botany work in which the students are currently engaged.

Mr. Yode has formed four groups of seven to eight students to route through his multitasking frame. He changes the group membership often to observe how students relate to and assist one another on tasks, and how they use home and school language. Today the groups' members are listed on different-colored papers posted on the board.

The instructional frame for this standard and phase shows that Mr. Yode has increased multitasking and continued mixed grouping. The groups move intact from one activity setting to the next. The activities in the frame include botany, the garden mural, library, and journaling. Mr. Yode introduces two continuing activity centers to the students. He is confident that the students can succeed in the two independent activities, library and journaling. Table 8.3 contains the instructional frame for these classroom continuing activity settings. Students will visit the library and journal several times every week for the rest of the school year.

The students and the teacher are comfortable with the instructional frame before they start the timed cycle. At this point Mr. Yode carefully checks on work products and ensures that all are traveling to the assigned activity settings with their groups. Every student must feel competent in the instructional frame.

Table 8.3 Instructional Frame: 110 Minutes					
Session 1	Session 2	Session 3	Session 4	Session 5	Session 6
Briefing	Teach Group 1	Group 1 Follow-up	Group 1 Journaling	Group 1 Library	
	Group 2 Library	Teach Group 2	Group 2 Follow-up	Group 2 Journaling	
	Group 3 Journaling	Group 3 Library	Teach Group 3	Group 3 Follow-up	
	Group 4 Preteach	Group 4 Journaling	Group 4 Library	Teach Group 4	Debriefing
10 minutes	20 minutes	20 minutes	20 minutes	20 minutes	15 minutes

Travel time: 5 minutes

Students: 30
Routing: Four mixed groups
Activity settings: (1) Teaching, (2) Follow-up, (3) Journaling, (4) Library

In each twenty-minute session there are four simultaneous activities, three of which are independent. The students sometimes finish their task before the end of the session. Mr. Yode reminds himself to bring up finishing activities at the next briefing, and reflects on improving timing.

Connecting Content to Students' Language

Mr. Yode briefs the students on the day's instructional frame, especially the new activity setting. The new setting is the classroom library, which students will visit often. In the briefing, the students discuss what they will do at the library. They say that there they will read alone, together, and for one another. They will create a log of their visits and their reading activity whenever they visit. They want Mr. Yode to help them make their own books for the library to share with peers and parents. The journaling activity setting is also introduced. Mr. Yode says that the journals are interactive so that he can write back to the students after they have made their entries. He asks them to use at least five botanical terms to describe how to plant a seed and take care of it. He reminds them to translate English and Latin terms into Spanish as they agreed to do. He requires them to count the number of terms they use from the three languages and report it in their journal.

The basic guidelines and recommendations for the third standard are as follows:

- Relate activity to students' lives.
- Maintain frame schedule.
- Introduce continuing activity settings: follow-up, library, and journaling.
- Change membership of student groups.
- Continue multitasking and rotating groups.
- Praise and promote success.
- Debrief on quality of independent work in products.

IMPLEMENTING PEDAGOGY STANDARD IV: TEACHING COMPLEX THINKING

Mr. Yode is encouraged that the class has progressed to this level of five-standards implementation in five weeks. The students are succeeding in the activities, following the schedule of the instructional frame, and attending the newly installed continuing activity centers—library, journaling, and computers. The students are performing the botany project activities independently; using the scientific terms; and producing beautiful products, such as the garden mural and lexicon notebook. Management is not a problem, although Mr. Yode continues to monitor and praise students at high levels. He chuckles when he realizes that such a positive management model has become his habit. He likes pretending that the students do not really need management.

Over the five weeks since school started, Mr. Yode has prepared his students for the challenge of the curriculum they will soon study. The students are building computer, vocabulary, mathematics, and other skills. Their new project work in the weather station is challenging them to integrate their skills and knowledge. They are learning scientific explanations of rain, wind, and other weather phenomena. Mr. Yode has developed the weather station as an interdisciplinary activity that includes tasks in all core content. Students read and write about the topic in a variety of genres using math, science, geography, computer, and meteorology skills to solve problems in tracking and predicting weather patterns in the local area. Some students are interested in spending more time at the station. Mr. Yode will arrange choice contracts with students after he has implemented the fifth pedagogy standard, on teaching through instructional conversation, so they can attend activities they prefer more often than the regular routing allows.

The student groups are productive on tasks, and the students willingly assist one another. Mr. Yode changes group membership often, knowing that once he has implemented the IC standard he will want to have stable groups for at least an eight-week quarter. After the quarter he will change group memberships on the basis of students' progress in relation to the content area standards.

The five groups that Mr. Yode has formed for implementing the fourth pedagogy standard, on challenging students' thinking, are organized by ability, although he is still thinking about shifting some of the students to balance social and academic skills within the groups. He has designed a multitasking frame for the five groups' activities (see Table 8.4). So far the students have moved from activity to activity in a round-robin fashion of intact groups. At this stage of standards implementation, Mr. Yode will start routing his students to his teaching activity setting and its follow-up in matched-ability groups. He will set his teaching goals to meet the student content standards, which he will address using the activities at the weather station and other student projects.

For grouping, he will cluster students to attend the independent activity centers in mixed groups to increase the variety of skills available for tasks, especially JPA. The worksheet for matched and mixed groups is in Appendix 8B2.

Mixing and Matching Students in Groups

Mr. Yode is conversing with six students from the red group at a small table. The students are studying categories of plants and trying to match their specimens. He has students summarize the chart displaying their discussion of the readings before assigning the group's follow-up activity. Mr. Yode assigns the students to identify the characteristics that scientists use to classify plants. They are planning a trip to the arboretum to increase their knowledge of plant classification. There they will meet with a guide who will review their classifications and provide corrective feedback. They

Table 8.4
Multitasking Instructional Frame: 140 Minutes

Session 1	Session 2	Session 3	Session 4	Session 5	Session 6	
Briefing	Blue Group to library	Blue Group to journaling	Blue Group to weather station	Blue Group to computers	Teach Blue Group	
	Orange Group to computers	Teach Orange Group	Orange Group to follow-up	Orange Group to journaling	Orange Group to weather station	
	Yellow Group to weather station	Yellow Group to computers	Teach Yellow Group	Yellow Group to follow-up	Yellow Group to journaling	
	Green Group to journaling	Green Group to weather station	Green Group to computers	Teach Green Group	Green Group to follow-up	
	Teach Red Group	Red Group to follow-up	Red Group to journaling	Red Group to weather station	Red Group to computers	Debriefing
20 minutes	20 minutes	20 minutes	20 minutes	20 minutes	20 minutes	14 minutes

Travel time: 6 minutes

Students: 30 fifth graders in five groups

Routing: Five matched groups go to (1) Teaching, (2) Follow-up. Mixed groups go to other activity settings.

Activity settings: (1) Teaching, (2) Follow-up, (3) Library, (4) Journaling, (5) Weather Station, (6) Computers will then discuss the data they are collecting at the weather station, which Mr. Yode has reviewed to give them corrective feedback on their work. Their follow-up activity at the weather station is to make corrections before continuing to collect data.

Mr. Yode has formed matched-ability groups to come to his teaching activity setting. He teaches skills for part of the time and develops conceptual understandings for the remainder. While he teaches each group, the other students assist one another in independent tasks at continuing activity settings around the classroom. Some students are reading and journaling alone; doing follow-up tasks assigned during the teaching session; participating in projects, including the preparation of a class botany dictionary; using listening skills (with headphones); doing content area writing and arts and crafts; and utilizing several computers. Mr. Yode reminds the students to use the class botany dictionary as a resource for designing tasks and games for their peers to complete, even simple word and other familiar games like Concentration and Fish are helpful for learning new words in three languages.

All of the continuing activity settings in the classroom need to be introduced before moving into the fifth standard. Additional activity settings can include assessment, observation stations, SGAs, vocabulary, arts and crafts, writing, mathematics, research, computers, and so on. To accommodate planning students' schedules and routing them from one activity setting to the next, every activity setting in the classroom must be numbered or named, and the number of students it accommodates must be clearly marked or noted.

The following list of activity settings suggests the variety of activities that can be included in a five-standards classroom. The activity settings marked with an asterisk are particularly recommended. Only the teaching and follow-up activities are required for teaching with dialogue using IC. Depending on their teaching goals and their students' needs, teachers may choose to make up their own content for activity settings.

1. Teaching*

2. Follow-up to teaching*

3. Journaling*

4. Library*

5. Vocabulary*

6. Computers*

7. Student-generated activity*

8. Assessment*

9. Games*

10. Integrated content focus (such as the weather station and settings for studying geodesy, the stock market, bridge building, and so on)*

11. Listening

12. Observation (inside or outside the classroom)

13. Research

14. Content area focus (such as mathematics, grammar skill practice, geography, and so on)

15. Arts and crafts

There is an exception to the sharing and talking that characterize all of the activity settings. In the setting reserved for assessment, students take quizzes and tests for practice and for real. They also prepare for standardized tests and need the same conditions that the tests require. The assessment setting needs to be placed in the quietest part of the classroom.

Mixed and Matched Student Groupings

By this time in the development of a five-standards classroom, most teachers use round-robin groups that stay together for all activities. One of the goals of five-standards classrooms is to ensure that all students work with every other student for some period. The rich resources of classroom diversity need to benefit all students. To ensure that students mix, teachers form teaching groups of those who will come to the teaching activity setting together and perform follow-up work together. The first groups for which membership is decided are the teaching groups. Teachers usually keep students grouped for a quarter or until data are available for deciding on different placements. Of course teachers may change students' group memberships at any time, but groups usually stay intact over a period of learning activity, which is usually about eight weeks, at least.

The worksheet on arranging activity settings provided in Appendix 8A, B1, and B2 helps teachers to plan.

Mixed and Matched Student Routing

When the students move away from the teacher to independent settings, they go in mixed groups. Appendix 8B2 is a worksheet for assigning students to independent settings. The worksheet informs the teacher who is where in the classroom at any time. The tracking worksheet also allows the teacher to assign students to groups by combining many factors to facilitate the group learning process, such as social skills (for getting along with peers), organizational skills, interests, logical thinking abilities, practical helpfulness, language proficiencies and needs, and many other characteristics discussed earlier in the book.

The basic guidelines and recommendations for the fourth standard are as follows:

- Set high standards in all activities.
- Introduce continuing (or permanent) activity settings: assessment, computers, observation, stock market, writing, SGA, games, arts and crafts, and so on.
- Increase practice opportunities.
- Provide corrective feedback.
- Use the frame routinely.
- Arrange students in mixed and matched groups.
- Use the instructional frame to route the groups to activity settings.
- Praise and promote success.

IMPLEMENTING PEDAGOGY STANDARD V: TEACHING THROUGH CONVERSATION

The frame for the fifth standard looks the same as the fourth standard's frame except that all of the activities are anchored in and assisted by IC between teacher and students (see Table 8.5). IC is the center of the classroom's teaching and learning activity. The instructional frame structures the instructional sequence that prepares students for IC. Students are grouped homogeneously for IC and heterogeneously to work together in the settings outside of the IC.

The frame for advanced IC may look different when teachers invite students to choose the activity settings they will attend. Mr. Yode introduces many activity

Table 8.5

Instructional Frame: 130 Minutes Instructional Conversation IC

IC: Teaching through dialogue.

Activity Centers: (1) IC; (2) IC follow-up; (3) Library; (4) Computers; (5) Weather Station; (6) Journals

Session 1	Session 2	Session 3	Session 4	Session 5	Session 6	
Briefing	Blue Group to follow-up or preparation for IC	Blue Group to journaling	Blue Group to weather station	Blue Group to computers	IC Blue Group	Debriefing
	Orange Group to computers	IC Orange Group	Orange Group follow-up	Orange Group to journaling	Orange Group to weather station	
	Yellow Group to weather station	Yellow Group to computers	IC Yellow Group	Yellow Group to follow-up	Yellow Group to journaling	
	Green Group to journaling	Green Group to weather	Green Group to computers	IC Green Group	Green Group to follow-up	
	IC Red Group	Red Group to follow-up	Red Group to journaling	Red Group to weather station	Red Group to computers	
Session Time 14 minutes	20 minutes	20 minutes	20 minutes	20 minutes	20 minutes	10 minutes

Travel Time = 6 minutes

settings to accommodate the focuses he uses throughout his teaching. When students choose, they may extend their stay at the settings in which they need more time to work. This means that they stay for more than one session—usually two that amount to forty minutes. All students must attend the teaching and follow-up activity settings, where they report to the teacher and to their assigned group on their progress in their independent activities. Students must be sensitive to the capacity of the activity settings, but in a class of thirty students with twelve settings, there will usually be space available to work as the students choose. A 'choice' instructional frame with the students' chosen destinations written in may be the regular frame for a week (see Table 8.6). Another example is provided in Appendix 8C.

Each student has a folder that holds his or her schedule. The student carries the folder and uses it to hold work in progress and completed work. At the end of the class or day the student deposits the folder in a designated place before leaving the classroom. The teacher will then check daily on the students' activity and work products. Homework assignments arise from the teaching activity center and are also discussed during briefing and debriefing.

The basic guidelines and recommendations for the fifth standard are cumulative of all the others and emphasize the following:

- Use IC daily to teach academic topics.
- Set high standards in all activities.
- Use the instructional frame to support IC.
- Coordinate all independent activity through IC.
- Stabilize teaching groups.
- Assess students' progress.
- Provide corrective feedback within IC.
- Offer students choice contracts to strengthen project activities.
- Reward students' success in the classroom community.
- Praise and promote students' academic success often.

RECOMMENDATIONS FOR IMPLEMENTING THE FIVE STANDARDS

The impact of the five standards on students' learning outcomes depends on the implementation of all of the standards. The standards are presented in this book in

Table 8.6.
Five Standards PHASE-IN

Standard	Phase 1 Week. Apply Standard I.	Phase 2 1 to 2 Weeks. Apply Standards I & II.	Phase 3 1 to 2 Weeks. Apply Standards I, II and III.	Phase 4 2 Weeks. Apply Standards I, II, III and IV.	Phase 5 On-Going. Five Standards IC Classroom
Teachers and Students:					
I Working Together in Joint Productive Activity – JPA	Build community: Produce class agreement.	Use language levers and strategies	Relate learning activity to students' lives and familiar themes.	Set high standards in all activities.	Use IC daily.
II Developing Language and Literacy	Use instructional frame.	Provide writing activities.	Use frame daily.	Increase activity challenge level.	Teach content-based standards in IC.
III Making Meaning – Contextualizing	Design tasks for student success.	Promote language expression in every activity.	Install continuing activity settings.	Base teaching on curriculum, content standards.	Assign independent activities to support IC.
IV Challenging Thinking To Complex Levels	Provide joint productive activity – JPA.	Use evidence based reading strategies.	Change group membership.	Provide corrective feedback.	Coordinate all student assignments and products in IC.
V Using Instructional Conversation (IC)	Develop students' independent work skills.	Use the instructional frame routinely.	Rotate small groups to continuing activity settings.	Make matched and mixed student groups.	Stabilize matched groups.
	Group students for joint activity.	Design leveled and timed tasks for independent student work.	Increase multitasking. Praise and promote	Route matched groups to teaching activity setting.	Adjust mixed group membership.
	Rotate groups to different tasks.	Arrange student groups. Introduce continuing activity centers	Debrief on quality independent work products. Praise success.	Route mixed groups to other settings.	Continue routing students to activity settings in mixed and matched groups.
	Use positive management like SCIIP.	Multitask by rotating groups to activity settings.		Praise and promote routing success.	Assess students' learning.
		Debrief on independent work.			Praise and promote learning community's academic success.

Note: Each standard establishes the foundation for subsequent pedagogy standards.

a sequence that teachers are recommended to follow for implementation. Each standard inserts a layer of the system that is vital to the functioning of the whole. When the standards are fully installed and working together, teachers are assisting students' learning in an extraordinarily powerful way.

Teachers are encouraged to take the time they need—up to seven weeks at the beginning of the school year—to develop a five standards classroom, especially if the teacher and students are new to using the system. Teachers decide how much time to devote to the implementation of each standard in response to the students' needs and their own. For example, some teachers implement the first standard in order to carefully build the foundation for the other standards. Then they present each of the other standards individually until everyone is comfortable. These teachers might be described as using a stage for each standard. However, once the teacher implements the fifth standard on a regular basis, the system is implemented.

Other, more experienced teachers combine, for example, the second and third standards. The second standard's language levers use the contexts in the third standard to make meaning. This process makes for a three-stage implementation schedule. A teacher typically practices IC with selected students during the implementation of the fourth standard. The teacher practices student grouping and routing to bring students into the instructional activity setting for IC. When the teacher shifts into routine IC use, the standards are in full implementation. Table 8.6 contains recommendations for standards implementation with prioritized emphases for each standard.

Dialogue, such as IC, is essential to learning. As a premier teaching strategy since the Greeks first recorded its use, IC is based on centuries of effective teaching practice. The five standards support IC in contemporary classrooms with a system for organizing instruction and using routines. In addition to strengthening the predictability and coherence of classroom teaching, five-standards pedagogy prepares and assembles students for learning primarily through dialogue in IC. The power of the five-standards pedagogy for teaching and learning converges in the use of IC to teach.

Summary

Teachers welcome miracles, but their work is about effects—on students' language development, thinking levels, and academic achievement. Teachers who use the five pedagogy standards, especially IC, continually learn about their students'

Table 8.7
Recommendations for Five Standards Implementation

Standard I	Standard II	Standard III	Standard IV	Standard V
Build community.	Use language levers.	Relate activity to students' lives.	Set high standards in all activities.	Use IC daily.
Use an instructional frame.	Provide writing activities.	Maintain the frame schedule.	Introduce continuing activity settings: assessment, observation, stock market, writing, SGA, arts and crafts, etc.	Use the frame to support IC.
Provide joint productive activity.	Increase students' language skills.	Introduce continuing activity settings: follow-up, library, journaling.	Increase practice opportunities.	Anchor all activity in IC.
Begin multitasking.	Make the frame routine.	Change student group membership.	Provide corrective feedback.	Stabilize groups.
Build students' independence.	Maintain the schedule.	Continue multitasking.	Use the frame routinely.	Route students to activity settings in mixed and matched groups.
Praise and promote productive activity.	Form student groups.	Praise and promote success. Debrief: Focus on independent work.	Mix and match students in groups. Praise and promote success.	Offer students choice contracts. Assess students' learning.
Build students' independent work skills.	Increase independent work.			

learning progress. They use this knowledge to provide responsive assistance in their students' zones of proximal development.

The five pedagogy standards support teachers in doing what many already do, but more systematically and routinely. Many of the standards and their indicators reflect familiar approaches to classroom teaching, but the power of these approaches to support teaching may not previously have been clear. The indicators' purposes are clear and specific. With the implementation of each standard through the indicators, the teacher combines pedagogy with teaching to build a system. At first the system might seem to be merely an organizational improvement. Yet as teachers continue to install the standards, particularly IC, the benefits of pedagogy for teachers—knowing more about students—and for students—understanding more about how to work with the teacher and their peers—are clear. When IC is routine, teachers listen to and guide every student, and students know that they will receive responsive assistance from their teacher.

When the five standards are in place, the system is charged for teaching that is not only upgraded but also substantively different from other models. The standards support teachers in making possible conditions in which teachers may teach using many approaches—most beneficially, dialogue with every student. The system's increased academic dialogue opportunities, instructional routines, and joint productive activities with teacher and peers combine to make teaching and learning more robust. Five-standards teachers can set goals for students' learning with the confidence and satisfaction that come from having both tools and a system for accomplishing those goals.

CONCLUSION

Teaching and pedagogy are ordinarily associated with instruction in classrooms. The extraordinary power of their association to influence learning is less commonly noted. Even at the level of increasing the frequency and predictability of teaching, the benefits of pedagogy are clear. At the level of inclusive teaching that uses responsive assistance, pedagogy's benefits may be surprising. When teaching's influence on students' higher order cognitive development is recognized, pedagogy's role in supporting teaching becomes profound.

To ensure students' language, literacy, numeracy, and cognitive competency for handling complex problems both now and in the future, teaching must provide robust learning experiences for all students. Teaching is strengthened for the goals it sets when pedagogy is intentionally installed to support it. The transmission model demonstrates an association of teaching and pedagogy that is powerful and persistent. The five pedagogy standards provide the same power for aligning teaching with modern understandings about how knowledge is acquired and who is to acquire it.

Teaching has overshadowed pedagogy for centuries. The traditional transmission model has been in place for so long that pedagogy disappeared—or so it seemed. Now that teaching seeks new and effective forms for meeting students' vast array of needs—from varied backgrounds and talents to differing cultures and languages—pedagogy, and even lack of pedagogy, is more visible—if teachers know how to see it.

The following chart shows elements of teaching and pedagogy that are involved in the shift from a transmission to a transformative model:

Transmission Teaching	Transformative Teaching
Individual/psychological	Interactive/social/community
Ability/IQ-based expectations	Content standards
Anecdotally driven decisions	Data-guided decisions
Curriculum based	Language and activity based
Outcomes vary	Outcomes produced

Transmission Pedagogy	Transformative Pedagogy
Cemetery model	Interactive, social model
Individual tasks	Joint productive tasks
Whole group	Small groups
Monotasking (single session): students in lockstep learning	Multitasking: students varying learning tasks
Abstract	Contextualized
One size fits all	Differentiated instruction
Teacher-controlled talk	Responsive dialogue
Recitation/memorization	Complex thinking
Lecture	Instructional conversation (IC)

The chart shows that the elements of teaching and pedagogy change dramatically in the shift from one model to another. Transformed teaching that is interactive, activity based, and outcomes oriented continually provides teachers with information about students' learning progress. Through students' participation and work products, teachers collect a variety of data on which to base their decision making. They shift their pedagogy from assigning solitary tasks to designing collaborations and sustained dialogue in manageable, teacher-assisted groups. They tailor tasks both individually and by groups to suit students' differentiated learning needs. They encourage students to interact over learning material in academic conversation with both the teacher and their peers. JPA and contextualization ready students for assistance in their zones of proximal development. In the IC, teachers responsively assist all students in taking their language and cognitive skills to more complex levels.

Five-standards pedagogy has yet to serve K–8 or K–12 teachers in the ways in which it has the power to do so. This pedagogy has mostly been used in graduate education programs in America's prestigious universities. It is also familiar in the nation's preschools, where students' cognition and language are nurtured in activity-based settings. But in the educational settings between kindergarten and graduate school, effective pedagogy has rarely been called on to support teaching to the degree to which it is capable. Where there is no system or where pedagogy is ignored, the impediment to classroom teaching and learning is practically insurmountable. Instead of being dismissed to an incidental or content-limited role, pedagogy must be recognized and applied as influential assistance for teaching.

The five standards are research based, anchored in psychology and education theory, and affirmed by effective practice. They express the powerful relationship between teaching and pedagogy in a set of principles or standards that every teacher can understand and apply as a system in the classroom. Teachers who begin to use the pedagogy standards can expect to feel a surge in the power of their teaching—that's what pedagogy does. The experience of teaching with pedagogy calls to mind the popular song about eagles flying high on the wind beneath their wings. Teaching's wings are what pedagogy safely lifts for soaring.

Five Standards of Pedagogy with Classroom Indicators

PEDAGOGY STANDARD I:

Teacher and Students Producing Together

Facilitate learning through joint productive activity among teacher and students using multiple classroom settings and student groupings.

Classroom Application Indicators

The teacher

1. Guides students to produce a classroom community agreement.

2. Designs suitable JPAs.

3. Uses an instructional frame to plan and organize instructional activity.

4. Arranges the classroom for interaction and joint activity.

5. Groups students for JPA.

6. Monitors student participation and production in positive ways.

PEDAGOGY STANDARD II:

Developing Language and Literacy

Develop competence in the language and literacy of instruction across the curriculum.

Classroom Application Indicators

The teacher
1. Affirms students' language preferences for all activities.
2. Listens and speaks to students on everyday and academic topics.
3. Uses language development levers in all interactions.
4. Provides phonics and comprehension activities that lead to all students' literacy.
5. Expands students' speech to include spoken and written academic language.

PEDAGOGY STANDARD III:
Connecting School to Students' Lives

Connect teaching and curriculum to students' experiences at home and in the community.

Classroom Application Indicators

The teacher
1. Links learning to students' lives.
2. Includes all students in instructional activities.
3. Contextualizes academic topics.
4. Matches activities to students' varied needs.

STANDARD IV:
Teaching Complex Thinking

Challenge students to think at increasingly complex levels.

Classroom Application Indicators

The teacher
1. Accesses and expands students' current understanding.
2. Sets high standards for all students' performance.

3. Assists student performance at increasingly advanced levels.

4. Teaches challenging content.

PEDAGOGY STANDARD V:
Teaching Through Conversation

Engage students in dialogue, especially instructional conversation.

Classroom Application Indicators

The teacher
1. Performs instructional conversation (IC) routinely within an instructional frame.

2. Guides students to full participation in IC.

3. Achieves academic outcomes in IC.

Timing Instructional Frames

The following instructional frame demonstrates how to calculate an hour-and-a-half, or ninety-minute, instructional period.

		Table 3.8 Instructional Frame: 90 Minutes		
Session 1	**Session 2**	**Session 3**	**Session 4**	**Session 5**
Briefing 11 minutes	Teaching 20 minutes	Teaching application 20 minutes	Teaching extension 20 minutes	Debriefing 15 minutes

Travel time: 4 minutes

CALCULATING THE SCHEDULE FOR A NINETY-MINUTE INSTRUCTIONAL FRAME

1. Subtract twenty-six minutes from the instructional frame time (IFT) to get the teaching activity time (TAT):

   a. IFT − 26 minutes = TAT
   - IFT = 90
   - 26 minutes =
     - Ten minutes for briefing (B)
     - Ten minutes for debriefing (D)
     - Six minutes estimated for travel time (T)
   - TAT = 64

   b. 90 minutes − 26 = 64 TAT

2. Divide the TAT by 20 (average time for a teaching activity in a frame). 64 divided by 20 = 3.2 instructional frame sessions are available.

Three twenty-minute sessions are available in sixty-four minutes, with four extra minutes left over. Extra minutes are usually used to extend debriefing or for cleanup, makeup, reading, or other finishing activity.

3. The formula for calculating the teaching sessions in the ninety-minute instructional frame follows:

$$\frac{\text{IFT} - 26}{20} = 3.2 \text{ teaching activity sessions}$$

The ninety-minute instructional frame has 3.2 sessions available for teaching activity in addition to briefing, debriefing, and travel. This means that four extra minutes are available in addition to two extra travel minutes. The teacher uses these minutes to expand the briefing or debriefing, or applies them to other tasks as needed. In Table 3.8, one extra minute is contributed to briefing and five extra minutes are contributed to debriefing.

Guidelines for Organizing Classroom Activity Settings

The following guidelines are designed to help you arrange the furniture and equipment into classroom activity settings. Each teacher and classroom will have special features to consider in addition to those listed here. Every teacher makes arrangements for student travel, materials management, and storage as needed.

- Assign every student a homeroom seat.

- Decide how students will store and carry their materials (folder, writing equipment).

- Make a setting available for large-group instructional activity. For elementary students, this may be a rug on the floor. In other classrooms, students must be able to look at the teacher easily from their seat. Avoid seating students with their backs to the place the teacher will occupy for large-group or other transactions.

- Arrange a setting in which the teacher can work regularly with a small group of students (three to seven) that has writing display areas (boards, charts) and materials storage space. This instructional setting should be in addition to and separate from the teacher's desk.

- Make several settings available for small-group work and individual instructional activity, accommodating groups of up to six students.

- Ensure that every setting's work area is visible from any position the teacher will occupy.

- Separate quiet settings from potentially noisy ones.

- In each setting, provide equipment such as task cards, bins, and boxes in which individual and group assignments can be placed, and storage for students' folders and texts.
- Match the furniture to the requirements of the setting:
  a. Most settings need seating for three or more students.
  b. Each setting needs easily accessible storage for and retrieval of materials.
  c. Art, listening, and other activities need a sink, an electric plug, or other preparation and cleanup facilities
  d. Games may be placed on the floor or on a rug or remnant.
  e. Technology requires electricity, hookups, supplies, and ease of access.
- Check that traffic patterns provide easy movement between settings.
- Provide students with folders for their work in progress and their routing plan and contract for the week. Students keep this folder with them during class.
- Designate a turn-in or storage place for students' folders.
- Provide mailboxes, a folder system, or other arrangement for returning work to students.

Directed Thinking Activity Cycles

DIRECTED THINKING ACTIVITY (DTA) CYCLE

1. *Present first evidence:* Have you ever seen or heard anything like this before?

2. *Elicit predictions:* What do you think the outcome could be?

3. *Present additional evidence:* Does the new information support your guesses?
   a. *Review previous predictions:* Which guesses still work and which will not now that you have additional evidence?

   b. *Validate predictions:* What guesses do you want to eliminate? Why can't it be that? Does everyone agree?

   c. *Elicit more predictions:* Now what do you think this will turn out to be?

4. *Review thinking direction:* What finally made your predictions accurate?

DIRECTED SEEING THINKING ACTIVITY (DSTA) CYCLE

Select a simple picture or drawing to use as a thinking stimulus. Divide the picture or drawing into chunks. For each chunk you present to students, prepare questions to help them predict what the final drawing will be. Prepare questions to help them validate their predictions using the evidence presented. Continue until the drawing is finished and the students' predictions are confirmed.

1. *Present first evidence:* Have you ever seen anything like this before?

2. *Elicit predictions:* What do you think the outcome could be?

3. *Present additional evidence:* Does the new information support your guesses?

    a. *Review previous predictions:* Which guesses still work and which will not now that you have additional evidence?

    b. *Validate predictions:* What guesses do you want to cross out? Why can't it be that? Does everyone agree?

    c. *Elicit more predictions:* Now what do you think this will turn out to be?

4. *Review thinking direction:* What finally made your predictions accurate?

DIRECTED LISTENING THINKING ACTIVITY (DLTA)

1. Select a story to read and discuss with students.

2. Decide what information (title, author, illustrations, other) to introduce and in what sequence prior to reading the story.

3. Chunk the story into reading portions.

4. Decide where to begin and end reading to promote discussion that encourages predictions.

5. Review and validate the predictions.

6. Encourage students to make more specific predictions focusing on a narrower range of possibilities.

7. Ask students what they already know about the story topic and book cover.

8. Identify vocabulary that students need to know in order to understand the story or simply need to learn.

9. Plan questions to promote student predictions for the first chunk and the following chunks of the story.

10. After the second chunk is read, prepare to guide students to review their previous predictions. At this point, avoid taking more guesses from students, which they will press you to do. Channel their energies into using the new evidence they have heard to validate or reject their previous guesses. Plan questions to guide review of the predictions they have already made.

11. Repeat step 10 as needed to get to the correct prediction.

12. Discuss with students how their thinking moved from broad and divergent to focused and convergent by asking, "What helped you make the correct predictions?"

DIRECTED READING THINKING ACTIVITY (DRTA)

As in the previous DTAs for listening and seeing, in DRTA students make predictions about what they will read on the basis of the book's title, illustrations, cover remarks and reviews, and their prior knowledge. Preparation for DRTA requires text chunking to support the DTA prediction and validation cycle.

1. Students are asked about their knowledge of the reading topic.

2. Students make predictions.

3. Students read the first section of text.

4. The teacher guides students in examining and analyzing the text.

5. Students revise and narrow their predictions in the DTA cycle of validation, using evidence from the story until their reading of the full text validates their thinking.

Web Sites

The following Web sites support activities presented in the book.

Curriculum-Based Visual-Literacy Programs
    Jacob Burns Film Center: http://www.burnsfilmcenter.com/Education/Docs/visual.html#curriculum

Developing Language over a Stimulus, Photo Analysis Guide
    Library of Congress, the Learning Page: http://memory.loc.gov/ammem/ndlpedu/educators/workshop/discover/guide4.html

Earth Science Curriculum Project
    Proposing Explanations for Fossil Footprints: http://www.nap.edu/readingroom/books/evolution98/evol6-e.html

Everyday Mysteries: Fun Science Facts from the Library of Congress
    http://www.loc.gov/rr/scitech/mysteries/archive.html

    Who invented Christmas Tree lights?
    http://www.loc.gov/rr/scitech/mysteries/christmaslights.html
    Why is it hot in summer and cold in winter?
    http://www.loc.gov/rr/scitech/mysteries/seasons.html
    What is the largest flower in the world?
    http://www.loc.gov/rr/scitech/mysteries/flower.html

Comic Books and Graphic Novels
    The Comic Book Project: http://www.comicbookproject.org

    Comics in the Classroom: http://www.comicsintheclassroom.net

National Association of Comics Art Educators: http://www.teachingcomics
.org

Hands-On Astronomy for Kids

Eyes on the Sky, Feet on the Ground: http://hea-www.harvard.edu/ECT/
the_book/index.html

History and Background

Humble Comics: http://www.humblecomics.com

Scott McCloud: http://www.scottmccloud.com

Magna Carta of King John of England, 1215

National Archives & Records Administration: http://www.archives.gov/
exhibits/featured_documents/magna_carta/index.html

Maps and Mapping

Library of Congress, Maps in Our Lives: http://www.loc.gov/exhibits/maps

Math Rappin' Teacher

http://blogs.edweek.org/teachers/webwatch/2006/07/rap_it_up.html?qs=
math+rappin+teacher

National Oceanic and Atmospheric Administration

National Ocean Service: http://oceanservice.noaa.gov/education/geodesy/
welcome.html

Learning Page for Teachers

Images of Our People—A Patchwork of Cultures: http://memory.loc.gov/
learn/lessons/index.html

The Branding of America—Teaching Ideas: http://memory.loc.gov/learn/
features/branding/teaching_ideas.html

Teacher Resources at the Library of Congress

http://www.loc.gov/teachers

Weather Activities

How seasons are affected by the axis and rotation of the earth: http://hea-www.harvard.edu/ECT/the_book/Chap2/Chapter2.html

Is it true that no two snow crystals are alike? http://www.loc.gov/rr/scitech/mysteries/snowcrystals.html

Online guide to snowflakes, snow crystals, and other ice phenomena: http://www.snowcrystals.com

Other Resources

Generation M: Media in the Lives of 8–18 Year-Olds: http://www.kff.org/entmedia/entmedia030905pkg.cfm

Alliance for a Media Literate America: http://www.amlainfo.org

Media Education Foundation: http://www.mediaed.org

Youth Radio: http://www.youthradio.org

Just Think: http://www.justthink.org

Curriculum packages: http://www.justthink.org/curriculum/index.html

George Lucas Educational Foundation: http://www.glef.org/foundation/lucas.php

Stock Market Math Activity

Instructional Period   Ninety minutes daily are recommended in the fifth grade classroom. The frame can be paused between any session, two through six, to suit scheduling requirements (see Appendix 6B).

Activity Type   Joint productive activity (JPA) involves students in forming clubs to develop portfolios of stocks with the capitalistic goal of profit. The students work on the portfolios daily, discuss them technically with the teacher each week, and report to the class weekly.

Class Size   Thirty students

Groups   Groups are mixed ability, membership is by student choice, and they comprise from three to seven students.

Routing   Students are routed through the five activity centers on a schedule. When they are familiar with the expectations and fully productive relative to the learning and content standards goals, they may shift to an instructional frame contract. The contract allows students to choose activity centers they will attend, but it requires attendance with the club for consultation and follow-up.

Classroom Activity Settings

1. *Teaching activity setting:* Small table for six to seven students and teacher, with board, chart paper, and book storage behind it. Located in the front of the room. The teacher uses one consultation session per week to discuss with students math and statistical concepts as they apply in stock market work. He assists students in problem solving and in understanding technical reading

261

material in the context of developing and monitoring their portfolios. The students and teacher discuss required and other readings, use "money talk" vocabulary, and decide on new readings. They prepare for weekly class and other reports. The teacher monitors the accuracy of students' spreadsheets, charts, and loss-gain claims, and provides corrective feedback.

2. *Teaching follow-up:* Students move as a club into a small-group work area, where they follow up and perform the teacher's assignments, which may involve a review quiz.

3. *Reading comprehension:* The reading comprehension activity setting is stocked with newspapers, magazines, and books on the study topic. The teacher-assigned readings and required summaries are posted for all students who attend the activity setting.

4. *Vocabulary development:* The fiscal lexicon activity center is stocked with dictionaries and financial resources. Students develop their personal fiscal dictionaries (see discussion of the Dictosaurus in Chapter Five) and prepare to use the vocabulary they learn in reports and discussions.

5. *Analysis:* The analysis activity setting requires computer access. Data are gathered and adjustments are made to the club's portfolio. All students are responsible for updating the club portfolio daily with profits and losses and alerts, both online and in the classroom.

Appendix 6.B
Stock Market Instructional Frame: 146 Minutes

Session 1	Session 2	Session 3	Session 4	Session 5	Session 6	Session 7
Briefing	*Teaching activity:* Teacher consulting with Aggressive Traders (AT) Stock Club	*Teaching application:* AT Club following up on consultant's advice	*Vocabulary development:* Unlocking fiscal lexicon and acronyms	*Reading comprehension:* Monitoring market news and alerts	*Analysis:* Tracking portfolio performance on spreadsheets	
	Tracking portfolio performance on spreadsheets	Teacher consulting with Blue Chip (BC) Investors Club	BC Club following up on consultant's advice	Unlocking fiscal lexicon and acronyms	Monitoring the market news	Debriefing
	Monitoring the market news	Tracking portfolio performance on spreadsheets	Teacher consulting with Mid-Cap (MC) Investors Club	MC Club following up on consultant's advice	Unlocking fiscal lexicon and acronyms	
	Unlocking fiscal lexicon and acronyms	Monitoring the market news	Tracking portfolio performance on spreadsheets	Teacher consulting with Small Cap (SC) Investors Club	SC Club following up on consultant's advice	
	Prepare spreadsheets for all sectors of stock in portfolio	Unlocking fiscal lexicon and acronyms	Monitoring the market news	Tracking portfolio performance on spreadsheets	Teacher consulting with Mixed (MX) Investors Club	
10 minutes	20 minutes	20 minutes	20 minutes	20 minutes	20 minutes	10 minutes

Travel time: 6 minutes

Note: Club reports are scheduled to occur either one per day after completing work on the frame or all on a single day instead of the frame. The instructional frame for stock market study can be used in any schedule. Even in a brief class period of forty-five minutes, at least one twenty-minute session can be completed under most circumstances. Teachers have reported students working on their activities on the school bus on their way to a field trip. The frame must always begin with the briefing and conclude with the debriefing. A debriefing can also be inserted whenever the class and teacher need to assess and review. If large issues arise that require more time to solve, the teacher pauses the instructional frame and shifts to a classroom meeting format.

Footprint Puzzle

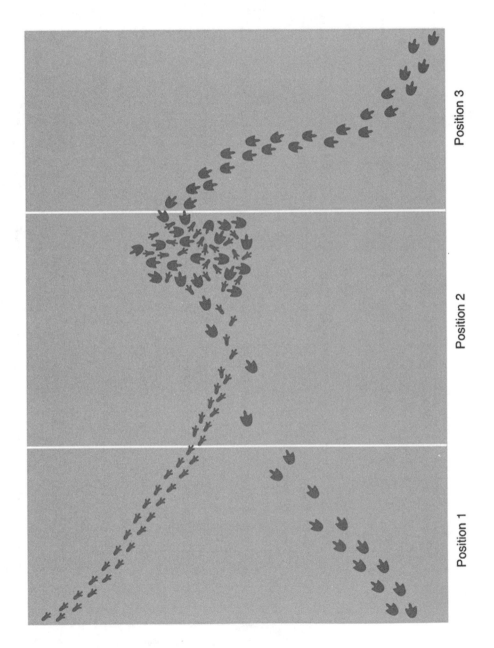

Position 3

Position 2

Position 1

Activity Settings Worksheet

A. To begin rotating students to activity settings in matched groups for the teaching settings and mixed groups for the independent settings, there must be at least seven settings in the classroom for students to attend. List the settings you plan to introduce. (You have already introduced some or all, but this will make their use more predictable and systematic.)

Activity Settings

1. Teaching activity setting

2. Teaching follow-up

3. _____ (Journaling)

4. _____ (Classroom Library)

5. _____ (Vocabulary Study)

6. _____ (Skill Practice)

7. _____ (Computers)

Add additional centers here; for example:

8. _____ (Science Observation Station)

9. _____ (Art)

10. _____ (Content Writing)

On the Scheduling and Routing Form (Appendix 8B), the preceding numbers are used to identify the activity settings that students will attend.

B. Check the activity settings for seating for six, supplies for all, and visibility for you from any place you may find yourself in the classroom.

C. Fill out the worksheet in Appendix 8B to divide your students into five matched-ability groups for teaching them at the teaching activity setting.

D. Prepare activities that students will find interesting for the settings. Plan to discuss their work at independent settings when they come to you at the teaching center.

E. Plan (if you have not done so already) to introduce each activity setting so that students will understand exactly what will be expected when they attend the setting.

F. Review the classroom agreement if needed, and update it if necessary.

G. After you have listed the students' names on the worksheet, enlarge the sheet and cut out the lines of numbers for each student. Or provide each student with the numbers of the activity settings he or she will attend during the sessions. Usually students use a folder with the schedule taped inside it to carry their work from one activity setting to another.

H. Remember that everyone is going to enjoy an active classroom.

Scheduling and Routing Form for Seven Activity Settings and Thirty Students

Activity Sessions	1	2	3	4	5	6	7	8	9	10
Student Names					Blue Group					
1	1	2	3	4	5	1	2	3	4	5
2	1	2	4	5	6	1	2	4	5	6
3	1	2	5	6	7	1	2	5	6	7
4	1	2	3	4	5	1	2	3	4	5
5	1	2	4	5	6	1	2	4	5	6
6	1	2	5	6	7	1	2	5	6	7
					Orange Group					
1	3	1	2	4	5	3	1	2	4	5
2	4	1	2	5	6	4	1	2	5	6
3	5	1	2	6	7	5	1	2	6	7
4	3	1	2	4	5	3	1	2	4	5
5	4	1	2	5	6	4	1	2	5	6
6	5	1	2	6	7	5	1	2	6	7
					Yellow Group					
1	3	4	1	2	5	3	4	1	2	5
2	4	5	1	2	6	4	5	1	2	6

3	5	6	1	2	7	5	6	1	2	7
4	3	4	1	2	5	3	4	1	2	5
5	4	5	1	2	6	4	5	1	2	6
6	5	6	1	2	7	5	6	1	2	7

Green Group

1	3	4	3	1	2	3	4	6	1	2
2	4	5	4	1	2	4	5	7	1	2
3	5	6	5	1	2	5	6	8	1	2
4	3	4	3	1	2	3	4	6	1	2
5	4	5	4	1	2	4	5	7	1	2
6	5	6	5	1	2	5	6	8	1	2

Red Group

1	2	3	4	5	1	2	3	4	5	1
2	2	4	5	6	1	2	4	5	6	1
3	2	5	6	7	1	2	5	6	7	1
4	2	3	4	5	1	2	3	4	5	1
5	2	4	5	6	1	2	4	5	6	1
6	2	5	6	7	1	2	5	6	7	1
# of students at settings	6	6	2–6	2–6	6	6	2–6	2–4	2–6	6

This form may be modified to include more activity settings and more or fewer students.

Activity setting 1: Teaching activity; activity setting 2: follow-up activity.

This scheduling and routing system uses matched groups for activity settings 1 and 2, and mixes groups for all others.

Each session is twenty minutes.

Teacher Assigned and/or Student Choice Activity Settings Grouping: 5
Matched Groups for Activity Settings 1 & 2; Choice or Mixed for Others

INSTRUCTIONAL FRAME SESSIONS: Briefing is #1; Debriefing is last.										
Session	**#2**	**#3**	**#4**	**#5**	**#6**	**#7**	**#8**	**#9**	**#10**	**#11**
Student Names										
Blue Group										
	*1	2				1	2			
	1	2				1	2			
	1	2				1	2			
	1	2				1	2			
	1	2				1	2			
	1	2				1	2			
Orange Group										
		1	2				1	2		
		1	2				1	2		
		1	2				1	2		
		1	2				1	2		
		1	2				1	2		
		1	2				1	2		
Yellow Group										
			1	2				1	2	
			1	2				1	2	
			1	2				1	2	
			1	2				1	2	
			1	2				1	2	
			1	2				1	2	

Green Group										
				1	2				1	2
				1	2				1	2
				1	2				1	2
				1	2				1	2
				1	2				1	2
				1	2				1	2
Red Group										
	2				1	2				1
	2				1	2				1
	2				1	2				1
	2				1	2				1
	2				1	2				1
	2				1	2				1

*=Number to identify Activity Setting in the classroom.

Instructional Frame: Student Contract and Choice Model

Session 1	Session 2	Session 3	Session 4	Session 5	Session 6	Session 7
Brief: Discuss performance expectations	Teach Blue Group	Blue Group Follow Up	Blue Group student chooses activity settings and sessions to attend	Blue Group student chooses activity settings and sessions to attend	Blue Group student chooses activity settings and sessions to attend	
	Orange Group student chooses activity setting	Teach Orange Group	Orange Group Follow Up	Orange Group chooses activity setting	Orange Group student chooses activity setting	
	Yellow Group student chooses activity setting	Yellows Group student chooses activity setting	Teach Yellow Group	Yellow Group Follow Up	Yellow Group student chooses activity setting	
	Green Group student chooses activity setting	Green Group student chooses activity setting	Green Group student chooses activity setting	Teach Green Group	Green Group Follow Up	
	Red Group Follow Up	Red Group student chooses activity setting	Red Group student chooses activity setting	Red Group student chooses activity setting	Teach Red Group	Debrief: Review products; class feedback, praise
Time: 12 mins	20 mins	20 mins	20 mins	20 mins	20 mins	12 mins

Travel Time = 6 minutes

Note: Teacher assigns and student chooses activity settings and sessions to attend. Student continues to attend teaching and follow-up activity settings.
Contract: Teacher and student discuss how many required and choice settings students will visit during the frame. Contract allows students to plan activities and combine settings. Contracting involves students in planning and managing their learning.

Allen, M. B. (2003). *Eight questions on teacher preparation: What does the research say?* Denver, CO: Education Commission of the States.

Au, K. H. (1980). Participation structures in a reading lesson with Hawaiian children: Analysis of a culturally appropriate instructional event. *Anthropology and Education Quarterly, 11*(2), 91–115.

Bloom, B. S. (Ed.). (1956). *Taxonomy of educational objectives, handbook I: Cognitive domain.* New York: David McKay.

Blumenfeld, P. C., Krajcik, J. S., Marx, R. W., & Soloway, E. (2001). Promising new instructional practices. In M. C. Wang & H. J. Wahlberg, *Tomorrow's teachers* (pp. 47–78). Richmond, CA: McCutchan.

Boaler, J. (1999). Participation, knowledge, and beliefs: A community perspective on mathematics learning. *Educational Studies in Mathematics, 40,* 259–281.

Borko, H. M., Brown, C. A., Underhill, R. G., Jones, D., & Agard, P. C. (1992). Learning to teach hard mathematics: Do novice teachers and their instructors give up too easily? *Journal for Research in Mathematics Education, 23,* 194–222.

Bransford, J. D., Brown, A. L., & Cocking, R. R. (2000). *How people learn: Brain, mind, experience, and school.* Washington, DC: National Academy Press.

Bruner, J. S. (1996). *The culture of education.* Cambridge, MA: Harvard University Press.

Chandler, M. A. (2005, September 5). The chalkboard's energetic new cousin: Interactive screens reshaping lessons. *Washington Post,* B01.

Chaney, B. (1995). *Student outcomes and the professional preparation of eighth grade teachers in science and mathematics.* Unpublished manuscript, prepared for National Science Foundation Grant RED-9255255 . Rockville, MD: Westat.

Clay, M. M. (1993). *Reading recovery: A guidebook for teachers in training.* Portsmouth, NH: Heinemann.

Cobb, P. (1994). Where is the mind? Constructivist and sociocultural perspectives on mathematical development. *Educational Researcher, 23*(7), 13–20.

Cohen, E. G. (1994). *Designing groupwork.* New York: Teachers College Press.

Coley, R. J., & Coleman, A. B. (2004). *The fourth-grade reading classroom.* Princeton, NJ: Educational Testing Service.

Dalton, S. S. (1995). *Developing teacher education for diversity: Review of preservice education for teachers of minorities (PETOM).* Invited paper for the University of Hawaii at Manoa and Kamehameha Schools/Bishop Estate Archives.

Dalton, S. S. (1998). Pedagogy matters (Research Report No. 4). Santa Cruz, CA: Center for Research on Education, Diversity & Excellence.

Dalton, S. S. (2002). How do preservice teachers learn? In L. Minaya-Rowe (Ed.), *Effective pedagogy and teacher training.* Greenwich, CT: Information Age Publishing.

Dalton, S. S., & Cramer, J. (1985, April). *Student-generated activities.* Paper presented at the American Educational Research Association, Chicago, IL.

Dalton, S. S., & Dowhower, S. (1985). *The directed seeing thinking activity (DSTA) and the directed listening thinking activity (DLTA)* (Early Education Bulletin No. 10). Honolulu: Center for Development of Early Education.

Dalton, S. S., & Moir, E. (1996). Text and context for professional development of new bilingual teachers. In M. McLaughlin (Ed.), *Teacher learning: New policies, new practices* (pp. 126–133). New York: Teachers College Press.

Dalton, S. S., & Sison, J. (1994). *Enacting instructional conversation in math with Spanish-speaking language minority students* (Research Report No. 12). Washington, DC: National Research Center on Cultural Diversity and Second Language Learning, Center for Applied Linguistics.

Dalton, S. S., & Tharp, R. G. (2002). Standards for pedagogy: Research, theory, and practice. In G. Wells & G. Claxton (Eds.), *Learning for life in the twenty-first century* (pp. 181–194). Oxford: Blackwell.

Dalton, S. S., & Youpa, D. (1998). School reform in Zuni Pueblo middle and high schools. *Journal of Equity and Excellence in Education, 31*(1), 55–68.

Darling-Hammond, L., Berry, B., & Thoreson, A. (2001). Does teacher certification matter? Evaluating the evidence. *Educational Evaluation and Policy Analysis, 23*(1), 57–77.

Davis, N. (2003) Technology in teacher education in the USA: What makes for sustainable good practice? *Technology, Pedagogy and Education, 12*(1), 59–73.

Delpit, L. (1995). Other people's children: Cultural conflict in the classroom. New York: Free Press.

Dictionary.com Unabridged (v. 1.1). Retrieved March 5, 2007, from http://dictionary.reference.com/browse/pedagogy.

Doherty, R. W., Hilberg, R. S., Epaloose, G., & Tharp, R. G. (2002). Standards performance continuum: Development and validation of a measure of effective pedagogy. *Journal of Educational Research, 96*(2), 78–89.

Doherty, R. W., Hilberg, R. S., Pinal, A., & Tharp, R. G. (2003). Five standards and student achievement. *NABE Journal of Research and Practice, 1*(1), 1–24.

Doyle, W. (1997). Whatever happened to all the research in classroom management? *Classrooms: Newsletter of the Classroom Management Special Interest Group of the American Educational Research Association.* Las Vegas: University of Nevada College of Education.

Earth Science Curriculum Project. (1973). *Investigating the earth* (Rev. ed.). Boston: Houghton Mifflin.

Echevarria, J., Short, D., & Powers, K. (2006). School reform and standards-based education: A model for English-language learners. *Journal of Educational Research, 99*(4), 195–210.

Echevarria, J., Vogt, M. E., & Short, D. (2000). *Making content comprehensible for English language learners: The SIOP model.* Boston: Allyn and Bacon.

Ellis, K. (2005, July 13). Media smarts. Available at http://www.edutopia.org/node/1321/print.

Epstein, J. (2001). *School, family and community partnerships: Preparing educators and improving schools.* Boulder, CO: Westview Press.

Entz, S., & Galarza, S. (2000). *Picture this.* Thousand Oaks, CA: Corwin Press.

Erickson, F., & Mohatt, G. (1982). The cultural organization of participation structures in two classrooms of Indian students. In G. Spindler (Ed.), *Doing the ethnography of schooling* (pp. 132–174). New York: Holt, Rinehart & Winston.

Estrada, P. (2004). Patterns of language arts instructional activity and excellence in first and fourth grade culturally and linguistically diverse classrooms. In H. Waxman, R. G.Tharp, & R. Hillberg (Eds.), *Observational research in U.S. classrooms: New approaches for understanding cultural and linguistic diversity* (pp. 122–143). Cambridge, MA: Cambridge University Press.

Estrada, P. (2005). The courage to grow: A researcher and teacher linking professional development with small-group reading instruction and student achievement. *Research in the Teaching of English, 39,* 320–264.

Ferguson, A. A. (2000). *Bad boys: Public schools in the making of black masculinity.* Ann Arbor: University of Michigan Press.

Finn, J. N., Pannozzo, G. N., & Achilles, C. M. (2003). The "whys" of class size: student behavior in small classes. *Review of Educational Research, 73*(3), 277–368.

Gay, G. (2002). *Culturally responsive teaching.* New York: Teachers College Press.

Getting tuned in iPod-enhanced reading a hit. (2005, October 16). *San Bernardino Sun.*

Godley, A. J., Sweetland, J., Wheeler, R. S., Minnici, A., & Carpenter, B. D. (2006). Preparing teachers for dialectally diverse classrooms. *Educational Researcher, 35*(8), 30–37.

Goldenberg, C. (2006, July 26). Improving achievement for English-learners: What the research tells us. *Education Week, 25*(43), 34–36.

Goldhaber, D. D., & Brewer, D. J. (2000). Does teacher certification matter? High school teacher certification status and student achievement. *Educational Evaluation and Policy Analysis, 22,* 129–145.

Gonzalez, N., Moll, L. C., & Amanti, C. (Eds.). (2005). *Funds of knowledge: Theorizing practices in households and classrooms.* Hillsdale, NJ: Erlbaum.

Gutierrez, K. D., & Rogoff, B. (2003). Cultural ways of learning: Individual traits or repertoires of practice. *Educational Researcher, 32*(5), 19–25.

Hart, B., & Risley, T. R. (1995). Meaningful differences in the everyday experience of young American children. Baltimore, MD: P. H. Brookes.

Hiebert, J., & Trends in International Mathematics and Science Study. Video Mathematics Research Group. (2003). Understanding and improving mathematics teaching: Highlights from the TIMSS 1999 video study. *Phi Delta Kappan, 84*(10), 768–775.

Hilberg, R. S., Chang, J. M., & Epaloose, G. (2004). *Designing effective activity centers for diverse learners: A guide for teachers at all grade levels.* Santa Cruz, CA: Center for Research on Education, Diversity & Excellence.

Hilberg, R., Doherty, R., Dalton, S. S., Youpa, D., & Tharp, R. (1998). Standards for effective mathematics education for American Indian students. In J. T. Hankes and G. R. Fast (Eds.), *Changing the faces of mathematics: Perspectives on indigenous people of North America* (pp. 25–35). Reston, VA: National Council of Teachers of Mathematics.

Hilberg, R. S., Tharp, R. G., & DeGeest, L. (2000). The efficacy of CREDE's standards-based instruction in American Indian mathematics classes. *Equity and Excellence in Education, 33*(2), 32–39.

Kajitani, A. (2006). *The rappin' mathematician, volume I* [CD-]. San Diego, CA: MathRaps.com.

Kamil, M. L., Manning, J. B., & Walberg, H. J. (2002). *Successful reading instruction.* Greenwich, CN: Information Age Publishing.

Kandel, E. R., & Hawkins, R. D. (1992). The biological basis of learning and individuality. *Scientific American, 267*(3), 78–86.

Kirschner, P., & Davis, N. (2003). Pedagogic benchmarks for information and communications technology in teacher education. *Technology, Pedagogy and Education, 12*(1), 125–147.

Kirschner, P., & Selinger, M. (2003). The state of affairs of teacher education with respect to information and communications technology. *Technology, Pedagogy and Education, 12*(1), 5–17.

Kirschner, P., & Wopereis, I. H. (2003). Mindtools for teacher communities: A European perspective. *Technology, Pedagogy and Education, 12*(1), 107–126.

Knezek, G., & Christensen, R. (2000). *Refining best teaching practices for technology integrations: KIDS project findings for 1999–2000.* Denton: University of North Texas.

Kuhn, M. R., & Stahl, S. A. (2003). Fluency: A review of developmental and remedial practices. *Journal of Educational Psychology, 95,* 3–21.

Ladsen-Billings, G. (2001). *Crossing over to Canaan: The journey of new teachers in diverse classrooms.* San Francisco: Jossey-Bass.

Lave, J., & Wenger, E. (1991). *Situated learning: Legitimate peripheral participation.* New York: Cambridge University Press.

Lee, C. D. (2006). *Every good-bye ain't gone.* New York: Routledge.

Levin, D., & Arafeh, S. (2002). *The digital disconnect: The widening gap between internet-savvy students and their schools.* Washington, DC: American Institutes for Research.

Marshall, J. (2003). Math wars: Taking sides. *Phi Delta Kappan, 85*(3), 193–200.

McDiarmid, G. W., & Wilson, S. M. (1991). An exploration of the subject-matter knowledge of alternate rout teachers: Can we assume they know their subject? *Journal of Teacher Education, 42,* 93–103.

National Reading Panel. (2000). *Report of the National Reading Panel: Teaching children to read.* Washington, DC: National Institute of Child Health and Human Development.

National Research Council. (1998). *Preventing reading difficulties in young children* (C. E. Snow, S. E. Burns, & P. Griffin, Eds.). Washington, DC: National Academy Press.

Padron, Y. N. (1992). The effect of strategy instruction on bilingual students' cognitive strategy use in reading. *Bilingual Research Journal, 16*(3 & 4), 35–51.

Pogrow, D. (2005). HOTS revisited: A thinking development approach to reducing the learning gap after grade three. *Phi Delta Kappan, 87*(1), 64–75.

Resnick, L. (1995). From aptitude to effort: A new foundation for our schools. *Daedalus, Journal of the American Academy of Arts and Sciences, 124*(4), 55–62.

Rivera, H., Galarza, S., Entz, S., & Tharp, R. G. (2002). Technology and pedagogy in early childhood education: Guidance from cultural-historical-activity theory and developmentally appropriate instruction. *Information Technology in Childhood Education Annual, (1)*, 181–204.

Rogoff, B. (1990). *Apprenticeships in thinking: Cognitive development in social context.* New York: Oxford University Press.

Rogoff, B. (1995). Observing sociocultural activity on three planes: Participatory appropriation, guided participation, and apprenticeship. In J. V. Wertsch, P. delRio, & A. Alvarez (Eds.), *Sociocultural studies of mind* (pp. 139–164). Cambridge, UK: Cambridge University Press.

Rosebery, A. S., Warren, B., & Conant, F. R. (1992). Appropriating scientific discourse: Findings from language minority classrooms. *Journal of the Learning Sciences, 2*(1), 61–94.

Rowan, B., Correnti, R., & Miller, R. J. (2002). What large-scale survey research tells us about teacher effects on student achievement: Insights from the Prospects Study of Elementary Schools. *Teachers College Record, 104*(8), 1525–1567.

Saunders, W. (1999). Improving literacy achievement for English learners in transitional bilingual programs. *Educational Research and Evaluation, 5*(4), 345–381.

Saunders, W., & Goldenberg, C. (1999a). *The effects of instructional conversations and literature logs on the story comprehension and thematic understanding of English proficient and limited English proficient students.* Berkeley: Center for Research on Education, Diversity & Excellence, University of California.

Saunders, W., & Goldenberg, C. (1999b). *The effects of comprehensive language arts/transition program on the literacy development of English learners* [technical report]. Berkeley: Center for Research on Education, Diversity & Excellence, University of California.

Saunders, W., & Goldenberg, C. (2001). Opportunities through language arts: Overview video, video guide, and program manual. Berkeley: Center for Research on Education, Diversity & Excellence, University of California.

Saunders, W., O'Brien, G., Lennon, D., & McLean, J. (1998). Making the transition to English literacy successful: Effective strategies for studying literature with transition students. In R. Gersten & R. Jimenez (Eds.), *Promoting learning for culturally and linguistically diverse students* (pp. 99–132). Monterey, CA., Brooks Cole.

Shaffer, D. W., Squire, K. R., Halverson, R., & Gee, J. P. (2005). Video games and the future of learning. *Phi Delta Kappan, 87*(2), 105–111.

Shanahan, T. (2002). *A sin of the second kind: The neglect of fluency instruction and what we can do about it.* PowerPoint presentation at A Focus on Fluency Forum, San Francisco, CA. Available at http://www.prel.org/programs/rel/fluency/Shanahan.ppt.

Spero, D. J. (1994). *Electricity current and static.* Monterey CA: Evan-Moor.

Stauffer, R. G. (1970). *The language-experience approach to the teaching of reading.* New York: Harper and Row.

Stigler, J. W., & Hiebert, J. (1997). Understanding and improving classroom mathematics instruction. *Phi Delta Kappan, 78,* 14–21.

Stigler, J. W., & Hiebert, J. (1999). The teaching gap: Best ideas from the world's teachers for improving education in the classroom. New York: Free Press.

Tafoya, M. (1983). *The red & the black: Santa Clara pottery.* Posterboard. Santa Fe, NM: Wheelwright Museum of the American Indian.

Tharp, R. G. (1989). Psychocultural variables and constants: Effects on teaching and learning in schools. *American Psychologist, 44*(2), 249–359.

Tharp, R. G., Dalton, S. S., & Yamauchi, L. (1994). Principles for culturally compatible Native American education. *Journal of Navajo Education, 11*(3), 33–39.

Tharp, R., Entz, S., & Galarza, S. (2002). *The Sheri Galarza pre-school case* [CD-ROM]. Provo, UT: Brigham Young University.

Tharp, R. G., Estrada, P., Dalton, S. S., & Yamauchi, L. (2000). *Teaching transformed: Achieving excellence, fairness, inclusion, and harmony.* Boulder, CO: Westview Press.

Tharp, R. G., & Gallimore, R. (1988). *Rousing minds to life.* New York: Cambridge University Press.

Tharp, R., Hilberg, S., Dalton, S., & Teemant, A. (2002). *Teaching alive! for the twenty-first century: The five standards for effective pedagogy in elementary settings* [CD-ROM]. Provo, UT: Brigham Young University.

Tharp, R. G., Jordan, C., Speidel, G. E., Au, K. H., Klein, T. W., Calkins, R. P., Sloat, K.C.M., & Gallimore, R. (1984). Product and process in applied developmental research: Education and the children of a minority. In M. E. Lamb, A. L. Brown, & B. Rogoff (Eds.), *Advances in developmental psychology,* vol. 3 (pp. 91–141). Hillsdale, NJ: Erlbaum.

U.S. Department of Education, National Center for Education Statistics. (2006). *The condition of education 2005* (NCES 2005–094). Washington, DC: U.S. Government Printing Office.

Valenzuela, A. (1999). *Subtractive schooling: U.S.-Mexican youth and the politics of caring.* Albany: State University of New York Press.

Valmont, W. J. (1976). *Seeing, listening, thinking activities kit.* New York: McCormick-Mathers.

Vygotsky, L. (1978). *Mind in society* (M. Cole, V. John-Steiner, S. Scribner, & E. Souberman, Eds.). Cambridge: Harvard University Press.

Wang, M. C., & Wahlberg, H. J. (2001). *Tomorrow's teachers.* Richmond, CA: McCutchan Corporation.

Wells, G. (2000). Dialogic inquiry in education: Building on the legacy of Vygotsky. In C. D. Lee & P. Smagorinsky (Eds.), *Vygotskian perspectives on literacy research: Constructing meaning through collaborative inquiry* (pp. 51–85). Cambridge, MA: Cambridge University Press.

Wilson, S. M., & Peterson, P. L. (2006). *Theories of learning and teaching: What do they mean for educators?* Washington, DC: National Education Association.

Wong-Fillmore, L., & Snow, C. E. (2000). *What teachers need to know about language.* Washington, DC: Center for Applied Linguistics.

NAME INDEX

E

Earth Science Curriculum Project, 179, 182
Echevarria, J., 35, 36
Edison, Thomas, 2
Ellis, K., 150
Entz, S., 25, 42, 61, 149
Epaloose, G., 65
Epstein, J., 39
Erickson, F., 45
Estrada, P., 24, 25, 26, 28, 30, 31, 32, 33, 39,
    40, 43, 45, 48

F

Ferguson, A.A., 40
Finn, J.N., 32

G

Galarza, S., 25, 42, 61, 149
Gallimore, R., 6, 22, 25, 26, 29, 30, 32, 38,
    40, 43, 45
Gay, G., 40
Gee, J.P., 44
Godley, A.J., 35
Goldenberg, C., 35, 37, 46, 47, 190
Goldhaber, D.D., 24
Gonzalez, N., 39, 141
Gutierrez, K.D., 34

H

Halverson, R., 44
Hart, B., 26, 36
Hawkins, R.D., 38
Hiebert, J., 23, 40
Hilberg, R.S., 25, 33, 43, 65, 213, 215

I

Institute of Education Sciences, 46
Iwan, ????, 42

J

Jones, D., 23
Just Think, 150

K

Kajitani, A., 99, 100, 135
Kamil, M.L., 44
Kandel, E.R., 38
Kirschner, P., 30, 41, 42, 44
Knezek, G., 44
Krajcik, J.S., 26
Kuhn, M.R., 37, 58

L

Ladsen-Billings, G., 34, 40
Lave, J., 30, 43
Lennon, D., 46
Levin, D., 44

M

McDiarmid, G.W., 23
McLean, J., 46
Manning, J.B., 44
Marshall, J., 135, 136, 161
Marx, R.W., 26
Media Education Foundation, 150
Miller, R.J., 24
Minnici, A., 35
Mohatt, G., 45
Moir, E., 24
Moll, L.C., 39, 40, 141

N

National Ocean Service, 184
National Oceanic and Atmospheric
    Administration, 150, 184
National Reading Panel, 30, 36, 37, 44, 115,
    217
National Research Council, 36

O

O'Brien, G., 46

P

Padron, Y.N., 45
Pannozzo, G.N., 32

SUBJECT INDEX

mathematics, 215–217; instructional conversations in social studies, 213–215

Continuing activity settings, 73

Corrective feedback, 166–168

Creative writing, 128

Cross Words, 116

D

Default pedagogy, 13–15

Dialogic instruction, 45–46

Dialogue teaching, 15–18

Dictosaurus, 102–103

Differentiated instruction, 155

Direct explanation, 44

Directed activity cycles: directed listening thinking activity (DLTA) cycle, 255–256; directed reading activity (DRA) cycle, 124; directed reading thinking activity (DRTA) cycle, 124–125, 256; directed seeing thinking activity (DSTA) cycle, 138–141, 254–255; directed thinking activity (DTA) cycle, 104–107, 138, 254

Diversity, 39–41

E

Early content themes, 59–64

ECT. *See* Early content themes

Engage, explore, explain, elaborate, evaluate approach, 179–182

English language learners (ELLs), 97–98

Equipment, guidelines for organizing, 252–253

Expanding students' current understanding, 160–163

F

Failed pedagogy, 14

Feedback, corrective, 166–168

Fifth grade stock market math activity, 260–262

Five-pedagogy-standards classroom, performance-based teaching in, 18–20

Fluency, 116–118

Frustration level, 58

Funds of knowledge, 39; community, 141–143; personal, 137–141

Furniture, guidelines for organizing, 252–253

G

Games, 145–146, 179

Grouping, 31–32; group membership, 88–90; group size, 88; mixed and matched, 237; routing student groups, 90–91, 238

H

Home teaching, 26–27

I

IC. *See* Instructional conversations

ICT. *See* Information communications and technology

Implementation indicators, 21

Independent level, 58

Information communications and technology, 41–42; and media, 148–150

Instruction, 4

Instructional conversations, 191–193; approaches to questioning, 203–206; assessment, 195; assisted performance, 196–197; balanced participation, 199–200; contextualizing in mathematics, 215–217; contextualizing in social studies, 213–215; goals, 194–195; how it works, 193–194; inclusiveness, 197–198; participation rights, 201–203; products, 217–218; research reports on, 46–47; responsiveness, 198–199; scheduling,

200–201; teaching, 207–208; teaching assistance in, 208–211; on text comprehension, 211–213. *See also* Pedagogy standard V

Instructional frames, 67–69, 175, 223; basic, 68; briefing, 69–71; classroom activity settings, 73–76; debriefing, 72–73; to foster language proficiency, 107, 108; multitasking classrooms, 76–85; ninety minutes, 72; sixty minutes, 69, 74; student contract and choice model, 269–270; teaching activities, 71–72; timing, 250–251

Instructional level, 58

Interaction, 85–87

Interactive journals, 128

J

Jigsaw puzzles, 117, 147

Joint activity content, 59

Joint productive activities, 57–67, 182–184

Journals, 127–128

JPA. *See* Joint productive activities

K

Knowledge development, 38

L

Language development, 36

Language diversity, 34–36

Language experience approach, 118–119

Language fluency, 116–118

Language preferences, 99–103

Language proficiency: instructional frames, 107, 108. *See also* Pedagogy standard II

Learning extensions, 147

Learning zones, 8

Linking learning to students' lives, 135–143

M

Management, 34

Mathematical party plans, 148

Mathematics, 43

Maze Game, 116

Metacognitive approaches, 28, 125–126

Methods, 4

Minority student enrollment, increases in, 3–4

Monotasking, 68, 72. *See also* Multitasking

Multitasking, 33, 76–79, 225; 110-minute instructional frame, 83; 60-minute instructional frame, 77; 90-minute instructional frame, 82, 86; developing the timeline, 84–85; expanding the instructional frame, 81–84; stocking activities for, 80–81. *See also* Monotasking

P

Parent-generated activity, 146–148

Participation, 91–93; forms of, 143–145

Pedagogy: defined, 4–6; failed, 14; research on, 24–25; role of in effective teaching, 8–20; and teaching, 5; transmission vs. transformative, 6. *See also* Default pedagogy

Pedagogy standard I, 30–34, 51–52; classroom application indicators, 51; community agreement (Indicator 1), 53–57; grouping for joint productive activities (Indicator 5), 87–91; implementing in a five standards classroom, 227–228; instructional frames (Indicator 3), 67–85; interaction and joint activity (Indicator 4), 85–87; joint productive activities (Indicator 2), 57–67; monitoring participation (Indicator 6), 91–93; rationale, 52–53

Pedagogy standard II, 34–37, 97–98; affirming students' language

Pedagogy standard II (*continued*)
preferences (Indicator 1), 99–103;
classroom application indicators, 97;
implementing in a five standards
classroom, 229–231; listening and
speaking to students (Indicator 2),
104–110; phonics and comprehension
activities (Indicator 4), 115–126;
rationale, 98; spoken and written
academic language (Indicator 5),
126–128; using language development
levers (Indicator 3), 110–115

Pedagogy standard III, 38–42, 133–134;
classroom application indicators, 133;
contextualizing academic topics
(Indicator 3), 151–155; implementing
in a five standards classroom, 231–233;
linking learning to students' lives
(Indicator 1), 135–143; matching
activities to students' needs (Indicator
4), 155–156; participation in
instructional activities (Indicator 2),
143–150; rationale, 134–135

Pedagogy standard IV, 42–45, 159–160;
assisting performance at advanced
levels (Indicator 3), 168–175;
challenging content (Indicator 4),
175–186; classroom application
indicators, 159; expanding students'
current understanding (Indicator 1),
160–163; implementing in a five
standards classroom, 233–238;
rationale, 160; setting standards for
performance (Indicator 2), 163–168

Pedagogy standard V, 45–47, 189–190;
academic outcomes in IC (Indicator 3),
206–218; classroom application
indicators, 189; guiding students to full
participation in IC (Indicator 2), 201–
206; implementing in a five standards
classroom, 238–240; performing IC

routinely within instructional frames
(Indicator 1), 191–201; rationale,
190–191

Pedagogy standards, 24–25; account of
five standards use in a classroom,
222–226; with classroom indicators,
247–249; developing a five standards
classroom, 226–227; and
implementation indicators, 21;
implementing standard I, 227–228;
implementing standard II, 229–231;
implementing standard III, 231–233;
implementing standard IV, 233–238;
implementing standard V, 238–240;
integrated, 47–48, 221–242;
recommendations for implementing,
240–242; research on, 29–30

Pedagogy theory, 25–26
Performance standards, 163–168
Performance-based teaching, 18–20
PGAs. *See* Parent-generated activity
Phonemic awareness, 116–118
Phonics, 116–118
Practice opportunities, 185–186
Prior knowledge, 38–39
Problem solving, 176–178
Project-based approaches, 155–156

Q
Quizzes, 147

R
Reading, 36–37, 43–44; and writing, 37
Reports, 128
Research: on pedagogy, 24–25; on
pedagogy standards, 29–30; on
teaching, 23–24
Research reports on instructional
conversation, 46–47
Responsive assistance, 190
Rubrics, 163–166

S

Scavenger hunts, 148
SCIIPP rubric, 92–93, 224
SGA. *See* Student–generated activity
Shared writing, 126–127
Stock market math activity (fifth grade), 260–262
Student contract and choice model, 269–270
Student–assisted performance, vs. teacher–directed performance, 15
Student–generated activity, 31, 146–148
Subtractive schooling, 39–40
Sudokus, 147–148

T

Task cards, 59
Task timing, 59
TAT. *See* Teaching activity time
Taxonomy, 169–171
Teacher–directed performance, vs. student–assisted performance, 15
Teaching, 4; content–driven teaching; dialogue teaching; transmission teaching; defined, 6–8, 29; and pedagogy, 5; research on, 23–24; role of pedagogy in effective teaching, 8–20; three processes of assistance, 7; timing of assistance, 7–8. *See also* Assisted performance
Teaching activity time, 84–85

Technology, 44–45

Technology, 44–45
Text comprehension, instructional conversations on, 211–213
Timing instructional frames, 250–251
Transactional strategy instruction, 44
Transformative pedagogy, vs. transmission pedagogy, 6
Transformative teaching model, 20–21; shifting to from transmission teaching model, 245
Transmission pedagogy, vs. transformative pedagogy, 6
Transmission teaching, 8–10; shifting to a transformative model, 245. *See also* Cemetery model
Trends in International Mathematics and Science Study (TIMMS), 10–11, 23

W

Web sites, 257–259
Word crosses, 103
Word finds, 103
Writing, 126–128
Written questions, 126

Z

Zone of proximal development, 7, 28–29
ZPD. *See* Zone of proximal development